WITHDRAWN
UTSA LIBRARIES

RACIST VICTIMIZATION

Racist Victimization
International Reflections and Perspectives

Edited by

JOHN WINTERDYK
Mount Royal College, Canada

GEORGIOS ANTONOPOULOS
University of Teesside, UK

ASHGATE

© John Winterdyk and Georgios Antonopoulos 2008

All rights reserved. No part of this publication may be reproduced, stored in a retrieval system or transmitted in any form or by any means, electronic, mechanical, photocopying, recording or otherwise without the prior permission of the publisher.

John Winterdyk and Georgios Antonopoulos have asserted their moral right under the Copyright, Designs and Patents Act, 1988, to be identified as the editors of this work.

Published by
Ashgate Publishing Limited
Gower House
Croft Road
Aldershot
Hampshire GU11 3HR
England

Ashgate Publishing Company
Suite 420
101 Cherry Street
Burlington, VT 05401-4405
USA

www.ashgate.com

British Library Cataloguing in Publication Data
Racist victimization : international reflections and
   perspectives
   1. Race discrimination - Cross-cultural studies 2. Race
   relations - Cross-cultural studies
   I. Winterdyk, John II. Antonopoulos, Georgios
   305.8

Library of Congress Cataloging-in-Publication Data
Racist victimization : international reflections and perspectives / edited by John Winterdyk and Georgios Antonopoulos.
      p. cm.
   Includes bibliographical references and index.
   ISBN 978-0-7546-7320-0
   1. Race discrimination--Cross-cultural studies. 2. Race relations--Cross-cultural studies.
I. Winterdyk, John. II. Antonopoulos, Georgios.

HT1521.R3773 2008
305.8--dc22

2007042468

ISBN 978-0-7546-7320-0

Library
University of Texas
at San Antonio

Mixed Sources
Product group from well-managed
forests and other controlled sources
www.fsc.org Cert no. SA-COC-1565
© 1996 Forest Stewardship Council

FSC

Printed and bound in Great Britain by
MPG Books Ltd, Bodmin, Cornwall.

Contents

List of Graphs		*vii*
List of Tables		*ix*
Notes on Contributors		*xi*
Acknowledgements		*xv*

Racist Victimization: An Introduction   1
John Winterdyk and Georgios Antonopoulos

1   Australia   19
       Nigel Stobbs

2   Canada   43
       Jo-Anne Wemmers, Lisette Lafontaine and Louise Viau

3   England and Wales   67
       Colin Webster

4   France   89
       Sophie Body-Gendrot

5   Germany   113
       Hans-Jörg Albrecht

6   Greece   139
       Vassiliki Petoussi-Douli

7   Japan   169
       Mark Fenwick

8   United States of America   185
       Ineke Haen Marshall and Amy Farrell

Epilogue   209
John Winterdyk and Georgios Antonopoulos

Index   *217*

List of Graphs

3.1	Ten year trend in reported racist incidents (England, Wales and London)	78
4.1	Evolution of racist and xenophobic 'threats' against North Africans in France since 1994	101
4.2	Evolution of racial violence since 1994 – racist acts in France – racist acts in Corsica – global threats	102
5.1	Extremist and xenophobic violence, 1982–2005	123
5.2	Trends in the number of asylum-seekers and xenophobic arson	125
5.3	Xenophobic crime in East and West Germany (2005)	126
8.1	Total hate crime incidents by year, 1995–2005	194
8.2	Reported hate incidents according to motivation 2005 UCR count and per cent of total incidents	195
8.3	Hate crime by motivation	197

List of Tables

1.1	Reported racial ancestry – Australian population 2001	24
1.2	Experience of racism in institutional settings	25
6.1	Number of reports per year and nationality of reporting persons, 1998–2004	152
6.2	Distribution of reporting foreigners per citizenship 1998–2004	153
6.3	Thematic categories related to matters of foreign citizens, 1998–2004	154

Notes on Contributors

Hans-Jörg Albrecht has been Director of the Max Planck Institute for Foreign and International Criminal Law in Freiburg/Germany (MPI) since March 1997. He teaches criminal law, criminal justice and criminology at the University of Freiburg. Professsor Albrecht obtained his PhD in 1979 and in 1991 he obtained the *venia legendi* for criminal law, juvenile criminal law, criminology, and prison law. From 1977 to 1991 Professsor Albrecht was a researcher fellow at the MPI. In 1991 he accepted an offer to lecture criminal law and criminology at the Law Faculty of the University of Konstanz. In 1993 he was offered the chair for criminal law, juvenile criminal law and criminology at the University of Dresden where he stayed until 1997. He has been given the status of guest professor at universities in China, United Kingdom, and Iran. In March 2005, the Law Faculty of the University of Pécs in Hungary awarded him the honorary doctorate.

Georgios Antonopoulos obtained his PhD from the University of Durham (UK) in 2005. He is now a lecturer in criminology at the University of Teesside (UK). His teaching and research interest include the criminality, criminalisation and victimisation of minority ethnic groups, qualitative research methods, and 'organised crime'.

Sophie Body-Gendrot is Professor of Political Science and of American studies, and Director of the Center of Urban studies at Sorbonne-Paris IV. She specialises in cross-national comparisons on minorities in cities, comparative public policy, ethnic and racial issues, urban disorders and empowerment. Her most recent books in English are: *The Civilization of Violence in Europe* (co-edited with P. Spierenburg), (Springer) (forthcoming); *The Social Control of Cities ? A Comparative Perspective*, (Blackwell 2000), and *Social Capital and Social Citizenship* (co-edited with M. Gittell) (Lexington Press, 2003).

Amy Farrell is currently a Principal Research Scientist and Associate Director of the Institute on Race and Justice at Northeastern University. Dr. Farrell's research focuses on disparate treatment of individuals within the criminal justice system. Primary areas of interest include analysis of racial and gender differences in traffic enforcement practices, disparate prosecution and sentencing outcomes in state and federal criminal justice systems and bias crime reporting. Over the past three years Dr. Farrell has led studies of racial and gender disparities in statewide traffic studies in Massachusetts and Rhode Island. Dr. Farrell is an active member of the Police Executive Research Forum panel of experts on racial profiling data collection and analysis. In addition to research on disparate treatment, Dr. Farrell has been actively involved in research on efforts by law enforcement to increase organizational integrity. Dr. Farrell is currently conducting research to help understand local law enforcement responses to trafficking in persons. Dr. Farrell has received funding from the National Institute of Justice, Bureau of Justice Assistance, Bureau of Justice Statistics, SOROS Foundation, Massachusetts Executive Office of Public Safety and the Rhode Island Attorney Gender. Dr. Farrell completed her doctorate from the Law, Policy and Society Program at Northeastern University in May of 2001.

Mark Fenwick is an Associate Professor at the Faculty of Law, Kyushu University, Fukuoka, Japan. His research and teaching interests include sociology of punishment, philosophy of criminal law and sociology of law.

Lisette Lafontaine was born in Montreal, Canada. She studied in Law and in Economics at the University of Montreal. She is a member of the Bar of the Province of Quebec and a career federal public servant who worked with the Department of Finance, the Privy Council Office and the Department of Justice. She is now a Senior Counsel in Criminal Law Policy with the Department of Justice in Ottawa, Canada.

Ineke Haen Marshall is a Professor in the College of Criminal Justice and the Department of Sociology at Northeastern University, Boston, USA. She has written in the area of comparative criminology, criminal careers, drug policy, juvenile delinquency and minorities. She edited *Minorities, Migrants, and Crime: Diversity and Similarity across Europe and the United States* (Sage, 1997), and she co-authored *Juvenile Delinquency in an International Perspective* (Kugler, 2003).

Vassiliki Petoussi-Douli is a Lecturer at the Department of Sociology, University of Crete, Greece. She received her PhD (1998) from Virginia Tech, USA. Her research and teaching interests include: Sociology of Law and Crime, Gender, Police and Policing and Bioethics. Her most recent publications include chapters on Greek police in Das, Dilip (ed.) *The World Police Encyclopedia* (New York, NY: Routledge Taylor and Francis Group, 2006) and in Sullivan, Larry E. (ed.) *Encyclopedia of Law Enforcement* (Thousand Oaks, CA: Sage Publications, 2005).

Nigel Stobbs is a lecturer in the Faculty of Law at the Queensland University of Technology. Prior to taking up a fulltime academic position, Nigel practised as a barrister of the Supreme Court of Queensland and of the High Court of Australia, practicing mainly in the criminal jurisdiction. He has researched and published in the areas of Indigenous human rights and public tolerance for sentencing reforms and has worked as a consultant to a number of human rights bodies. His doctorate focuses on the emerging field of therapeutic jurisprudence.

Louise Viau is a lawyer and full professor at the Law Faculty of the University of Montreal. Since 2004, she has been Secretary of the Law Faculty. She is a specialist in criminal law. She also teaches as a visiting professor at the Université Paris II since 1999.

Colin Webster is a Reader in Criminology at Leeds Metropolitan University, UK. He previously taught at the Universities of Teesside and York and has researched and written extensively on race, crime and social exclusion. He co-authored *Poor Transitions: Young Adults and Social Exclusion* (Policy Press, 2004) and recently published *Understanding Race and Crime* (Open University Press, 2007).

Jo-Anne Wemmers obtained her PhD from the University of Leiden (The Netherlands) in 1996. She worked as a researcher at the Research and Documentation Centre (WODC) of the Dutch Ministry of Justice. She is now a Professor at the School of Criminology of the University of Montreal (Canada) as well as Principal Researcher with the International Centre for Comparative Criminology, where she heads the research unit "Victimology and Restorative Justice".

John Winterdyk obtained his PhD in Criminology from Simon Fraser University (British Columbia in Canada) in 1998. He is the current Chair (2005–2009) of the Department of Justice Studies at Mount Royal College in Calgary, Alberta as well as the former Editor of the *International Journal of Comparative Criminology*. Since 2004, his textbook publications include: *Reader for Comparative Criminal Justice/Criminology*. Edited with Harry Dammer and Philip Reichel (Bochum Un. Press, Bochum, Germany, in press); *Qualitative and quantitative research methods reader: A Canadian orientation*. Edited with L. Coates and S. Brodie (Toronto: Pearson Education, 2006); *Canadian Criminology* (2nd ed.) (Scarborough: Pearson Education, 2005); *Issues and perspectives on young offenders in Canada* (3rd ed.). Editor. (Toronto: Harcourt Brace, 2005); *Lessons in Comparative/International Criminology*. Edited with Liqun Cao. (Toronto: de Sitter Publications, 2004); and *Adult Corrections: International perspectives*. Editor. (Monsey, NY: Willow Press, 2004).

Acknowledgements

We would like to heartily acknowledge each other's involvement. One of the most rewarding aspects of engaging in international and comparative criminological projects such as this one is the opportunity to meet, socialize and work with colleagues from around the world who have similar interests. We have collaborated on a number of articles over the years and this book represents our first joint effort of working on a book together. The process has been very rewarding and we would not have been able to complete the project without each others' assistance and keen interest in the study of racial victimization. We are also deeply appreciative of all the contributors who helped to make this book a reality. Without their expertise, the book would never have been written. Collectively they attended to our editorial requests and slight delays with commendable patience. John Winterdyk also remains indebted to his partner and dearest friend Rosemary who while always supportive regularly wonders about the enthusiam he has for his work. Thanks also to their two boys, Alex and Michael, who while often distracted by their teen years still find time to command distraction from John's desk. Georgios is also heavily indebted to Rena Vasilaki, John Tierney, Ben Bowling, Mark Simpson, Rob MacDonald and Tracy Shildrick for their support.

Finally, we express appreciation for Neil Jordan, Donna Elliott, Elaine Couper and the wonderful "team" at Ashgate, who not only saw the merit of producing this book but helped nurse our ideas into a publishable form.

Racist Victimization: An Introduction

John Winterdyk and Georgios Antonopoulos

> The death of 13-year-old Devin Brown, on Feb. 06/05, at the hands of the Los Angeles Police Department has generated a wide array of complicated emotions in the Black community, including shock and anguish, confusion and introspection. Why, people wondered, was this boy killed? Could his death have been prevented? Were the police rash and trigger-happy? Was there a racial overture to the killing? Or were they simply defending themselves?

The industrially advanced world has expressed a considerable concern over ethnicity, 'race,' and migration. In countries with a long colonial history such as Britain, France, the Netherlands, and in countries where the indigenous people were subjugated by a 'white majority' such as the United States, Australia and Canada, or even in countries where migrants have relatively recently come to attention such as Greece and Ireland, several social issues are intertwined with the issues of ethnicity, 'race,' and migration. The 9/11 bombing in New York and Washington, D.C., Madrid bombings in 2004 (also known as 3/11), and July 2005 bombings in London, fed debates about the relationship between minority ethnic groups and terrorism (see Wall, 2004). Meanwhile, the riots in Paris and other French cities, in the late 2005, brought abundant light onto the issue of integration of minority ethnic people in the 'mainstream' society (Graff, 2005; *The Economist*, 2005a). Similarly, Amnesty International has pointed out that since 9/11, 'racial profiling' has increased in the United States (Amnesty International, 2004).[1] For example, in response to an increase in the number of complaints from 'minority' groups,[2] a growing number of

---

1 Racial profiling refers to the discriminatory practice by member so of the criminal justice system: usually law enforcement officials, of targeting individuals for suspicion of crime based on the individual's race, ethnicity, religion or national origin.

2 By the sociological term 'minority ethnic groups' we mean groups, who share common cultural, genealogical and ancestry characteristics and consider themselves as a distinct group (Smith, 1987). By 'racial' minorities we mean groups of people with shared, inherited physical features such as skin colour and by shared nationality, religious affiliation, language use, etc. (see Abizadeh, 2001).

Wirth, L., "The Problem of Minority Groups," page 347 in Ralph Linton (ed.), *The Science of Man in the World Crisis*. New York: Columbia University Press, 1945. The political scientist and law professor, Gad Barzilai, has offered a theoretical definition of non-ruling communities that conceptualizes groups that don't rule and are excluded from resources of political power. Barzilai, G. *Communities and Law: Politics and Cultures of Legal Identities*. Ann Arbor: University of Michigan Press.

law enforcement agencies have recently conducted inquiries about racial prejudice towards Blacks and Hispanics being stopped by the police (Racial Profiling Data Collection Resource Centre, 2005). Sociologist Louis Wirth (1987–1952) defined a minority group as "a group of people who, because of their physical or cultural characteristics, are singled out from the others in the society in which they live for differential and unequal treatment and who therefore regard themselves as objects of collective discrimination." More recently, to this list could be added the shift in attitude towards Arabs, Muslims and South Asians (see Sardar, 2005). A term that is used by a number of activist groups that epitomizes their concern about racial profiling is "DWB" – Driving While Black or Brown! For example, a 2001 US Gallup poll reported that 55 per cent of whites and 83 per cent of Blacks believed that racial profiling is widespread.

Crime in particular has historically been one of the most important social issues identified with ethnicity, 'race,' and migration and in many countries certain crimes have been associated with certain minority ethnic groups in the majority's social consciousness. At the same time however, the status of minority ethnic people as *victims* has been relatively neglected in a large number of countries. Yet, as Goodey (2005: 1) observed: "most of us do not experience crime as criminals but as victims"; however even fewer of us experience being the victim of racism, gender, religion, or any other personal, cultural, or social differences. After 1990 however, the public, political and academic concern about the issue has increased and this is partly due to a number of high profile cases of racist violence like the death of a Black youngster, Stephen Lawrence, in 1993 in London by a gang of white youth (see Macpherson, 1999), and the brutal killing of James Byrd, a 49-year-old black man from Texas by racists (see Winterdyk, 2006). Yet, our world history is replete with documented accounts of the experiences of racial and ethnic oppression, segregation, subordination, and an array of prejudice shared by minority groups. Nevertheless, relative to the escalating conflictual relationships (see above); within the criminal justice system, particularly policing, there remains a dearth of information on racist victimization. For example, a Canadian literature search on the dual topic of 'crime and race' will reveal an appalling scarcity of material for a country which prides itself as a multicultural society and which has played a major role in the international movement for human rights and justice. Yet, one need to reflect on such recent racially based cases such the as Marshall Inquiry in Nova Scotia, the Aboriginal Justice Inquiry in Manitoba, the Caswey Report in Alberta, etc., to see the there is much work still to be done in the area of racist victimization (see Chapter 2 for further details).

There has been some confusion as to what constitutes 'racist' victimization and what its difference is to 'conventional,' criminal victimization. Nugent et al. (1989) suggest that the difference is the *motivation* behind the actual act. Racist victimization, as opposed to 'conventional' victimization involves that interaction of the offender(s) and the victim(s), who are not being victimized in their capacity as individuals but in their capacity as representatives of the community they belong (Witte, 1996). In racist victimization, whole communities are the 'collective victims' (Karydis, 1994). According to Björgo and Witte (1993b), racist violence is distinguished into three types depending on the form it takes and its severity: a) terrorist incidents (e.g., armed attacks, and arson), b) street violence incidents (e.g., assaults), and c) vandalism, threats and verbal abuse (see below for further discussion). Many of these incidents do not by themselves constitute a crime, although, as Smith (1994: 1106) argues, "some crime may occur in the sequence" something that imposes great constraints on the victims' (and potential victims') life (see Webster, 1995).

According to Godrej (1994), racism is not just a bad behaviour on a personal level. Racist victimization has been perpetrated by a range of individuals and/or by groups. For example, there is the plight of Black people and Native Americans in the United States of America, Aboriginal people in Australia, the Maori in New Zealand, Roma in Romania, or the ethnic cleansing in the Darfur region of Sudan, the killing of Muslims by Hindu in Godhra, India in 2002, or the relatively recent killing of Mayan Indians in Guatemala, the race riots throughout France in 2005, to the various forms of discrimination that take place in various work and occupational settings around the world. Other forms of human rights infringement and victimization include marriage fraud; a rapidly growing problem in such countries as India, or the exploitation of children from impoverished locations are being exploited for the sex trade industry, for labor, etc.

The perception that racist acts are perpetrated exclusively by groups like the Ku Klux Klan is a mistaken one (see Brazier, 1985). Most of the times these individuals and groups see their actions as legitimate because their views and attitudes are shared by the wider community in which they belong (see Sibbitt, 1997). Racist acts can also be perpetrated by the state and its conveyors. Racist victimization has enormous consequences to the (quality of) life of minority ethnic groups. It should be noted that in this Introduction, and indeed in this collection, a number of 'related' terms appear. Some of these terms, and specifically those related to ethnicity and 'race' need to be clarified, and are presented in Box 1 below.

Box 1: Racist Victimization Terminology

Prejudice: "refers to opinions or attitudes held by members of one group towards another. A prejudiced person's preconceived views are often based on hearsay rather than on direct evidence, and are resistant to change even in the face of new information" (Giddens, 1997: 212–213).

Discrimination: "consists of unequal, unfavourable and unjustifiable treatment based on a person's sex, gender, 'race,' ethnicity, culture, religion, language, class, sexual preference, age, physical disability or any other improper ground" (Bowling and Phillips, 2002: 38).

Ethnocentrism: is a form of prejudice. It is considered as "a set of beliefs that judges other groups as inferior to one's own" (Bowling and Phillips, 2002: 36).

Xenophobia: "the fear of hatred of anything that is foreign or outside of one's own group, nation or culture. Xenophobia is an overt form of prejudice and ethnocentrism …" (Herbst, 1997: 235).

Hate crime: "the violence of intolerance and bigotry, intended to hurt and intimidate someone because of their race, ethnicity, national origin, religion, sexual orientation or disability" (US Department of Justice, 2005).

Racism: "the belief that certain groups are innately, biologically, socially, morally superior to other groups based upon what is attributed to be their racial composition" (Kleg, 1993: 95).

Institutional racism: "refers to the processes – intentional and unintentional – by which criminal justice agencies systematically discriminate against certain social groups on grounds of race or ethnicity" (McLaughlin, 2001: 151).

The association of crime and victimization with ethnicity and 'race' has to be examined as a part of a wider historical context in which the 'convergence' of strangers has occurred and generated "... imagery, beliefs and evaluation about the 'Other'" (Miles, 1989: 11). The emergence of the ideas about ethnicity and 'race' especially in the nineteenth century, interacted with the newly developed then criminology and pseudo-science of eugenics and in their attempt to control the 'Other,' inflicted great suffering, which was inherited in the twentieth century too. The belief that the world is composed of different 'races' of varied 'capacity' led to the perception that humans can be categorized in each of these categories, and that different groups possess several and specific characteristics, which make a group be considered superior or inferior to the other(s), and which is the quintessence of racism (see Tierney, 1982). 'Scientific racist' views, such as this by the 'father of criminology,' Cesare Lombroso, who advocated for the atavists, individuals not fully evolved were predominant (coupled with the need to subjugate people in the colonies), and were leading to prejudice, acts of discrimination, and the (violent) victimization of members of minority ethnic groups. After the abolishment of slavery in the United States, Black people were not only segregated, excluded, and discriminated against, but also experiencing harassment and violence by white people who were "... resistant to any changes they suggested blacks were their equals" (Barri Flowers, 1988: 8–9). In the nineteenth and twentieth centuries Britain the anti-immigrant sentiment was strong enough to cause disturbances and violence against the 'Other' (see Panayi, 1996), and in Eastern Europe the programs against the Jews and the Gypsies were commonplace (Klier, 1993).

Today, as Hargreaves (2000: 52) suggests, examples of racist crime are omnipresent, and sometimes are "nourished" by the media. Countries like Germany, Rwanda and former Yugoslavia have all experienced genocide as a result of ethnic differences. Shaw (2002) reports on an account of Moroccan farm laborers being attacked in Spain in 1999, the vandalizing of Jewish cemeteries and more recently the attacks of people of Arab ancestry in France, attacks on Turkish immigrants in Germany, and the 2005 attacks on persons of Middle-Eastern appearance in Australia, among numerous other accounts. Another form of victimization of minority people includes the exploitation of migrant children in the sex trade, for labor, etc. In particular, the organization Global Watch Against Child Labour reports that in 2005 some 20,000 child were sold into some form of slavery, 38,000 children were involved in the sex-trade in South Africa, and Kenya acknowledges that it doesn't have any laws preventing the illicit trafficking of children (Global March Against Child Labour, 2005). The link between racism and trafficking for the financial exploitation of one's sexuality, or for labour, may not be as clear in a first look; but there exists and it is "racist ideology [that] fuels trafficking" (United Nations, 2001: 2).

In fact, as is evident in this Introduction and the contributions included in this anthology, one is hard pressed to identify a country that is completely free of conflict around ones' ethnic/racial background. As Joe Hicks (2003) recently observed, racism has become "institutionalized instead of withering away," and can be viewed in many areas of social life from education to health to housing to employment to policing. For example, according to Dodd (2005), 27 per cent of the people stopped and searched by the police in London after the 7 July 2005 bombings were Asian, although Asian representation in the population of the city in only 12 per cent. In addition, although the police have denied that they target ethnic minorities, stops of vehicles under anti-terrorism powers rose by 193 per cent for Asian drivers (Dodd, 2005). Finally, relatively new forms of racist victimization constitute the racial abuse through the internet (see Stobbs in this collection) and the abuse of Black footballers in European stadia (Garland and Rowe, 2001; Jacques, 2005).

It should be noted however, that not *all* minority ethnic groups are in the same position when it comes to being victims of racism and discrimination. It is *some* minority ethnic groups that are subjected to different official policies than other (e.g., EU nationals vs non-EU nationals within the European Union), and it is *some* ethnic groups that are subjected to social exclusionary policies, attitudes and practices. Moreover, it is *some* groups whose ethnicities do not correspond to 'progress' but 'cultural backwardness,' something that is relative since, as it is evident from the chapters that follow, racist victimization changes focus.

There are a number of sources of data on racist victimization. Over the years, the number of regional, national, and even international surveys has grown dramatically. And while the use of official crime data sources such as the Uniform Crime Reports (UCR) was the dominate source of crime data or police data for metropolitan centres (e.g., London), victimization surveys allow researchers to access different populations (either offenders or victims). These and other national, regional and local surveys have helped to enrich our knowledge and understanding of the extent and impact of crime as well as spawned an 'awakening' to such issues as racist victimization, and guided policy around these issues. Official crime statistics and victimization surveys are not however, the exclusive sources of data on the topic. There are, for instance, some studies that are based on a number of sources (e.g., Bowling, 1999).

The theoretical framework(s) in relation to racist victimization is very narrow and the theoretical enquiry on the issue is extremely limited. This is certainly the case as to the causes of racist crime. Green et al. (2001) identified a number of theories from the literature to explain racist victimization. They include five macro-level and one micro-level theory: a) historical-cultural, b) sociological, c) economic, d) political, e) psychological, and f) synthetic. The responses to racist victimization have also been a very important part of the racist victimization nexus. Bowling and Phillips (2002) put all responses into four categories: a) self-defense, b) state responses, c) police responses, and d) multi-agency responses, whereas Hopkins Burke and Pollock (2004) suggest that there are three types of interventions that can be largely viewed, namely law, situation prevention of racist crime and social prevention of racist crime. Needless to say, the legal responses are by far more than the other two types. Before we discuss some of the issues surrounding racist victimization we will provide a brief historical overview of the study of victimology since without this sub-discipline research into racist victimization might not have emerged.

Brief History of (Racial) Victimology

As various authorities on the subject of victims have noted, 'victims' have come increasingly to play a major role in discussions about crime and its control. The historical heritage of victimology has been traced back to the Middle Ages and German common laws (Winterdyk, 2006). German law included a system of "composition" (compensation) or *wergild* in which victims were to be compensated in some manner (usually in financial terms) for the harm or injury incurred. While Benjamin Mendelsohn (1900–1998) is recognized as the pioneer of victimology, it was the German scholar Hans von Hentig (1887–1974) who "wrote tellingly in theory about the role of the victim in the duet of crime" (Schafer 1968: v). Most of the early work involving the study of victims focused on theoretical issues around a theme generically described as "the art of blaming the victim" (Winterdyk 2006: 354). However, by the 1980s, due to changing political and ideological changes, the focus shifted towards victim's rights and concern in particular about such crimes as rape, sexual assault, domestic violence, and to a lesser extent the victimization of gays and lesbians. The shift from theoretical issues to empirically testing of the relationship between victims and offenders led to the flourishing of the victimization survey.

Over the years, the number of regional, national, and even international surveys has grown dramatically. And while the use of official crime data sources such as the Uniform Crime Reporting (UCR) was the dominate source of crime data, victimization surveys allow researchers to access different populations (either offenders or victims), and they make different assumptions from such sources as the UCR. Some of the more established victimization survey sources include, among others: the *British Crime Survey* (BSC) starting in the 1980s, the *National Survey of Ethnic Minorities*, the 1984 *Canadian Urban Victimization Survey* which was replaced with the *General Social Survey* in 1988, the American *National Crime Victimization Survey* (NCVS) which has been conducted since 1973, and the *International Crime Victimization Survey*. These, and other national and regional surveys, have helped to enrich our knowledge and understanding of the extent and impact of crime as well as spawned an 'awakening' to such issues as racist victimization, hate motivated crimes, and racial profiling. The findings have also helped to guide policy around 'law and order' and crime prevention strategies. In addition to generic based surveys, there have also been a growing host of specialized surveys on such topics as violence against women, repeat victimization, racial profiling, and to a lesser extent racist victimization. For example, while the NCVS collects data on race and ethnicity, it does not do so with the intent of providing profiles on racist victimization *per se*. But, it is possible to obtain information on hate crime. By contrast the BSC does ask if its respondents believe their victimization was racially motivated. And while Canada has legislation pertaining to hate crime (see Chapter 2), the Department of Justice does not collect in any reliable manner information pertaining to hate crime, let alone data on racial motivation in spite of the fact that there have been an increasing number of such incidents reported in the media in recent years.

While there are a number of different definitions of the meaning of victimology, for the general purpose of this reader, we will use the definition offered by the World Society of Victimology (cited in van Dijk, 1997: 4). They define victimology as:

> The scientific study of the extent, nature and causes of criminal victimization, its consequences for the persons involved and the reactions thereto by society, in particular

the police and the criminal justice system as well as voluntary workers and professional helpers.

Having provided a general overview on the history and nature of victimology and racist victimization, we will now discuss the relevance of why researchers, policy-makers, and criminal justice officials need to understand and respond to the problem of racist victimization within the general context of victim's rights.

The Application of Victimology: The Emergence of Victim's Rights

> *Justice isn't served until crime victims are* – Colorado Organization for Victim Assistance, 2005.

Where once the victim was essentially the "forgotten actor" or element in the criminal justice process (Baker, 1994), they are now major consideration in criminal justice policy reforms in most parts of the world. Perhaps the most significant international document relating to victim's rights has been the 1985 UN Declaration of Basic Principles of Justice for Victims of Crime and Abuse of Power (see: www.unhchr.ch/html/menu3/b/h_comp-49.htm). In addition, many countries now have 'Victims Rights Week' which is, in principle, intended to create awareness and commemorate victim's rights and services across all sectors of their society. In addition most of the countries represented in this collection have various types of 'victims' services' programs and/or policy which include one or more of the following principles and are intended to ensure the fair and equitable treatment of victims:

- Victims of crime should be treated with courtesy, compassion and respect.
- The privacy of victims should be considered and respected to the greatest extent possible.
- All reasonable measures should be taken to minimize inconvenience to victims.
- Information should be provided to victims about the criminal justice system and the victim's role and opportunities to participate in criminal justice processes.
- The views, concerns and diversity of victims should be considered in the development and delivery of programs and services, and in related education and training.
- Information should be provided to victims about available options to raise their concerns when they believe that these principles have not been followed (Winterdyk 2006: 371).

While considerable in-road has been made with regard to victim's rights in general, there has been little work done to directly address the specific rights of victims of racially based acts.

Victim Impact Statements

In addition to the emergence of victim's rights, victims in many countries have now also been permitted the opportunity to offer their impression to the court during the decision-making process. This presents a unique set of challenges since most people when victimized do not expect it and their responses tend to be unpremeditated and unplanned. Hence, as Fattah (1991: 29) has noted: "the reaction of different victims to the victimization experience is varied." O'Connell (2004) observes that victims' reactions can evolve from fright, to anxiety and ultimately despair and helplessness but for some victims they may react favourably towards their victimizer(s) (e.g., the Stockholm Syndrome). Considerable research has been conducted in this general area but very little within the context of racist victimization.

Formally known as victim impact statements (VIS), these (usually) written statements (in some jurisdictions such statements can be presented orally or via video) allow the victim to describe to the court the effect that crime has had on them. The United States was the first country to introduce the use of VIS in the mid–1970s. Although there are mixed findings in the literature as to the effect of VIS, they represent an attempt by the legal system to acknowledge the victim and to provide them with an opportunity to participate in the case involving them. There is a virtual void in the literature as to the extent, effect and impact of VIS involving racist victimization and how it is being addressed within the criminal justice system. Yet, there is a plethora of research and policy-based measures that allow victims of 'hate crime' to provide VIS. For example, most Canadian provinces have specific legislation that allows VIS for anti-hate and anti-racism acts. Most provinces also have specific agencies such as CASSA (Council of Agencies Servicing South Asians) that provide various support services to victims of hate-crime.

Purpose of the Reader

They cannot represent themselves, they must be represented – Karl Marx

Although the research and academic study of crime and the criminal justice system is well established as a science and disciplinary area of study, the role of the victim is a relatively new area of interest and study, and has not, as Goodey (2005: 1), notes, "enjoyed the same status as criminological research, policy and practice on crime and criminals." Relatively recently, as various authorities on the subject of victims have noted, 'victims' have come increasingly to play a major role in discussions about crime and its control (see Winterdyk, 2006). However, as we mentioned earlier, there has still been *relatively* little interest in the racist victimization, of minority ethnic groups and racial minorities. The international research has mainly focused on the issues of criminality of minority ethnic groups and racial minorities, or the relationship between minority ethnic groups and racial minorities and the criminal justice system (see Phillips and Bowling, 2003). We decided to edit this collection on racist victimization in an attempt to contribute to the efforts made especially after the 1990s.

The purpose of this book is to look at the available research on the issues relating to racist victimization in a number of countries which tend to exhibit different cultural, historical, social and geographical characteristics in relation to who, and why certain individuals/groups are being victimized. Minority ethnic groups and racial minorities differ not only in the countries appearing in this collection but throughout the world. However, there is a link among these countries: although not the same minority and migrant groups live in the countries of the western (and eastern) world, the trend of exclusion, persecution and victimization remains the same. Whether Afro-Caribbean, Aboriginal people, Black, Asian, Moroccan, Turkish, Chinese, Roma or Gypsy, all these groups have something in common. Although they belong in different types of 'ethnic-making situations,' as Fenton (1999: 32) would suggest, they constitute the 'Others,' who have been identified with danger, fear, and (national) insecurity and, as a consequence they have been – among 'Other' – prejudiced against and victimized. This is why, as Tonry (1997b) suggests, the combination of data and accounts on all minority ethnic groups and racial minorities can teach us a great deal on the topic. It should also be mentioned that, although the collection refers primarily to minority *ethnic* groups, some data, information and discussions are offered around *religion*. This is primarily for two reasons: a) religion *is* an integral part of the ethnicity, and b) even if religion was not an integral part of one's ethnicity, it would have been extremely difficult to distinguish between *ethnic* and *religious* minorities. As Perry (2003) suggests:

> ... it is not transparently clear whether [anti-Semitic and anti-Muslim] violence is motivated by presumed differences in religious beliefs, or antipathy towards Jews and Muslims as distinct ethnic groups. Does the fact that much anti-Semitic violence is directed toward synagogues imply a predominantly religious motivation? Or does the fact that violence is directed at dark-skinned people – taken to be Middle-Eastern – imply that such assaults are grounded in racial rather than religious bias?

In bringing together this collection of articles, by recognized experts in the field, we want to provide – among other – a clear account of the extent, nature, characteristics, and reactions towards racist victimization within an international context. Although there are a number of books on racist violence and victimization most of these books tend to focus on racist victimization within a local or national context (see, for example, Gabbidian and Greene, 2005; Panayi, 1996; Bowling, 1999; Chakraborti and Garland 2004; Waldrop and Zelden, 2001). Of the very few remarkable books on racist violence and victimization that have an international context, each of the chapters focuses on different aspects of the issue (see, for example, Bjorgo and Witte, 1993). To the best of our knowledge no previous attempt has been made to write, or edit, a book with the specific orientation found in this text. However, there has been a report published by the European Monitoring Centre on Racism and Xenophobia (2005) providing findings from 15 EU countries on the issues and synthesizing some data (see Helpful web links below). Therefore, we believe that this collection represents a worthy and needed contribution to the growing body of literature on criminology/victimology and in particular to the material on racist victimization.

In addition to providing a descriptive overview of racist victimization a number of the chapters provide some insight into the possible social, political and historical contexts which can be used to explain the persistence and entrenchment of (violent) racist victimization. While the following questions are not answered directly in any of the chapters, to varying degrees they collectively should encourage/enable to reader to explore some of the deeper issues surrounding racial victimization. For example:

- Why are younger minority ethnic and/or racial youth more likely to be the victim of racially based conflict?
- Why are certain areas more prone to racial conflict than others?
- What are the mechanisms and processes that predispose certain individuals to racist victimization?
- What are some of the key factors that impact the likelihood of victims of racist violence not reporting their victimization to criminal justice officials?
- How and why are racist victimization incidents occurring? And, what policies appear to work?

This text has been written and edited for researchers and academics within the fields of criminology, victimology and race relations, as well as for the undergraduate and postgraduate students pursuing courses on the above subjects and taking up modules on ethnicity, 'race' and crime. It should allow those interested in the general subject areas of criminology, victimology and race relations to identify (new) areas of research both at a national and international level. Finally, given that prejudice, discrimination and racism are issue that concerns *all* of us, we hope that the text will be proven interesting to a general audience.

Framework of the Chapters and the Book

Upon soliciting the eight contributors we identified a series of questions and themes which we asked all the authors to address to the best of their ability.[3] This helps to ensure some uniformity between the contributions and enables a richer degree of comparability between two or more of the countries represented in the book. Each of the contributors was asked to provide:

- some a historical overview of racist victimization in their country
- a discussion of racism and racist crime within the legal context of their country
- a description of the extent and nature of racist victimization in their country
- an overview of the social, cultural, and political reaction to racially motivated victimization in their country, and
- a conclusion with some general observations about the plight and direction of racist victimization within their country.

---

3 Authors were identified through their recognized expertise in the area based on related publications, presentations, etc.

While a set of basic guidelines was provided, the contributors were encouraged to present 'their' accounting of the situation rather than impose a standardized definition of racist victimization and/or other relevant aspects to the subject matter.

Collectively, the book is international in perspective (and to a much lesser extent comparative). In so doing, it allows the reader to broaden their range of knowledge about the subject matter as well as provide "perspective for results yielded by one national case study, and control the extent to which these results can be generalized to other regions" (della Porta, 1995: 210). However, we acknowledge that there are problems with our collection, just as with other collections, which are comparative and international in perspective. These problems arise because, as Nelken (2000) suggests, most of the international and comparative texts on criminology and criminal justice are 'national reports' on the given issue, since it is relatively difficult to conduct empirical or theoretical research in different contexts, and thus have an insight into the deeper issues that affect a social phenomenon. As Sztompka (1990: 47) argues "one of the most perennial methodological riddles of comparative sociology is the incommensurability of concepts." Øyen (1990), an established authority in the theory of comparative social research, similarly suggests that there is a non-equivalence of concepts among different geographical and/or historical contexts that makes comparison difficult. However, Winterdyk, Reichel, and Dammer (forthcoming) suggest that as the interest in comparative and international research grows researchers as developing/refining techniques that enable more reliable and valid comparisons.

Brief Overview of the Chapters

This collection includes representation from eight different countries. As noted above, the authors were asked to address a common set of themes which can serve to allow for single or multiple comparisons. As we saw no reason for prioritizing the order of appearance, we present the countries in alphabetic order. They include: Australia, Canada, England and Wales, France, Germany, Greece, Japan, and Unites States of America. As much as we tried to standardize the format for each chapter, it should be noted that the nature and level of detail covered across the chapters is not always consistent. The variability in coverage is primarily attributable to the phenomenology of racist victimization, the different experiences the countries have with (different) minority ethnic groups, differences in the collection of relevant data and empirical research on the topic as well as the way the issue has been treated by different countries. Inevitably, as it is the case in most edited collections some repetition is present.

Chapter 1 by Nigel Stobbs focuses on *Australia*, where tension and friction among ethnic groups has been an integral element of the country's history. Stobbs suggests that there is "an apparent disparity between the way Australia perceives itself as tolerant and accepting of cultural diversity and the way in which large sectors of the migrant and ethnic population perceive themselves as marginalized and victimized." Simultaneously, the responses of the Australian state government have not contributed greatly towards the reduction in racist victimization, though there is some evidence that relevant legislation may be effective when it comes to individual cases of racist victimization in the country.

Chapter 2 by Jo-Anne Wemmers, Lisette Lafontaine and Louise Viau focuses on another multi-ethnic society, *Canada*. Despite the country being a multi-cultural one, prejudice against specific ethnic groups has not been absent. However, relevant legislation has only recently been introduced although the issue of racism and discrimination has been prohibited by Human Rights legislation. Data on racist victimization in Canada do not provide a clear picture due to numerous limitations and very little data is available in relation to the perpetrators of racist crimes that have great physical and psychological effects not only on the individuals but also to the ethnic community to which the victim belongs.

Chapter 3 by Colin Webster focuses on *England and Wales*, where publicity and a campaign about the racist murder of a young Black man in London, Stephen Lawrence, in the early 1990s and the findings of a subsequent inquiry (the Macpherson inquiry) into the failed police investigation, transformed the debate on the issue. This chapter pursues the wider implications for the changes in the law, and reflects on the history, trends and patterns of racist victimization in Britain. According to Webster, the motivations of perpetrators of racist violences as well as the situational factors that contribute to hate crime are key aspects in understanding racist victimization. This chapters attempts at addressing this issue and concludes with an assessment of whether understanding of, and policing and criminal justice responses to racist victimization have improved and been sustained.

Chapter 4 by Sophie Body-Gendrot focuses on *France*, a country in which racism against minority ethnic groups, particularly those from the former French colonies, is not a new phenomenon. However, the issue has been rather neglected, and it was the riots in parts of Paris and other French cities in the end of 2005 that revived debates about the position of minority ethnic groups in France and the treatment they received from State agencies. According to Body-Gendrot, the absence of political and public debate on racism and racist victimization is a characteristic of French culture, and the laws against racism that exist in the country have been primarily used to combat anti-semitism and discrimination in general.

Chapter 5 by Hans-Jörg Albrecht casts light on racist violence in *Germany*. This is a context which in the past was associated with extreme violence against specific ethnic groups. Although, some data from a number of sources exist (e.g., police and judicial statistics, surveys and academic research, NGOs, media and international organisations), these sources suffer from a number of limitations and are largely inadequate to provide a clear picture as to the incidence, prevalence and trends in racist violence in the country. In addition, very little is known about the actual effectiveness of anti-racist legislation and policies in Germany, which, as Albrecht suggests, "are not led by scientific information but are rather guided by normative theory and ideology." The author of this chapter urges for a rigorous research agenda to be set.

Chapter 6 by Vassiliki Petoussi-Douli focuses on *Greece*, a country which was transformed from a country of emigration to a country of immigration in the early 1990s. Migrants, according to the author, are primarily the victims of racist victimization in the country although this type of victimization is experienced by other groups as well (e.g., Roma). The lack of an *effective* legal framework of immigration and of appropriate strategic planning and management led to the state employing reactive measures, which frequently provided for the victimization of large numbers of migrants by the state agencies and the Greek public. As Petoussi shows in her chapter, while significant changes have been made in recent years in the legislative, administrative, educational levels, as well as efforts to facilitate social integration of immigrants; problems still remain. Among those issues discussed is the general lack of official and publicly available data on racist victimization.

Chapter 7 by Mark Fenwick provides a discussion of racist victimization in *Japan*. Japan is a country different from the counties presented in the rest of the collection, and one in which the 'myth of homogeneity' has been promoted and the existence of minority groups (and consequently their rights) denied. In addition, as Fenwick suggests, there is a wider perception of the foreigner-as-criminal in the Japanese context, which has legitimized discrimination and victimization against foreign residents. Indeed, despite the denial of the issues of racist victimization in Japan, the media, academic and NGOs evidence suggests that forms of racial discrimination and victimization are a routine feature of everyday life in the country.

Chapter 8 by Ineke Haen Marshall and Amy Farrell is dedicated to a country that has been seen as a melting pot (or a 'salad bowl,' see Millet, 2004) of a number of minorities, and a country in which these minorities have been victimized because of their background, the *United States of America*. There are broadly four main groups that have been the victims of racism: African Americans, Hispanics, Native Americans, and – after 9/11 – people of Arab origin. In contrast to other contexts (see Greece, Chapter 6) data on the issue is not a problem in the United States. As Marshall and Ferrell show, the 1990 *Hate Crime Statistics Act* made it a federal requirement to collect data on racist victimization, and agencies such as the FBI and the National Crime Victim Survey have been collecting relevant data since then. This is presented in the US chapter along with data from state and local-level reports. The fourth section of their chapter zeros in on the social, cultural and political reaction to racially motivated victimization, with particular emphasis on racial profiling.

All of the chapters are, of course, based on past data, research and literature. However, all contributing authors directly, or indirectly, provide directions for future research in each country and internationally. In addition, all authors identify direction towards solving (part of) the problem, from identification of perpetrators and action actions them to a development of a range of policies and strategies to prevent racist victimization (see also Sibbitt, 1997). However, what appears to be the resultant force is that criminal justice responses – no matter how effective – and although they constitute the first an integral part of an integrated approach against racist victimization, they are extremely limited (see Levin and McDevitt 1993; Jabbour, 2001).

References

Abizadeh, A. (2001), 'Ethnicity, Race and a Possible Humanity,' *World Order*, 31(1): 23–34.

Amnesty International (2004), *Threat and Humiliation: Racial Profiling, Domestic Violence and Human Rights in the United States* (NY: Amnesty International).

Antonopoulos, G.A. (2006), 'Greece: Policing Racist Violence in the 'Fenceless Vineyard,' *Race & Class*, 48(2), 92–100.

Antonopoulos, G.A. (2007), 'Ethnotikes kai 'Fyletikes' Meionotites, kai Metanastes Os Thymata' [Ethnic and 'Racial' Minorities, and Migrants as Victims], *Poiniki Dikaiosyni*.

Baker, D. (1994), *Reading Racism and the Criminal Justice System* (Toronto: Canadian Scholars' Press).

Barri Flowers, R. (1988), 'Minorities and Criminality.' *Contributions in Criminology and Penology No.21* (Westport, CT.: Greenwood Press).

Björgo, T. and Witte, R. (1993), 'Introduction,' in Björgo, T. and Witte, R. (eds.), *Racist Violence in Europe* (London: Macmillan), 1–16.

Bowling, B. (1999), *Violent Racism*, revised edition (Oxford: Clarendon Press).

Bowling, B. and Phillips, C. (2002), *Racism, Crime and Justice* (London: Longman).

Brazier, C. (1985), 'The White Problem,' *New Internationalist*, Issue 145.

Collins, D. Excerpted from *The Collins Column*, 19 September 2001, *Vancouver Sun* –www.canada.com/vancouver/vancouversun/ retrieved October 18/05.

Dobson, R.B. (1974), *The Jews of Medieval York and the Massacre of March 11/90* (York: St Anthony's Press).

Dodd, V. (2005), 'Surge in Stop and Search of Asian People After July 7,' *The Guardian*, 24 December.

Della Porta, D. (1956), *Social Movements, Political Violence, and the State: A Comparative Analysis of Italy and Germany* (Cambridge: Cambridge University Press).

European Monitoring Centre on Racism and Xenophobia (2005), *Racist Violence in 15 EU Member States – A Comparative Overview of Findings from the RAXEN NFP Reports 2001–2004*, European Monitoring Centre on Racism and Xenophobia.

Fattah, E. (1991), *Understanding Criminal Victimization* (Scarborough, ON: Prentice-Hall).

FitzGerald, M. and Hale, C. (1996), *Ethnic Minorities, Victimization and Racial Harassment*, Research Findings No.39 London: Home Office.

Frances Reid, S. and Smith, R.G. (1998), 'Regulating Racial Hatred,' *Trends and Issues in Crime and Criminal Justice*, No. 79 (Canberra: Australian Institute of Criminology).

Gabbidian, S.L. and Greene, H.T. (2005), *Race and Crime* (Thousand Oaks, CA: Sage).

Gall, T.L. and Lucas, D.M. (1996), *Statistics on Crime and Punishment* (Detroit, MI.: Gale Research Inc).

Garland, J. and Chakraborti, N. (2004), 'Racist Victimisation, Community Safety and the Rural: Issues and Challenges,' *British Journal of Community Justice*, 2(3): 21–32.

Garland, J. and Rowe, M. (2001), *Racism and Anti-Racism in Football* (Basingstoke: Palgrave).

Gardner, J. (1990), *Victims and Criminal Justice.* Office of Crime Statistics, Attorney Generals Department, South Australia (Series C, No. 5).

Giddens, A. (1997), *Sociology.* 3rd edition (Cambridge: Polity Press).

Global March Against Child Labour, (2005), Available online at www.globalmarch.org retrieved on 23 October 2005.

Godrej, D. (1994), 'Race: Unlocking Prejudice,' *New Internationalist*, Issue 260.

Goodey, J. (2005), *Victims and Victimology: Research, Policy and Practice* (Essex, England: Pearson).

Graff, J. (2005), 'Streets of Fire,' *Time*, 14 November, 22–33.

Green, D., McFalls, L. and Smith, J. (2001), 'Hate Crime: An Emergent Research Agenda,' *Annual Review of Sociology*, 27, 479–504.

Hamm, M. (1994), 'Conceptualising Hate Crime in a Global Context,' in Hamm, S. (ed.), *Hate Crime: International Perspectives on Causes and Control* (Cincinnati, OH.: Anderson), 173–194.

Hargreaves, I. (2000), 'How the Newspapers Nourish Racial Intolerance,' *New Statesman*, 24 April, 52.

Herbst, P. (1997), *The Colour of Words: An Encyclopedic Dictionary of Ethnic Bias in the United States* (Boston, Ma.: Intercultural Press).

Hicks, J. (2003), Nation could, did change. *Los Angeles Daily News*, July 13, http://www.latimes.com, retrieved on 25 January 2006.

Hopkins Burke, R. and Pollock, E. (2004), 'A Tale of Two Anomies: Some Observations on the Contribution of (Sociological) Criminological Theory to Explaining Hate Crime Motivation,' *Internet Journal of Criminology.* Available online at: http://www.internetjournalofcriminology.com/ijcarticles.html, retrieved on 12 January 2006.

Husband, C. (1982), 'The East End Racism 1900–1980: Geographical Continuities in Vigilantist and Extreme Right-wing Political Behaviour,' *London Journal*, 8(1), 3–26.

Institute of Race Relations (2005), 'Protecting Ethnic Minorities,' *European Race Bulletin*, No.53, 15–30.

Jabbour, R. (2001), Policing Partnership in a Multicultural Australia: Achievements and Challenges: An Australian Arabic Perspective. Australian Institute of Criminology, Brisbane, 25–26 October.

Jacques, M. (2005), 'The Shame in Spain,' *The Observer Sport Monthly*, No.63 (May), 26–31.

Kleg, M. (1993), *Hate Prejudice and Racism* (Albany, N.Y.: State University of New York).

Klier, J.D. (1993), 'The Pogrom Tradition in Eastern Europe,' in Björgo, T. and Witte, R. (eds.), *Racist Violence in Europe* (London: Macmillan), 128–138.

Klug, F. (1982), *Racist Attacks* (London: Runnymede Trust).

Levin, D.M. and McDevitt, J. (1993), *Hate Crime: The Rising Tide of Bigotry and Bloodshed* (New York, NY: Plenum Press).

Macpherson, Sir William of Cluny (1999), *The Stephen Lawrence Inquiry*, Cmnd 4262–1 (London: HMSO).

Mcguire, M. (1985), 'Victims Needs and Victims Services,' *Victimology*, 10: 539–559.

McLaughlin, E. (2001), 'Institutional Racism,' in Mclaughlin, E and Muncie, J. (eds.) *The Sage Dictionary of Criminology* (London: Sage), 151–153.

Miles, R. (1989), *Racism* (London: Routledge).

Millet, J. (2004), 'Understanding American Culture: From Melting Pot to Salad Bowl,' *Cultural Savvy*, available online at: http://www.culturalsavvy.com/understanding_american_culture.htm, accessed on 22 December 2006.

Nelken, D. (2000), 'Just Comparing,' in Nelken, D. (ed.), *Contrasting Criminal Justice: Getting from Here to There* (Aldershot: Ashgate), 3–22.

Newburn, T. (1993), *The Long-term Needs of Victims: A Review of the Literature*. Research and Planning Unit Paper 80, Home Office, London.

Nugent, S., Wilkie, M. and Iredale, R. (1989), *Racist Violence*, No.8 (Canberra: Australian Institute of Criminology).

O'Connell, M. (2004, July), Personal communication with John Winterdyk. Victims of Crime Co-ordinator, Government of South Australia, Melbourne, Australia.

Øyen, E. (1990), 'Comparative Research as a Sociological Strategy,' in Øyen, E. (ed.), *Comparative Methodology: Theory and Practice in International Social Research* (London: Sage), 1–18.

Panayi, P. (1996), *Racial Violence in Britain* (Leicester: Leicester University Press/Pinter).

Perry, B. (2003), 'Where Do We Go From Here? Researching Hate Crime,' *Internet Journal of Criminology*, available online at: http://www.internetjournalofcriminology.com/ijcarticles.html, retrieved on 11 January 2006.

Phillips, C. and Bowling, B. (2003), 'Racism, Ethnicity and Criminology: Developing Minority Perspectives,' *British Journal of Criminology*, 43, 269–290.

Racial Profiling Data Collection Resource Centre, 2005, available online at www.racialprofilinganalysis.neu.edu/, retrieved on 23 October 2005.

Sampson, A. and Phillips, C. (1992), *Multiple Victimisation: Racial Attacks on an East London Estate*, Crime Prevention Unit Series Paper No. 36 (London: Home Office).

Sardar, Z. (2005), 'The Next Holocaust,' *New Statesman*, December, 16–19.

Schafer, S. (1968), *The Victim and his Criminal: A Study in Functional Responsibility* (Upper Saddle River, NJ: Prentice-Hall).

Shaw, M. (2002), *Preventing Hate Crimes: International Strategies and Practices* (Montreal: International Centre for the Prevention of Crime).

Sibbitt, R. (1997), *The Perpetrators of Racial Harassment and Racial Violence*. Home Office Research Study 176 London: Home Office.

Smith, A.D. (1987), *The Ethnic Origins of Nations* (Oxford: Blackwood).

Smith, C. (ed.). (1997), 'Lyons,' in Commission for Racial Equality. *Racially Motivated Crime: Responses in Three European Cities* (London: Commission for Racial Equality), 67–97.

Smith, D.J. (1994), 'Race, Crime, and Criminal Justice,' in Maguire, M., Morgan, R. and Reiner, R. (eds.), *The Oxford Handbook of Criminology* (New York: Oxford University Press), 1041–1117.

Sztompka, P. (1990), 'Conceptual Frameworks in Comparative Inquiry: Divergent or Convergent?' in Albrow, M. and King, E. (eds.) *Globalization, Knowledge and Society* (London: Sage), 47–58.

The Economist (2005a), 'After the Riots,' 17 December, 37–38.
The Economist (2005b), 'On the Beach,' 17 December, 63.
Tierney, J. (1982), 'Race, Colonialism and Migration,' in Tierney, J. (ed.), *Race, Migration and Schooling* (London: Holt, Rinehart and Winston Ltd), 1–43.
United Nations (2001), *The Race Dimension of Trafficking in Persons – Especially Women and Children* (United Nations Department of Public Information).
U.S. Bureau of Justice Statistics (2005), retrieved December 16/05: http://www.ojp.usdoj.gov/bjs/abstract/cvus/definitions.htm.
Van Dijk, J.J.M. (1997), 'Towards a Research-based Crime Reduction Policy: Crime Prevention as a Cost-effective Policy Option.' *European Journal on Criminal Policy and Research*, 5(3): 13–27.
Waldrop, C. and Zelden, C.L. (2001). *Racial violence on trial: A handbook with cases, laws, and documents.* ABC-Clio. Inc.
Wall, T. (2004), 'Police State UK,' *New Statesman*, 22 November, 12–13.
Webster, C. (1995), 'Researching Racial Violence: A Scientific Realist Approach.' Paper presented in the British Criminology Conference, Loughborough University, 18–21 July.
Winterdyk, J. (2006), *Canadian Criminology* (2nd ed.) (Toronto: Prentice Hall).
Winterdyk, J., Reichel, P, and Dammer, H. (forthcoming), *A Guided Reader in Comparative Criminology/Criminal Justice Research* (Bochum, Germany: Bochum University Press).
Witte, R. (1996), *Racist Violence and the State* (London: Longman).

Helpful websites

http://eumc.eu.int/eumc/index.php European Monitoring Centre on Racism and Xenophobia.
http://ruljis.leidenuniv.nl/group/jfcr/www/icvs/ International Crime Victimization Survey based in (Leiden, The Netherlands).
http://www.minorityrights.org/ - Minority Rights Group International.

Chapter 1

Australia

Nigel Stobbs

Introduction

Australians regard themselves as tolerant – a characteristic of the national psyche referred to as giving people 'a fair go'. This is a nation, which is overtly proud of an alleged heritage of embracing social and ethnic diversity. Its Federal government claims to have developed one of the world's most successful multicultural policies. *Multicultural Australia: United in Diversity*, the seminal policy document which seeks to set the multicultural agenda for the next few years, declares that:

> Australians have embraced respect for cultural diversity, making our nation one of the most harmonious societies in the world. Australia's multicultural policy promotes acceptance of and respect for our cultural diversity. It supports the right of each Australian to maintain and celebrate, within the law, their culture, language or religion (Department of Immigration, and Indigenous and Multicultural Affairs, 2003: 3).

How can this claim be reconciled, then, with observations such as this, from an Arab Muslim Australian explaining his experience to representatives of the Human Rights and Equal Opportunity Commission's (HREOC) 2004 investigation into prejudice against Arab and Muslim Australians (HREOC, 2004):

> Everywhere you go you have a constant fear that someone's going to attack you, or you expect that everywhere you go someone's going to be racist to you. We are citizens of Australia, not strangers. We just want security because we are not feeling safe or secure at all. We walk in the street and we are afraid, we go into train stations and we are afraid… wherever we go we are afraid (HREOC, 2004: 8).

Does the stark disparity in these two observations mean that one of the observers is greatly mistaken about the actual level of interracial harmony in Australia or is the disparity more a matter of perception? In a recent study Johnson (2005) found in a survey of Vietnamese and Middle Eastern migrants that although these groups of migrants did not report higher levels of actual victimisation than the wider surveyed sample in the ICVS, and in fact reported lower rates of personal crime, it was significant that this group was more likely to believe that offences and threats directed at them were motivated by race.

Racial and ethnic tensions are perhaps an inevitable outcome of the social and political factors which have shaped Australian history. From the sudden and violent confrontation of two acutely disparate cultures which resulted from the colonisation of the continent as a consequence of eighteenth century British penal policy, through the mass intake of foreign labour after the Second World War to the recent influx of refugees and asylum seekers from Asia, the Middle East and Africa, Australia has always been, as we shall see in this chapter, an incubator for such tension. The public policies and government responses to these tensions have often been overly idealistic and optimistic, sometimes informed by a simplistic and two-dimensional view of both the nature and causes of racist victimisation. Even today, as we shall see, there is a lack of understanding of the categorical confusions and blurring of distinctions between concepts of race, ethnicity and religion in some strategies designed to combat the ideology and practice of racist victimisation. Poynting et al. (2004) observe that as a result of various terror attacks across the globe, the moral panic over so-called 'race rapes' in Sydney and the influx of asylum seekers from the Middle East, we are seeing the emergence of an 'Arab other' who is "becoming the pre-eminent folk devil in contemporary Australia".[1] It is probably fair to say that the increasing complexity of the social, political, cultural and economic contexts in which racist victimisation has been experienced in Australia requires more sophisticated and research informed responses than have been adopted in the past. There is some doubt as to the adequacy of current strategies (which are largely reactive in nature) to address the problem and this may well be the result of a lack of sufficiently framed research (Johnson 2005: 6).

Historical Background of Racist Victimisation in Australia

The Interaction of Indigenous and Colonial Cultures

Racial hatred and racial vilification have a long history in Australia. The island continent was colonised (or invaded, depending on one's perspective) by Britain in 1788. Perhaps unsurprisingly, the inevitable tension between a colonising European culture and an Indigenous population of hundreds of diverse hunter gatherer communities has influenced the Australian cultural and racial ethos in fundamental ways ever since.

The first European settlers were 736 convicts deported from England for fairly minor property offences arising largely out of desperate poverty, guarded by about 200 Royal Marines. For about thirty years after the arrival of these first English colonists in Australia the embryonic colonial government was mostly concerned with basic survival and the management of the European population. It gave little thought to relations with the Indigenous inhabitants, and in this policy vacuum probably

---

[1] Poynting and Noble (2004: 4) would agree with the view that this categorical confusion tends to hinder responses to racism. In a submission to HREOC's Isma-Listen investigation, Poynting suggests that "The extent to which categories of race, ethnicity (culture) and religion are conflated in the 'common sense' of racism is an aspect which needs to be studied, especially in as much as it determines the scope of legislation and the targeting of anti-racist initiatives and resources" (HREOC 2004:4).

occurred the darkest days of Australian history. Although Aboriginal people[2] were technically British subjects and entitled to all the rights and protections of any subject of the Crown, in reality there were no mechanisms to protect those rights. Agriculture and rural expansion took precedence. By the mid 1880s the Aboriginal population on the mainland had been reduced from about 300,000 to a mere 60,000.

Deliberate violence and imported diseases were the main causes of this drastic drop in population. The smallpox virus had never been seen in Australia before 1788, and so there was no natural immunity to it among the Indigenous population. The response to the levels of disease and aggression from farmers was to appoint local protectors of Aborigines who had only vague powers and did little more than distribute some blankets and medicines and try to mediate in disputes between Indigenous people and pastoralists.

Despite this initial devastation, however, it became apparent in the first few decades of the twentieth century that Indigenous Australian civilization was not going to disappear – the Indigenous population was in fact growing. A naïve Social Darwinism which had informed earlier policies of protection predicted that the continent's original culture should have been eradicated by the more pervasive and colonial culture of the Europeans. A renewed commitment to human rights as a result of the two world wars in some sense stimulated a renewed concern for the welfare of Indigenous people. Policy became focused on assimilation. The 1961 Native Welfare Conference of Federal and State Ministers declared that:

> The policy of assimilation means that all Aborigines and part-Aborigines are expected to attain the same manner of living as other Australians and to live as members of a single Australian community, enjoying the same rights and privileges, accepting the same customs and influenced by the same beliefs as other Australians.

A number of commentators have argued that this policy of assimilation was an act of cultural and even racial genocide. At the very least, a policy of assimilation must have been motivated by some desire for homogeneity of culture – and was, according to Broome (1994: 171), "absorption and naive social engineering to change Aborigines into Europeans with black skins". Indigenous Australians were given access to the mainstream social security system in 1960 and the right to vote as late as 1962. A 1967 referendum sought and received the authority of the citizen body to include Indigenous people for the first time in census data. In a practical sense, then, Australia only recognised its Indigenous peoples as being fully human as recently as 1967.

A number of wide ranging public enquiries in recent years (such as HREOC's *Bringing them Home*, 1997) have exposed the consequences of deplorable public policy decisions of the mid to late twentieth century which caused extensive dislocation of Aboriginal families and communities. Indigenous people were

---

2 Researchers should note that there are many different indigenous cultures still present in Australia. The term 'Aboriginal' is sometimes used to refer collectively to all the mainland indigenous cultures and tribes. Its use is not always appropriate when referring to the indigenous Australian population as it may be seen as excluding the Torres Strait Islander People.

forcibly removed in large numbers from their traditional homelands and relocated to missions and other settlements based on the purported rationale of centralising the delivery of essential services such as health and education. What this in fact meant was that contrived and artificial communities emerged consisting of peoples from very different Indigenous cultural backgrounds who were forced to integrate into amorphous cultural groups with little chance of meaningful employment. Indigenous workers were press-ganged into working for pay which was grossly inadequate for their needs and substantially less than what the public purse paid to non-Indigenous employees. Even half a century later, many Indigenous people are still seeking compensation for the money that was either not paid to them, or withheld by public officials for dubious community welfare purposes. Children were regularly removed from the care of their parents and either orphaned out to white families or raised in dehumanising institutions which left many scarred for life. These children are collectively known as 'The Stolen Generation' and despite widespread public outrage and the numerous recommendations of the Human Rights and Equal Opportunity Commission's report *Bringing Them Home* the Federal government in Australia still refuses to compensate these dislocated children and families.

The result of these devastating public policies, and the failure of successive Australian governments to come to grips with their fiduciary duties and human rights obligations to the Indigenous population, has ensured that racial tensions between Indigenous and non-Indigenous groups have remained high. A nation wide effort at reconciliation has seen some progress made at a local level, but in the light of statistics which show alarming disparities in infant mortality rates, life expectancies, employment opportunities, rates of imprisonment and health standards, the treatment of Indigenous Australians remains the most serious issue of racist victimisation today.

In the early history of the nation there are a number of other examples of overtly racist government policy enforced through legislation. The Australian Constitution (s.51 (xxvi)) has always contained a provision allowing the Federal government to make special laws for "the people of any race, for whom it is deemed necessary to make special laws". This legislative power was often relied upon to enact laws making it legal to employ Chinese and Pacific Island workers on pay and conditions significantly worse than those afforded to those of European descent.

Migration and the Multicultural Nature of Contemporary Australian Society

In the early 1900s there is no doubt that the poor treatment of the Indigenous population was the most significant issue of racism facing the developing nation. But Australia is now one of the most multicultural societies on Earth. Patterns and incidents of racist victimisation have tended to follow the patterns of immigration and the cultural and ethnic blend of the overall population. According to the Australian Bureau of Statistics (2005) only 76 per cent of Australians are actually born in Australia, and that figure has been stable since the first national census in 1901.

One recent commentator, Luke McNamara (2002), agrees that the nature and extent of racial vilification in Australia has fluctuated over time, in response to a number of political, economic and demographic factors. Wakim (1992) reports that during the first Gulf War, for example, there was a marked increase in the reporting of incidents of racial vilification and racist violence against Australians of Arab descent. Historically, the greatest percentage of immigrants arriving in Australia was skilled Caucasian labour from the UK.

The infamous "White Australia policy" of the 1900s was designed to ensure that only English speaking Europeans were accepted as residents. A dictation test required prospective migrants to respond in a designated European language (by writing out 50 words spoken by the assessor) – and the language was chosen by the person giving the test to ensure that those of an 'undesirable' ethnic origin would fail. Andrew Fraser (2005b) describes the underpinning rationale of the policy as a view that:

> ethnic homogeneity was one of the great strengths of the Australian nation, one that ought to be preserved and not squandered or thrown away in pursuit of utopian visions of universal harmony in which lions could be re-educated to lie down with lambs.[3]

Drastic labour shortages as a result of the ravages of war saw a significant influx of Eastern European people and Jews immediately following the end of the Second World War and this began an era in the mid-twentieth century during which these people suffered significantly from racist attitudes and practices. It was quite common in those times for European immigrants to be employed in conditions much inferior to those enjoyed by the Australian mainstream population. Many of these immigrants worked in appalling conditions on large scale construction projects such as the Snowy Mountains Hydro-Electric scheme. The Snowy Mountains scheme was conceived to create irrigation reserves to expand the agricultural outputs that were increasingly fuelling a booming post-war economy. The Commissioner of the scheme, Sir William Hudson toured Europe recruiting workers, telling them: "You will not be Balts or Slavs – you will be men of the Snowy", illustrating an assimilationist approach to ethnicity under which migrant workers were expected to develop fluency in the English language as quickly as possible and were discouraged from retaining their traditional cultural practices. Although this scheme is now considered to be the 'birthplace' of Australian multiculturalism, a number of commentators suggest that a national, romantic myth has developed in relation to this era in which a false image of multicultural harmony developed. Brook Thomas (2001:8), for instance, argues that the Australian "attempt to link multiculturalism with a tradition of social justice indulges in a flattering national myth".

The Nature and Extent of Racist Victimisation in Australia

As alluded to in the Introduction to this book, quantitative certainty about the extent of racial victimisation in most, if not all, countries is elusive. Clearly, not all

---

3 This quote comes from the paper "Rethinking the White Australia Policy", discussed later in this chapter that was accepted for publication in the October 2006 edition of the peer reviewed *Deakin Law Review*, but then blocked from publication on the strength of legal advice obtained by the University's management.

incidents of racist victimisation are reported, neither is there a universally accepted definition of which behaviours comprise racism. A 2003 survey by Kevin Dunn of the University of New South Wales began with the observation that although a number of Federal government inquiries into the extent of racism in Australia had been commissioned, the results of these inquiries had often not been released (Dunn, 2003). As we saw above, Australia is a highly multi-cultural nation – and in fact in the 2001 national census only 39 per cent of the population identified themselves as being of Australian ancestry. It would be surprising, therefore, if the 61 per cent of the population comprising the balance did not report a significant incidence of racist attitudes or some experience of racial tension. In Table 1.1 it can be seen that a large section of the population which identifies as being of non-Australian ancestry comes from a great diversity of ethnic origins.

Table 1.1 Reported racial ancestry – Australian population 2001

Number of people reporting a particular ancestry	Ancestries in descending order of numbers identifying
6.7 million	Australian
6.4 million	English
1.9 million	Irish
500,000 – 999,999	Italian, German, Chinese, Scottish
150,000 – 499,999	Greek, Dutch, Lebanese, Indian, Vietnamese, Polish, Maltese, Filipino, New Zealander, Croatian, Serbian, Australian Aboriginal, Welsh, Macedonian, French, Spanish, Maori, Hungarian, Russian, Sinhalese, Turkish, South African
20,000 – 49,999	American, Korean, Danish, Austrian, Portuguese, Ukrainian, Japanese, Indonesian, Samoan, Egyptian, Swedish, Jewish, Swiss, Chilean, Khmer, Thai, Canadian
10,000 – 19,999	Latvian, Iranian, Assyrian/Chaldean, Malay, Finnish, Bosnian, Mauritian, Norwegian, Czech, Fijian, Romanian, Tongan, Armenian, Slovene, Pakistani, Afghan, Anglo-Indian, Lithuanian, Iraqi, Burmese, Albanian, Syrian, Lao
5,000 – 9,999	Torres Strait Islander, Bengali, Papua New Guinean, Cook Islander, Tamil, Estonian, Slovak, Palestinian, Salvadoran, Argentinean, Timorese, Uruguayan, Somali
2,500 – 4,999	Peruvian, Kurdish, Taiwanese, Bulgarian, Sudanese, Brazilian, Colombian, Australian South Sea Islander, Coptic, Ethiopian, Nepalese, Zimbabwean, Jordanian, Hispanic (North American)
Less than 2,500	70 other ancestries

Source: Australian Bureau of Statistics (2001)

Over a three year period, between 1989 and 1991, the Human Rights and Equal Opportunity Commission (HREOC, 1991) concluded that although racist violence on the basis of ethnic identity in Australia is nowhere near the level that it is in many other countries, it nonetheless exists at a level that causes concern and it could increase in intensity and frequency unless firmly dealt with.[4] The Inquiry did conclude, however, that "racist attitudes and practices (conscious and unconscious) pervade our institutions, both public and private" (HREOC, 1998: 1).

Although the Inquiry reported that incidents of actual violence stemming from racism were usually in the form of 'one-off' unprovoked attacks from strangers, there was a clear indication that the greatest perceived threat to people of different ethnic backgrounds was a lack of institutional tolerance and understanding.

Dunn (2003) conducted a survey of 5,056 people in New South Wales and Queensland to collect data on the experience of racism and racial discrimination in both institutional and social settings. His survey found, conversely, that the frequency of overtly racist behaviours seemed to be greater in social rather than institutional settings and that most racism was experienced in settings such as shops, sporting events, restaurants and in the street. His research suggested that the most common forms of racism were name calling, disrespectful treatment and lack of trust. As we shall see later in the chapter, most of the legislation and government responses in Australia target the incidence of racism in institutional settings as these sorts of behaviours are obviously the easiest to verify and to regulate in the sense that those employed in institutional settings have legal obligations in relation to how they treat clients and other members of the public.

A summary of Dunn's data is presented in Table 1.2. The table shows respondents' responses in relation to personal instances of racial discrimination within institutional settings in Australia:

Table 1.2 Experience of racism in institutional settings

Experience of racism	In the workplace	In education	In housing	In policing
Speakers of a language other than English	35.6%	22.9%	16.3%	15.8%
Born overseas	35.2%	24.5%	15.9%	15.0%
Indigenous Australians	28.7%	36.2%	21.3%	23.4%

Source: Dunn (2003: 9)

As the Federal inquiries have noted (HREOC 2002: 2) it is very difficult to quantify the extent of racist victimisation based solely on reported incidents or even on the basis of surveys. Government agencies tend to collect data and compile reports on incidents which involve actual violence and racial violence is not the whole extent of racial victimisation or vilification. But if we accept that racial violence is the most extreme form of victimisation or vilification then we can readily see that racism

---

4 What constitutes a 'firm dealing with' of racist victimisation is a matter of conjecture.

is of course a problem in contemporary Australian society. The HREOC Inquiry cited above recorded 1,447 incidents of racially motivated violence and harassment (HREOC, 1998). Of course we could also argue that incidents of racist violence may act to encourage, or incite, others to behave in racist or intolerant ways. Two high profile cases of alleged racist behaviour and attitudes in recent years may help to indicate the ways in which racism is perceived and construed.

At a rugby league football ground in the rural Queensland town of Toowoomba there is a stand which carries the sign "The E.S. 'Nigger' Brown Stand". This sign was erected in memory of a local footballing hero whose name was Edward Stanley Brown, the stand having been named after him in 1960. An Australian aboriginal man, Steve Hagan attended a match at this ground with his family and was deeply offended at both the sign and the continued use of the word 'Nigger' by commentators at the ground to describe events happening in that stand during the match. Hagan wrote to the Trustees of the ground asking that they remove the offending sign. After they refused he pursued the matter in the Human Rights and Equal Opportunity Commission, the Federal Court and ultimately the High Court of Australia. At each stage he was unsuccessful. One High Court judge, Mary Gaudron, responded to the complaint by saying: "But your argument comes to this, does it not? Any person of any colour – let us assume pink persons who are offended because of any material, including for example, a pink truck, cement mixer, they think you should not use the pink – and it is called 'Pinky's Cement-Mixer' would automatically make out a complaint?" (*Hagan v. Trustees*, 2002).

Although Justice Gaudron was making a comment about the interpretation of a particular legislative provision I think we can identify a typical sort of public response to some issued of alleged racism. And that response is often that people of particular races are often overly sensitive to perceived racial slurs whether they are intended or not, or that we should avoid over-regulation of our behaviours for the sake of political correctness. But as a result of a successful complaint by Hagan to the UN's Committee on the Elimination of Racial Discrimination, some carefully considered and mature comments were made by the Committee about this particular issue and about the relationship between contemporary community standards and perceptions of racism. The Committee acknowledged that the original Mr. Brown (who was of Anglo-Saxon descent) had never objected to the sign in his lifetime, and that no complaint had been registered by any other member of the Toowoomba community in the 39 years that the sign had been displayed. But the Committee then advised that the Convention on the Elimination of All Forms of Racial Discrimination was a living document which must be interpreted by taking into account all the circumstances of contemporary society. In this context, the Committee advised, they had a duty to recall the increased sensitivities in respect of words such as the offending term appertaining today. They added that the memory of a distinguished sportsperson could be honoured in ways other than by maintaining and displaying a public sign considered to be racially offensive – and the Australian government was advised to take the necessary measures to secure the removal of the offending term from the sign in question, and to inform the Committee of what action was taken (*Steven Hagan v. Australia*).

Although the Trust which owned and managed the ground was a private body, the government could have taken a range of steps to implement the Committee's recommendation. Legislation could have been enacted to target that particular ground, or all similar sporting facilities, or a simple letter to the Trust strongly urging the removal of the sign could have been drafted. No action whatsoever was in fact taken by the Australian government in response to this recommendation. In fact, on a number of occasions the Australian government has criticised this UN body for unduly intruding in Australian domestic affairs. The lawyer who acted *pro bono* for Mr. Hagan in these proceedings, Willheim (2003:128) observes that "continuing display of the 'Nigger Brown' sign in the face of the clear recommendation from the Committee will serve to diminish Australia's standing as a nation that respects human rights".

Another high profile matter involving alleged racial vilification was that which involved arguably Australia's most listened to radio broadcaster, Alan Jones (*Western Aboriginal Legal Service Limited v. Jones*). During his daily 2UE radio program, Jones made comments about a case involving alleged discrimination against an Aboriginal woman seeking rental accommodation in the rural town of Dubbo. The Aboriginal woman went into a local real estate agency and asked for a list of available rental accommodation. She was told that nothing was available. The woman then asked a white friend to go into the office and make the same enquiry. The white woman was given information about available rental units. Jones comment, on air, was:

> So the Aboriginal woman argued discrimination and she got an award of $6,000. Now I think that it's a joke. And I tell you why I think it is. If I owned the only property on the real estate agent's list, the only property for letting, and a bloke walked through the door, and I don't care what colour he is, looking like a skunk and smelling like a skunk, with a sardine can on one foot and a sandshoe on the other, and a half drunk bottle of beer under the arm, and he wanted to rent the final property available and it was mine, I'd expect the agent to say 'no' without giving reasons. What discrimination would the agent be guilty of then?

Jones was pursued by an Indigenous advisory body on alleged charges of racial vilification. Although the matter was ultimately dismissed by the Administrative Appeals Tribunal on a technicality, the tribunal assigned to hear the evidence found that the ordinary reasonable listener would not have been incited to hatred by the remarks of Mr. Jones, but "would have been incited to serious contempt for and severe ridicule of Aboriginal persons in New South Wales on the ground of their race".

This matter touched on a raw nerve in the Australian community and was quite divisive at the time. There was a significant sector of the community who thought that racial vilification charges were extreme and a decision to pursue Jones was an attack on free speech. In the Australian legal and social environment, the purported right to free speech has always been a very influential factor in limiting the extent to which anti-discrimination and anti-racism laws are effective. But in this case, the Tribunal held that Jones's use of the words "and I don't care what colour he is" were not exculpatory, nor evidence that he was being overtly non-racist. The Tribunal looked behind the actual words used and said the ordinary reasonable listener would have understood the disclaimer to be a mere artifice – a shield behind which the broadcaster could say what he really felt about some potential aboriginal tenant. It is common knowledge that such a disclaimer is often used by many people to 'shield' the full force of their remarks in the event that they are called upon to account for them.

In another recent development, members of the Muslim community in Australia have expressed deep concern that the recently enacted *Anti-Terrorism Act 2005*, will unfairly penalise and discriminate against Muslims and people of Middle Eastern descent and ethnicity (Nettle, 2004). Control orders issued pursuant to this new law will enable police to put a person under house arrest, to force them to wear a tracking device, to prevent access to telephones or the internet and limit personal and civil rights in a number of other ways. These control orders can stay in place for up to one year, but can be immediately replaced with a subsequent order, meaning that a person could be subject to such restrictions on their liberty on a permanent basis. To issue the order, a judge needs to be convinced of its necessity simply on the balance of probabilities and not the usual criminal standard of beyond reasonable doubt. Muslim community leaders fear that this may lead to racial stereotyping and racial profiling.

Unfortunately Australia's main race protection law, the *Racial Discrimination Act*, was drafted more than 30 years ago and did not anticipate the political and demographic nature of the current era – and the *Anti-Terrorism Act* is unlikely to be challenged on the basis of that legislation. The terrorism legislation allows for random stop and search powers and it is not difficult to see why the Muslim and Middle Eastern community would fear that members of their community would be more likely to be subject to these 'random' searches. This sort of racial profiling, it is feared, could lead to community backlash against the Muslim population. In the parliamentary debates related to this legislation, Senator Kerry Nettle (2004) revealed that eight representatives of the Muslim community had visited her to report that many members of their community, especially women and children, were afraid to leave their homes or to be involved in Muslim cultural organisations for fear of being identified by ASIO (Australian Security Intelligence Organisation) as supporters of radical organisations and therefore vulnerable to incarceration under the Act.[5]

There is nothing in the Act to prevent racially and culturally inappropriate behaviour on behalf of officials – women who wear hijaab or niqaab who are required to partially disrobe to facilitate a search have no recourse or protection from insulting or discriminatory behaviour.

---

5 The Senator points out that these people "would not be caught under the scope of this terrorism legislation by picking up the phone and talking to their friends, going to a protest or giving money to Islamic community organisations" but treated these representations as evidence of the fear and *perceptions* of racial profiling that are genuinely felt. In the same report she notes that a non-Muslim offender convicted of exploding a bomb near a Sydney mosque was tried under the general criminal law, yet every Muslim person accused of similar offences had been pursued under the terrorism laws.

The potential marginalisation and demonising of the Muslim community in Australia is already being realised. Serious rioting involving the bashing of people of 'Middle Eastern appearance' and the burning of cars and buildings in the Eastern suburbs of Sydney in late 2005 were the first of their kind seen in Australia, sparked as they were by backlashes against the Sydney Muslim population. Large scale and violent demonstrations against people of other racial or religious backgrounds have been almost unheard of in modern Australia prior to this.

The rioting began as a protest by mostly local residents at Cronulla beach in Sydney's Eastern suburbs – which consists of a largely Caucasian population – but the beach is also popular with younger members of the large Muslim population of the Western suburbs. A large crowd of approximately 5,000 assembled in the area on 11 December 2005 in response to both extensive media coverage of an allegedly race motivated assault on three local volunteer lifeguards, and a series of SPAM-type mobile phone text messages broadcast in the week leading up to the riot.[6] The Sydney and national media had described the alleged assailants as "a number of Lebanese Muslim youths from the suburbs of Western Sydney" (*Sydney Morning Herald*, 2005: 1). A number of people identified as being of "Middle Eastern appearance" were chased and assaulted by the mob. Over the next few days the media reported incidents of retaliatory violence involving bashings by "people of Lebanese ethnicity", which included the burning of over 100 cars. Attacks were also reported on both Christian churches and on mosques (Leys and Box, 2005).

These emerging demonstrations of racism seen in the Sydney riots are based on conceptions of nationhood which are seen to be somehow antithetical to racial and cultural diversity. It was suggested in the introduction to this chapter that Australians see themselves as 'tolerant', but perhaps only to the extent that those to be tolerated are not perceived as a threat. Stereotypical views of what it means to be an Australian leave little room for divergence from the racial norm, which in Australia has traditionally been the Anglo-Saxon.

As we saw earlier in this chapter, the remnants of the White Australia policy, recently revived, modified and championed by the academic Andrew Fraser, seem to stem from a belief in a national culture in which minority cultures and ethnic groups are seen as a threat to the traditional identity of Australians. Inevitably there is a tendency to evaluate the credibility and acceptability of other ethnic groups on the basis of how closely they conform with the dominant national identity, however contrived or narrow that identity may be.

The fear and distrust bred by misconceptions about other races are at the heart of the HREOC's (1998: 1) definition of racism:

---

6 The sending of these mobile text messages (SMS – Short Message Service) to incite racially based violence would be an offence under the *Racial Hatred Act 1995* and several people have subsequently been charged with this offence as a result of the Cronulla riots. This is an emerging vehicle and platform for the dissemination of racial vilification content deserving of quantitative research – especially in SMS saturated jurisdictions such as Australia and Europe.

Racism is an ideology that gives expression to myths about other racial and ethnic groups that devalues and renders inferior those groups that reflects and is perpetuated by deeply rooted historical, social, cultural and power inequalities in society.

In very recent years there has been a marked increase in the number of people entering the country from Sudan, Afghanistan, Iraq and a number of Asian countries. One in five Australians now has at least one parent who was born in Asia (Australian Bureau of Statistics, 2005). An increase in African migration levels is a direct result of Federal government policy to target this area in filling its annual quota for the intake of refugees and asylum seekers. This recent change in migrant demographics has again seen an upsurge in racist victimisation and vilification, sometimes from surprising quarters. On 29 June 2005, the Sydney newspaper the *Paramatta Sun*, ran a front page story with a photo of a Sudanese couple being granted Australian citizenship, with a caption purporting a quote from their young daughter of "Now mum and dad are Aussies like me" (Heary, 2005). In response to this story, Andrew Fraser, a controversial associate professor in the Department of Public Law at Macquarie University wrote a letter to the Editor of the paper in which he is reported as saying that; "Experience practically everywhere in the world tells us that an expanding black population is a sure-fire recipe for increases in crime, violence and a wide range of other social problems" (Dick, 2005:1). Fraser articulates beliefs that sub-Saharan immigrants to the local area are more likely to commit criminal offences due to factors such as lower IQ's, heightened testosterone levels and poor 'impulse control'. Commenting upon the results of Asian students in his state's final year examinations he is reported as writing:

> Look at the annual HSC (Higher School Certificate) results – the consequence of which is that ... (Australia) ... is creating a new heavily Asian managerial-professional, ruling class that will feel no hesitation ... in promoting the narrow interests of their co-ethnics at the expense of white Australians (Dick, 2005: 1).

He concludes that: "The fact is that ordinary Australians are being pushed down the path to national suicide by their own political, religious and economic elites". Fraser urges Australia to withdraw from refugee conventions to avoid becoming 'a colony of the Third World'.

Although these comments would surely appear to many as being overtly racist, a number of Australian academics claim that they are misconceived and often misinterpreted but do not constitute racial vilification. This is despite the fact that the Deakin University Vice-Chancellor Sally Walker ordered that an article by Fraser be removed from the Deakin Law Review on advice that it was in breach of the *Racial Discrimination Act 1975*.

Despite Fraser's claims that race and ethnicity *simpliciter* have some causal correlation with levels of criminal behaviour, there is of course ample research to suggest that ethnicity is a less valid or useful predictor of crime than the social and economic environment of the offender. Mukherjee (1999) surveys the results of five major publications related to ethnicity and crime in 30 countries, including Australia, and points to a number of reasons why researchers ought to be wary of either statistical or anecdotal evidence which suggests a relationship between ethnicity and criminal behaviour. Migrants tend to have lower levels of education and training and therefore fewer life chances, and are forced by necessity to dwell in "poorer and disadvantaged city neighborhoods" (1999: 1). Mukherjee also reminds us that there are clear statistical correlations in many jurisdictions between unemployment and over-representation in arrest and imprisonment levels (1999: 6).

Over-representation is still a significant issue for Australia's Indigenous peoples. The Royal Commission into Aboriginal Deaths in Custody (RCIADIC) found that there was a very significant over-representation of Indigenous Australians in the criminal justice system in Australia, particularly in prisons. RCIAIDC found that approximately 2 per cent of the Australian population is of Aboriginal or Torres Strait Islander descent, yet close to 25 per cent of the prison population is comprised of Indigenous Australians (RCIADIC, 1991) and that an Indigenous person was 29 times more likely to be incarcerated in a police watch house or prison during their life time than a non-indigenous Australian. High visibility of Indigenous people and a substantial problem of 'over-policing' were found to be a important factors in this distressing trend.

Another focus of research in recent years has been the purported problem of so-called 'ethnic youth gangs', particularly in large metropolitan areas such as the Western suburbs of Sydney and Melbourne. Several high profile cases with very extensive levels of media coverage may have contributed to the perception that ethnic gangs are a persistent and chronic problem. The arrest and prosecution of a number of young ethnic men for a series of five brutal rapes in Sydney in 2000 and 2002 are illustrative. All those charged and convicted with the rapes were of 'Middle Eastern appearance' (in the first four rapes those charged were of Lebanese descent and in the fifth rape of Pakistani descent – all victims were women of European descent). These matters were noteworthy in terms of the political response to the perception that such offences were widespread. The New South Wales Premier, Bob Carr, named the offenders and identified the ethnic communities from which they came in the Parliament, attracting responses from the Lebanese community that this would lead to increased inter-racial tensions in the area. The Carr government went so far as to enact new legislation to create the offence of "aggravated sexual assault in company" to create significantly higher penalties for these offences.[7] It also enacted a new provision[8] preventing a person who was charged with a prescribed sexual offence, and not represented by a lawyer, from cross-examining certain witnesses themselves.[9] The right of an accused person to cross-examine those making allegations against them is usually considered to be one of the cornerstones of the adversarial system.

A major study sponsored by both the Australian Multicultural Foundation and the National Police Ethnic Advisory Bureau (White, Peronne, Guerra and Lampubnani, 1999) set out to investigate whether and to what extent such gangs existed, why they formed and how active they were. The study was motivated by "media and

---

7 Section 61JA *Crimes Act 1900* (NSW).

8 Section 294A *Criminal Procedure Act 1986* (NSW) – inserted 2003.

9 The offenders in these matters were at times unrepresented due to their belief that non-Muslim lawyers would not act impartially or in their best interests.

political concerns over 'ethnic youth gangs' in Melbourne in the early 1990's" (4). Perhaps predictably the report concluded that the perception that there were a significant number of ethnic 'gangs' with some sort of formal hierarchy and criminal objectives appeared spurious (although some gang activity, particularly related to drug distribution was clearly evident). One interesting finding was that even the young people surveyed found it difficult to comprehend what was meant by a 'gang' – and that there was a common conflation between being a member of a gang and being a member of some other social group with common ethnicity of members (such as a simple group of friends). Those surveyed for the report pointed to the problems associated with migration including lack of employment and vocational training, poor English language skills and lack of support services as contributing to the marginalisation and victimisation of ethnic youth in urban areas (White, Peronne, Guerra and Lampubnani, 1999).

The perception of a problem with 'ethnic youth gangs' represents a kind of racial victimisation in itself, especially given the increased police attention, adverse media coverage and racial profiling which is bound to ensue. Further, such a perception is symptomatic of a wider racial stereotyping which can lead to other forms of victimisation, such as racially-based violence and vilification, and risks inciting the kind of backlash that was seen in Cronulla in 2005.

The uncertainty as to the precise size of the problem of racially inspired violence in Australia has traditionally been attributed to two factors – the lack of published statistical data and a reluctance by victims to report attacks. The National Inquiry into Racist Violence (HREOC, 1991) found that police in all Australian jurisdictions failed to keep any statistics on racially motivated crimes. Although it may be administratively difficult for police services to do this, given that most offences are reported to them in terms of the type of offence committed rather than whether it was racially motivated, Johnson (2004) points out that an attempt to make some sort of statistical record would help communities to gauge whether perceptions of the racial motivation behind behaviour directed towards them are accurate.[10] Johnson recommends that statistics on ethnicity and crime should be collected at all stages of the criminal justice process including arrest and cautioning, prosecution and corrections.

The Emerging Specter of Cyber-racism in Australia

Apart from racial and economic demographics, another key factor in the incidence and targets of racial discrimination and victimisation in Australia has been the development of faster and more far reaching modes of mass communication and publication. McNamara (2002) notes that in its 1998 Annual Report into Anti-Semitism in Australia, the Council of Australian Jewry found that for that year there had been 324 reports of anti-Semitic violence, physical harassment, vandalism and intimidation. The Council further observed that an upsurge in anti-Semitic material

---

10 Johnson does, however, include some raw data collected by the Victorian Police Service in the period 1996–1997 relating to the country of birth of offenders. Data on the ethnicity of victims is much harder to come by.

was directly attributable to the accessibility of the internet. Although anti-Semitic groups and pseudo-political activists who espouse the deportation of non-Anglo Saxon people are certainly not unique to Australia, the lack of a binding Internet Code of Conduct for internet service providers (ISPs) and a strong tradition of free speech stemming from the vigorous politics of its colonial past, means that the development of the internet has seen a new and worrying expansion of racial vilification on a platform which virtually guarantees wide dissemination. The Race Discrimination Unit of HREOC believes that the internet represents the most prolific and potentially damaging forum for racist crime and vilification in Australia, noting that this may include material published on websites, in computer games, uploaded music with racist lyrics, open publishing sites and interactive media such as chat rooms and discussion forums (HREOC, 2002). At its 2002 Symposium on Cyber-Racism, HREOC published this example of racist content created by an Australian and posted on an Australian based website: (http://www.hreoc.gov.au/racial_ discrimination/cyberracism/examples.html).

> ...look at the bizarre form of transvestitism that (non Muslim) Arab Women practice. No amount of 'big hair', tight skirts, pancake makeup and electrolysis can conceal the fact that they are not attractive Women. They end up looking like cheap drag queens, a parody of Woman. I personally prefer a Woman with less facial hair than myself! The Birka, or full Arab headdress has far less to do with Muslim female modesty than it has to do with the embarrassment of the Muslim Arab male at his wife's ugliness.... (HREOC, 2002).

HREOC admits that legal regulation of the internet in Australia has so far been ineffective in responding to and eradicating racism in cyberspace. There have been some high profile investigations and prosecutions of individuals and organisations who publish cyber-racism, but very often the response is that this material is either transferred to file servers in other jurisdictions or the interaction of the people involved switches to the more private elements of the internet (such as password protected chat rooms) which may be outside the scope of current racial discrimination and vilification laws.

Legal, Agency and Social Responses to Racist Victimisation in Australia

Australia has implemented both Federal and State legislation to meet its obligations under the *International Convention on the Elimination of all Forms of Racial Discrimination*. The primary means of meeting these obligations was the enactment of the *Racial Discrimination Act 1975*, which has been used to successfully combat a large number of overtly racist behaviours and has even been used by the High Court of Australia to strike down legislation, which it considers to be in breach of the Act (although as discussed above this is unlikely to affect the validity of the new *Anti-Terrorism Act*).

All States and Territories in Australia have anti-discrimination legislation which prohibits discrimination in some areas (such as education, accommodation and employment) on the grounds of race. While this legislation has been moderately successful in combating high profile and obvious examples of racial discrimination, on the everyday and systemic levels it is less effective. A key addition to Australian law was the insertion of a provision into this Act, in 1995 which outlaws acts of "racial hatred" in public. This makes it unlawful for a person to commit an act which is reasonably likely to offend, insult, humiliate or intimidate another person or group of people, where the act is done because of the race, colour or national or ethnic origin of those people. The sorts of acts which can comprise racial hatred include speaking, singing, making gestures in public, displaying drawings or images in public or publishing in newspapers, leaflets or websites. It is interesting to note that when recently interviewed about the need for laws to criminalise acts of religious violence in Australia, the current Prime Minister John Howard was reported on a number of occasions as expressing his belief that racial vilification laws don't work.

Despite the Prime Minister's scepticism, these racial vilification laws have been effective on a number of occasions and demonstrate that they provide a legal remedy against some overtly racist activities which were not available in the past. A good example of this was the prosecution of Frederick Toben (*Toben v. Jones*) who posted material on the internet which claimed that there was doubt that the holocaust had occurred, that is was untrue that there had been gas chambers constructed for the purpose of executing Jews at Auschwitz and that a number of Australian Jews were deliberately exaggerating the extent of the 'alleged' holocaust for their own financial gain. The Federal Court found these acts of publication to be in breach of the racial hatred provisions and the website was ordered to be removed. Toben was subsequently imprisoned in Germany in relation to the same internet material, despite the fact that the website was created and uploaded in Australia. This is an indication that transnational racist behaviour can be effectively combated, at least in relation to publication on the internet.

The anti-discrimination and anti-racism laws may not be so effective, however, in combating institutional or government behaviour or policy, which unfairly discriminates against people based on their ethnic origin.

A current issue of concern to many commentators in Australia is the policies which are being implemented to deal with the increasing numbers of refugees and asylum seekers arriving in the country without following the regular refugee or immigration protocols. Although desperate situations and fearful threats to personal and family security often encourage people to flee their own countries to seek shelter elsewhere, there is a tendency in Australian government circles to label these people, if they do not or are not able to access Australian consular offices in their own countries as 'queue jumpers'. While it is reasonable to assume that a person living in the developed world or in a region which is not disrupted by war or civil unrest may be able to access consular offices to arrange appropriate visas and to file applications for immigration, those who live in the poorest and most fraught parts of the world surely do not have this luxury.

In order to try and avoid the operation of international human rights agreements and to deny some refugees the opportunity to apply for asylum, the Australian government enacted legislation to remove the regions of Christmas Island and the Ashmore Reef Islands from Australia's migration zone (DIMIA, 4) – a practice referred to as the 'Pacific Solution'. This meant that refugees arriving on these islands would no longer be considered as being within Australian territorial waters and therefore unable to lodge asylum applications (without the express permission of the Minister for Immigration).[11]

The move was prompted by the fact that an increasing number of people were arriving at these locations without entry visas after long and dangerous sea voyages from South Asian countries. Government policy was then to forcibly move these people to various other Pacific nations where there applications could then be made and considered, but without entering Australian territory and without the option of appeal to Australian courts. In return for housing these asylum seekers, the Pacific nations involved were offered huge aid packages. Complaints about the effects of these policies and the psychological effects of years in mandatory detention for those who were actually successful in reaching Australian territorial jurisdiction have been made to a number of United Nations bodies, including the Commission on Human Rights. The policies implemented by the Australian government in response to the increased numbers of people seeking asylum and refugee status in Australia have done little to foster attitudes of tolerance and acceptance towards people of different races and cultures. Rather, they have provoked increased distrust of refugees and asylum seekers, and of people of ethnic backgrounds generally, among the wider Australian community and have contributed to reinforcing racial stereotypes. One recent commentator goes so far as to suggest that these policies ought to be seen as instances of 'State crime' in which the sovereign state itself is the perpetrator of racist victimisation (Pickering, 2005).[12]

HREOC, the body charged with investigating and prosecuting cases of racism under the *Racial Discrimination Act*, has strong concerns that the regulation of racist victimisation in Australia is not currently effective enough to combat the underlying social issues which give rise to racist behaviour. A number of commentators have suggested that the original absence of criminal sanctions from the anti-racism legislation significantly weakened its deterrence value (the Act only provided for civil fines to be imposed). It is unlikely however, that criminal sanctions will have any far reaching or broad social effects, and the criminal provisions of the legislation, for serious racial vilification, have been virtually unused. Furthermore, there has been continual opposition to allowing police to investigate matters of serious vilification on the grounds that various police services in Australia have, in the eyes of some, a poor record when it comes to modeling values of racial, ethnic and religious tolerance (Nugent et al., 1989).[13] Legislation aimed at bolstering multiculturalism and promoting ethnic, racial or religious tolerance has obviously been effective in

---

11 According to Adrienne Millbank of the Australian Parliament's Social Policy Group (2000), the proportion of people arriving in Australia as unlawful asylum is seekers (often referred to colloquially as 'boat people') is less than 10 per cent of the overall number of illegal residents and immigrants – which the Group calculated to be 53, 143 persons.

12 Pickering argues that "the intensive regulation of the new regulatory state through increasing securitisation and control….undermines the rule of law whereby the law no longer operates in its ordinary sense but is an empowering agent for officials as regulators of citizens and non-citizens" (at p.207).

13 These researchers report a number of respondents to the National Inquiry into Racist Violence claimed that police had treated them as if they (the victims) were the real problem or that the violence must have been provoked by them in some way.

the prosecution of some matters, mostly those involving the mass media, but the fact is that laws and regulations are unlikely to create paradigmatic shifts in the community wide values and levels of intolerance which may be an expression of social, political and economic conditions. Perhaps the Australian Prime Minister's poor opinion of racial and vilification laws is inspired by observations of this nature. Thornton (1995: 89) suggests that in Australian (as in perhaps many developed nations) there is a: "latent racism that resides just beneath the social surface ever ready to erupt, particularly when the economy declines and competition for jobs is sharpened".

The continued emphasis placed on notions and implied rights of freedom of speech by legislators, judges, academics and media commentators also acts to limit the effectiveness of racial vilification laws. The belief that some expressions of intolerant attitudes, even if offensive in nature, ought to be protected on the grounds of these rights makes it unsurprising that criminal sanctions for racist behaviours are rarely, if ever, imposed. Avenues for complaint and enforcement are overwhelmingly those involving the initiation of proceedings with human rights bodies and tribunals. This places a heavy procedural and evidential burden on the victims of racist victimisation who require the confidence and ability to bring their matter before these civil authorities.

Law enforcement agencies in Australia have incorporated a peak body to advise the police services of each State and Territory on issues related to cultural, ethnic and linguistic diversity and to promote partnerships between ethnic communities and police. The Australian Police Multicultural Advisory Bureau (APMAB) has existed in some form since1993 and has a research as well as advisory role. One objective of the body is to: "encourage, support and conduct (where appropriate) research on relevant aspects of police and ethnic matters and practices; to monitor and evaluate policies, programs and other initiatives related to police-community issues for possible adoption by police jurisdictions" (APMAB, 2005). The need to forge meaningful partnerships between police services and local ethnic communities has long been recognised amongst senior police (see Palmer, 1992) and most jurisdictions now train and employ members of these communities as unsworn uniformed officers (usually lacking powers of arrest) who accompany regular officers on their duties in ethnic neighbourhoods and to incidents involving people of various ethnic communities.[14] Virtually no research is available on the success of these liaison officers, but the fact that the programs are still operating after nearly twenty years and their numbers are generally increasing[15] seems to indicate that they are of benefit.[16]

---

14 In Queensland these officers are called 'Police Liaison Officers'(PLO) and in New South Wales as 'Ethnic Community Liaison Officers'. In Queensland the PLO's work mainly with the Indigenous and Vietnamese communities.

15 A table listing full details of the numbers and focus of ethnic liaison officers in each State is available at http://www.apmab.gov.au/mlo/index.html.

16 The author has been involved in some training activities for Queensland PLO's and anecdotal evidence suggests that lack of training and career progression may be the main problems faces by these officers.

A number of ethnic peak bodies and advisory councils have also had some success in lobbying for responses and reform to racial victimisation. In 2003, the Australian Arabic Council (AAC) was able to convince the Victorian Police Service to abandon the term 'of Middle Eastern appearance' as an ethnic descriptor altogether from its operational manuals. The Victorians reduced the number of ethnic descriptors from 14 to just 4 (Aboriginal, Caucasian, Asian and 'other'). The AAC argued that the phrase was a creation of European cartographers and involves an assumption that those reporting and investigating crime can discriminate differences in appearance between Egyptians, Iranians and Yemenis (for example) and Greeks, Italians and Maltese (AAC, 2003). The Council noted that when a suspect is described as being "of Middle Eastern appearance" it encourages the perception that people with a Middle Eastern heritage are more likely to be involved in crime, but when the suspect is subsequently discovered to have no connection with these ethnicities, no apology to the relevant communities, or correction to the original description is forthcoming. It is worth noting that APMAB guidelines advise the use of these four ethnic descriptors only.

Conclusion

We began this chapter by observing an apparent disparity between the way Australia perceives itself as tolerant and accepting of cultural diversity and the way in which large sectors of the migrant and ethnic population perceive themselves as marginalised and victimised. We have seen that racial and ethnic tensions have been a persistent issue throughout Australian history, and that policy responses of the Australian government have done little to ease these tensions or to reduce the experience of racist victimisation.

As a result of some of the discussion throughout the chapter we might conclude that the term 'multicultural' is now used pejoratively in this country. In the major report on ethnicity and crime prepared by the Australian Institute of Criminology for the Department of Immigration and Indigenous and Multicultural Affairs, Mukherjee (1999: 115) makes the concluding observation that responses by various components of the criminal justice system to: "a few incidents of hate and bias is hardly the solution that will change a pervasive social enigma". Mukherjee advises, perhaps somewhat tritely, that the elimination of racist victimisation will require widespread acceptance of ethnic diversity by the Australian community.

What can be done to resolve this disparity and to promote this widespread acceptance is beyond the scope of this chapter. But effective responses to the problem of racist victimisation will require, at the very least, clear explications of its nature, causes and prevalence – and these clear explications have not yet emerged in the Australian literature. We discussed in the introduction to this chapter the problem of category confusion between race, ethnicity and religion and Mukherjee also observes that attempts to explain the interrelationships between ethnicity and crime rarely consider variables beyond the country or region of a person's origin (1999). And if we are to engage in cross-jurisdictional collaborative research we need to have some common ground as to what constitutes such fundamental characteristics 'ethnicity'[17] and 'victimisation', let alone what we conceive of as being 'indigenous', 'Muslim' or 'of Middle Eastern appearance'. Is it indeed useful or possible to separate concepts of ethnicity, race and religion when investigating the marginalisation of the 'Other'?

Many of the responses to issues of ethnicity and crime are reactive and not based on wide community consultation (such as the NSW government's legislative reforms in response to the spate of rapes in 2002). We also looked at evidence that although racial discrimination and racial hate legislation may be effective in dealing with individual cases of racist victimisation, their ability to effect systemic or community wide change is doubtful. If the answer to racist victimisation is indeed community acceptance and a true spirit of multiculturalism then punitive and reactive measures in isolation are clearly inadequate.

References

Australian Arabic Council – AAC. 2003. *Ethnicity & Crime in NSW: Politics, Rhetoric & Ethnic Descriptors*. Available online at: http://www.aac.org.au/print.php?ArtID=24 (retrieved 21 January 2006).

Australian Bureau of Statistics – ABS. 2001. *Census of Population and Housing 2001*. Available online at: http://www.abs.gov.au/ausstats/abs@census.nsf/4079a1bbd2a04b80ca256b9d00208f92/7dd97c937216e32fca256bbe008371f0!OpenDocument (retrieved 12 December 2005).

Australian Bureau of Statistics – ABS. 2005. *Migration Australia*. Report #3412.0 Canberra: Australian Bureau of Statistics.

Australian Police Multicultural Advisory Bureau – APMAB. 2005. *Corporate Philosophy*. Available online at: http://www.apmab.gov.au/bg/philosophy.html (retrieved 19 January 2006).

Broome, R. 1994. *Aboriginal Australians*. 2nd ed. Sydney: Allen and Unwin.

Department of Immigration, Multicultural and Indigenous Affairs – DIMIA. 2003. *Multicultural Australia: United in Diversity*. Canberra: Australian Government Printing Service.

Department of Immigration, and Multicultural and Indigenous Affairs – DIMIA. 2004. *Fact Sheet 81 – Australia's Excised off-shore Places*. Available online at: http://www.immi.gov.au/media/fact-sheets/81excised.htm (retrieved 8 January 2005).

Dick, T. 2005. 'Academic Stirs Fight Over Race', *The Sydney Morning Herald*, 16 July. Available online at: http://www.smh.com.au/news/national/academic-stirs-fight-over-race/2005/07/15/1121429359329.html?oneclick=true# (retrieved 12 December 2005).

---

17 Mukherjee (1999: 6) suggests, for instance, that although we might define 'ethnicity' to include first, second and third generation immigrants, data from virtually all available jurisdictions suggests that second and third generation immigrants are about as likely as those born in the country surveyed to be involved in crime (although the argument here may be that this relates to the person's involvement as a perpetrator, rather than as a victim, of crime).

Dunn, K. 2003. *Racism in Australia: findings of a survey on racist attitudes and experiences of racism.* National Europe Centre Paper No.77. Sydney: University of Sydney.

Fraser, A. 2005a. 'Rehabilitating (and Denaturing) the White Australia Policy: A Leftist Defence of Asian Exclusion', *American Renaissance* (February): 9–12.

Fraser, A. 2005b. 'Rethinking the White Australia Policy', unpublished paper.

Hagan v. Trustees of the Toowoomba Sports Ground Trust B17/2001 (19 March 2002). Transcript available online at: http://www.austlii.edu.au/cgi-bin/disp.pl/au/other/hca/transcripts/2001/B17/1.html?query=%5e+%20%28%2819+march+2002%2c+the+high+court+of+australia+%29+and+%28on%29%29

Steven Hagan v. Australia. United Nations Committee on the Elimination of Racial Discrimination, Communication No. 26/2002, UN Doc CERD/C/26/D/2002 (31 May, 2002).

Heary, M. 2005. 'Now Mum and Dad Are Aussies Like Me', The *Parramatta Sun*, June, 29:1.

Human Rights and Equal Opportunity Commission – HREOC. 1991. *Report of the National Inquiry into Racist Violence in Australia.* Available online at: http://www.multiculturalaustralia.edu.au/doc/racediscrimcomm_2.pdf (retrieved 18 November 2005).

Human Rights and Equal Opportunity Commission – HREOC. 1997. *Bringing them Home.* Sydney: HREOC.

Human Rights and Equal Opportunity Commission – HREOC. 1998. *Race for Business: A Training Resource Package.* Sydney: HREOC.

Human Rights and Equal Opportunity Commission – HREOC. 2002. *Cyber-Racism Symposium – Summary Report.* Available online at: http://www.hreoc.gov.au/racial_discrimination/cyberracism/ retrieved November 21, 2005).

Human Rights and Equal Opportunity Commission – HREOC. 2004. *Isma-Listen: National consultations on eliminating prejudice against Arab and Muslim Australians. Independent Research part 1: The Survey.* Available online at: http://www.hreoc.gov.au/racial_discrimination/isma/research/index.html#11 (retrieved 12 January 2006).

Johnson, H. 2005. 'Experiences of Crime in Two Migrant Communities' *Trends and Issues in Crime and Criminal Justice* (Issue 302). Canberra: Australian Institute of Criminology.

Leys, N. and Box, D. 2005. 'Church Attacks Spark Fears', *News Limited Online.* 15 December. Available online at: http://www.news.com.au/story/0,10117,17570541-2,00.html_(retrieved 12 January 2006).

McNamara, L. 2002. *Regulating Racism: Racial vilification laws in Australia.* Monograph Series No. 16. Sydney: Sydney Institute of Criminology.

Millbank, A. 2000. *Boat People, Illegal Migration and Asylum Seekers in Perspective*, Commonwealth of Australia Department of the Parliamentary Library, Current Issues Brief 13/1999–2000.

Mukherjee, S. 1999. *Ethnicity and Crime.* Trends and Issues in Crime and Criminal Justice. Paper No.117 Canberra: Australian Institute of Criminology.

Native Title Welfare Conference. 1961. 'The Policy of Assimilation'. Decisions of Commonwealth and State Ministers at the Native Welfare Conference, Canberra, 26–27 January 1961.

Nettle, K. (Senator). 2004. *Anti-Terrorism Bill 2004: Second Reading Debate*. Senate of Australia Hansard – June 17.

Nugent, S, M. Wilkie and R. Iredale. 1989. *Racist Violence*. Paper No.8 of a series of papers on violence, National Committee on Violence. Available online at: http://www.aic.gov.au/publications/vt/ (retrieved 21 January 2006).

Palmer, M. 1992. 'Policing in Partnership with a Multicultural Australia : The Challenge of the 1990's'. *Australian Journal of Public Administration*, 51(2): 244–247.

Pickering, S. 2005. *Refugees and State Crime*. Sydney: Federation Press.

Poynting, S. and G. Noble. 2004. 'Living with Racism: The experience and reporting by Arab and Muslim Australians of discrimination, abuse and violence since 11 September 2001'. Submission to HREOC's Isma-Listen: National consultations on eliminating prejudice against Arab and Muslim Australians, 19 April 2004.

Poynting, S., G. Noble, P. Tabar and J. Collins. 2004. *Bin Laden in the Suburbs: Criminalising the Arab Other*. Sydney: Institute of Criminology/Federation Press.

Royal Commission into Aboriginal Deaths in Custody. 1991. *National Report Volume 1* . Available online at: http://www.austlii.edu.au/au/special/rsjproject/rsjlibrary/rciadic/national/vol1/12.html (retrieved 11 December 2005).

Sydney Morning Herald (2005) 'Sydney's racist mob violence spreads', December 11: 1.

Thomas, B. 2001. 'Civic Multiculturalism and the Myth of Liberal Consent: A Comparative Analysis'. *The New Centennial Review*, 13: 1–35.

Thornton, M. 1995. 'Revisiting Race' in Race Relations Commissioner (ed). *Racial Discrimination Act 1975: A Review*. Canberra: Australian Government Publishing Service: 88–100.

Toben v. Jones [2003] FCAFC 137 (27 June 2003).

Wakim, J. 1992. 'The Gulf War Within the Australian Community and Arab Australians: Villains, Victims or Victors?' In G. Bird (Ed), *Racial Harassment*. Melbourne: Monash University, Melbourne National Centre for Cross-cultural Studies in Law: 51–58.

Western Aboriginal Legal Service Limited v. Jones & anor [2000] NSWADT 102 (31 July 2000).

White, R., S. Peronne, C. Guerra and R. Lampugnani. 1999. 'Ethnic Gangs in Australia: Do They Exist?' Report to the Australian Multicultural Foundation. Available online at: http://www.amf.net.au/rsch_youth_ethnicYouthGangs.shtml (retrieved 4 December 2005).

Willheim, E. 2003. 'Australia's Racial Vilification Laws Found Wanting? The "Nigger Brown" Saga', *Asia-Pacific Journal on Human Rights and the Law*, 1:86–129.

Helpful web links

In addition to the internet based documents specifically referenced above, researchers may also find the following more general sites useful:

http://www.hreoc.gov.au/racial_discrimination – Human Rights and Equal Opportunity Commission's racial discrimination portal.
http://www.immi.gov.au – Department of Immigration and Multicultural Affairs.
http://www.austlii.edu.au/au/other/IndigLRes/ – Indigenous law resources hosted by the Australian Legal Information Institute.
http://www.aic.gov.au/ – Australian Institute of Criminology.
http://www.indigenous.gov.au/ – Australian Government's Indigenous Portal.
http://www.abs.gov.au – Australian Bureau of Statistics.
http://www.racismnoway.com.au/ – Racism No Way. A national educational resource collection.
http://www.fecca.org.au/index.html – Federation of Ethnic Community Councils of Australia.
http://www.aiatsis.gov.au/ – Australian Institute of Aboriginal and Torres Strait Islander Studies.
http://www.refugeecouncil.org.au/ – Refugee Council of Australia.
http://www.rrt.gov.au/ – Refugee Review Tribunal.

Chapter 2

Canada

Jo-Anne Wemmers, Lisette Lafontaine and Louise Viau

Introduction

Canada is known internationally as a multi-ethnic and multi-cultural society. However, it is relatively recent that non-Europeans have begun to enter Canada in large numbers. While in 1961, almost 97 per cent of Canada's population was of European extraction, by 1991, this percentage dropped to only 60 per cent (Stenning, 2003). In the 1960s, changes to Canadian immigration policy put an end to national origin as a screening criterion and as a result immigration from different regions of the world such as the Caribbean, Central and South America, Asia and the Middle East, began to increase substantially (Silver et al., 2004). Thus, during the last 40 years, there have been major changes in the make-up of Canadian society.

Racial victimization refers to the victimization of an individual or a group because of their race or ethnic group (also, see Introduction to this text). Victimization is defined as a violation of the human rights of an individual or a group, including criminal victimization, by another individual or group of individuals. This definition places victims at the heart of our object of study. It encompasses both criminal and non-criminal offences such as name calling and insults. In addition, it covers victimization by fellow citizens (i.e., hate crimes) as well as victimization by authorities such as the police.

In this chapter we will examine the history of racial victimization in Canada and the legislation combating it. This is followed by a discussion of the research on the extent and the nature of racial victimization in Canada. Finally, the impact of racial victimization is addressed. The chapter closes with recommendations for policy and research.

Historical Background

Canada's history of immigration, has not been free of prejudice and intolerance. For example, in the late 19th century a 'head tax' was introduced for Chinese immigrants in order to discourage Chinese immigration to Canada (Backhouse, 1999). The immigration of European Jews fleeing the Holocaust in the middle of the 20th century was accompanied by growing anti-Semitism in many parts of Canada (Backhouse, 1999). During World War II, Japanese immigrants on the west coast were transported, interned, and dispossessed (Adachi, 1976) as were Italians and

Germans in Ontario and Quebec (Iacovetta et al., 2000). It wasn't until the 1970s that Canada adopted its first legislation against racial victimization.

While the federal government was slow to act, certain provinces took the lead. In 1947 under the leadership of former Premier Tommy Douglas, the province of Saskatchewan adopted the first general law prohibiting discrimination in Canada. The *Saskatchewan Bill of Rights Act* affirmed fundamental rights and prohibited various forms of discrimination, but lacked enforcement mechanisms and remedies necessary to enforce it. The first comprehensive legislation prohibiting discrimination and providing for an enforcement mechanism was the *Ontario Human Rights Act* adopted in 1962. It created the Ontario Human Rights Commission to oversee compliance with the Act. Prior to 1962, various laws dealt with different kinds of discrimination but there was no national or uniform policy in Canada.

In 1960, the federal Bill of Rights was adopted. This was a precursor to the *Canadian Charter of Rights and Freedom*. The Bill of Rights aimed to specify the rights of Canadians. However, it was not part of the Canadian Constitution and no remedy was provided in case of violation. This problem was corrected when, following the repatriation of Canada's Constitution from Great Britain, the *Canadian Charter of Rights and Freedom* was adopted. The Charter, which came into force on 17 April 1982, guarantees the right to equality. The Charter applies to all levels of government. As a result, discriminatory legislation, regulation or government policy or program would be found inconsistent with the Charter and therefore unconstitutional. The only exception to this rule is positive action, which allows minority groups to receive preferable treatment. After the coming into force of the Charter, all legislation was placed under judicial scrutiny to make sure that it does not contravene one of the constitutional rights (see *Canada Act 1982*, sec. 52).

In 1977, the federal government passed the *Canadian Human Rights Act*. The Act created the Canadian Human Rights Commission to administer the Act. The Act applies to the federal public sector and the private sector under federal jurisdiction. By 1979, all provinces had passed a human rights Act, applying to the public and private sector under their jurisdiction.

Inciting Hatred

The great immigration boom in the 1950s and 1960s generated concerns about racial and religious intolerance. At the same time, hate propaganda, and in particular anti-Semitic and anti-Negro literature, was perceived by many as being on the rise. Most of this hate propaganda came from the United States and was mainly disseminated as written material sent to Canada by mail (Kaplan, 1993). By 1964, many organizations concerned about respect for human rights were arguing in favour of new legislation prohibiting hate propaganda before it became a serious concern because of the perverse influence it might have in the long run. However, as the government tried to come to terms with its growing multiculturalism and egalitarian social values as well as the value of freedom of expression there was considerable debate and concern as to whether it would be possible to effectively and fairly define and articulate material intended to incite and/or promote racial discrimination within the Canadian socio-political context.

In January 1965, the then Minister of Justice of Canada, the Honourable Guy Favreau appointed a *Special Committee on Hate Propaganda in Canada* to study the question and report on the importance of the problem and the need for a legislative response to it. The Committee, chaired by Professor Maxwell Cohen, Dean of the Faculty of Law of McGill University, had also as members a representative of the Canadian Jewish Congress, Mr. Saul Hayes, and a representative of the media, Mr. Shane MacKay, executive editor of the *Winnipeg Free Press*. Some prominent members of the academic world were also on the Committee: Prof. Pierre-Elliott Trudeau, who would in 1968 become the Leader of the Liberal Party of Canada and Prime Minister of the Country; Prof. Mark R. MacGuigan, who would be elected as a member of Parliament in the coming years. Both of them were then associate law professors, Prof. Trudeau at the University of Montreal and Prof. MacGuigan at the University of Toronto. Also sitting on this Committee was Father Gerard Dion, professor at the Faculty of Social Sciences of the University Laval whose influence was great in convincing the other members of the Committee to look at the question in a broad way rather than from a strict legalistic point of view.

On 10 November 1965, the Special Committee presented its report to the then Minister of Justice of Canada, the Honourable Lucien Cardin. The Committee concluded that the existing legislation could not offer an appropriate answer to the problem of hate propaganda. Although the Committee was aware of the importance of the freedom of expression, it nonetheless concluded that:

> [t]he triumphs of Fascism in Italy, and National socialism in Germany through audaciously false propaganda have shown us how fragile tolerant liberal societies can be in certain circumstances. They have also shown us the large element of irrationality in human nature which makes people vulnerable to propaganda in times of stress and strain. Both experience and the changing circumstances of the age require us to look with great care at abuses of freedom of expression (Cohen, 1966, pp. 16–17).

After a perusal of the legislation that already existed in the *Criminal Code* and elsewhere in the federal laws, the Committee concluded that the current provisions of the *Criminal Code* concerning defamatory libel were too limited to prohibit the kind of harm being caused by hate propaganda. The Committee recommended that the *Criminal Code* be amended to introduce two new offences. The first one would prohibit the advocacy of genocide whereas the second one would prohibit public incitement of hatred against an identifiable group likely to occasion breach of the peace and group defamation. The Committee also proposed the inclusion in the Code of a broad definition of the expression "identifiable group" to encompass "any section of the public distinguished by religion, colour, race, language, ethnic or national origin" (Cohen, 1966, p. 115).

Nearly a year later, in 1966, the government tabled Bill S-49 in the Senate. A Special Joint Committee of the Senate and of the House of Commons was put in place to study the Bill that was almost identical to the draft legislation included in the Cohen Report. However, the parliamentary session ended before this Committee reported on its work. Thus, the Bill was not adopted. Between 1967 and 1969, the Bill returned to Parliament three times before it was finally adopted. Although the bill was strongly supported by the then Minister of Justice, the Honourable John

Turner, the proposed new criminal offences raised many concerns among members of Parliament. It was finally adopted in 1969 by a deeply divided House of Commons on a vote of 89 to 45, with 127 abstentions. The Bill had then to be adopted by the Senate: 39 senators voted in favour of the Bill and 24 voted against it. The new legislation entered into force in 1970 as sections 281.1 and 281.2. These sections are sections 318 and 319 of the current *Criminal Code*. We will return to these sections in our discussion of current legislation.

Sentencing Hate Crimes

The law regarding hatred was subsequently revisited by a Special Committee of the House of Commons in 1984 and the Law Reform Commission of Canada in 1986, both of which recommended improvement, including the addition of racial hatred as an aggravating factor in sentencing (Stenning, 2003). Section 718.2 of the *Criminal Code* was introduced by Bill C-41. It was tabled before Parliament in 1994. Assented to on 13 July 1995, the new legislation came into force on 3 September 1996. Considered by some to be the most significant statutory sentencing reform in Canada's history (Roberts and Hastings, 2001), the Bill introduced into the *Criminal Code* new sections describing the purpose and principles of sentencing judges would have to take into account in the determination of any sentence to be imposed on an offender. Among those principles, section 718.2a)i) of the *Criminal Code* prescribed that judges have to take into consideration: "evidence that the offence was motivated by bias, prejudice or hate based on race, national or ethnic origin, language, colour, religion, sex, age, mental or physical disability, sexual orientation, or any other similar factor." The honourable Allan Rock, then Minister of Justice, had to fight criticism from numerous Members of Parliament, particularly Members belonging to the Reform Party, and explain the reasons why the government considered it important to stipulate sentencing principles and in particular the adoption of "sexual orientation" to the list of hate-based factors.

Section 718.2a)i) of the *Criminal Code* distinguishes national and ethnic origin and, also, stipulates that language is a factor that has to be taken in account for sentencing purposes. Comparing this section with the definition of "identifiable group" for the purpose of sections 318 and 319 *Criminal Code*, a judge would have to conclude that the scope of the hate crimes created by these sections is more limited than the situations that have to be taken into account during the sentencing process for whatever offence that might have been motivated by hate. It is also more limited than the motives of discrimination included in the *Canadian Human Rights Act, 1985* which is somewhat different from the scope of section 718.2a)i) Cr. Code. This is because these sections interfere with freedom of expression guaranteed by section 2b) of the *Canadian Charter of Rights and Freedoms*.

Canadian Legislation Against Racism

Racism, understood as an opinion or belief, is not prohibited in Canada. However, manifestations of racism are prohibited by human rights legislation and, for the most extreme forms, by the criminal law. Criminal law prohibits inciting genocide or hatred. As well, the criminal law makes it an aggravating factor for sentencing purposes when any offence is motivated by bias, prejudice or hate based on enumerated factors which include race.

Protection from Institutional Racial Victimization

Equality before the law The right to equality is guaranteed by the *Canadian Charter of Rights and Freedoms*, which is part of the *Constitution Act*, 1982. Section 15 of the Charter provides that: "(e)very individual is equal before and under the law, and has the right to the equal protection and equal benefit of the law without discrimination and, in particular, without discrimination based on race, national or ethnic origin, colour, religion, sex, age or mental or physical disability." Although sexual orientation was NOT expressly protected by this section, the Supreme Court of Canada held in a 2000 ruling that it is: "clearly an analogous ground to the listed personal characteristics" (Little Sisters Book case). The Canadian Parliament had already added sexual orientation to the grounds of discrimination in the CHRA in 1996, and in 2000 it passed legislation to extend to same-sex couples the federal benefits available to heterosexual couples and impose the same obligations.

With respect to the protection against institutional racism within the criminal justice system, it is important to mention the *Canadian Multiculturalism Act* of 1988. This statute contains a declaration that multiculturalism is the policy of the Government of Canada and in particular, that it is the Government's policy to ensure that all individuals receive equal treatment and equal protection under the law, while respecting and valuing their diversity, and that all federal institutions (including the federal police force, the RCMP) shall generally carry on their activities in a manner that is sensitive and responsive to the multicultural reality of Canada.

Prohibition of discrimination in the Canadian Human Rights Act The *Canadian Human Rights Act*, which applies to the federal public and private sectors, is particularly important regarding discrimination in the private sector, such as non-criminal racial harassment in the workplace. The purpose of the *Canadian Human Rights Act*, stated in section 2 of the Act, is to provide equal opportunity without discriminatory practices based on prohibited grounds. The Act prohibits discriminatory practices, provides remedies to the victims and a mechanism for redress.

Discrimination is prohibited when it is based on one of the following grounds: race, national or ethnic origin, colour, religion, age, sex, sexual orientation, marital status, family status, disability and conviction for which a pardon has been granted (section 3).

Discriminatory practices are defined in sections 5 to 14.1 of the Act and include, when based on a prohibited ground, denying goods, services, facilities or accommodation that are available to the general public; refusing to employ a person; excluding a person from an employee organisation; publishing or displaying any notice or representation that implies discrimination; communicating repeatedly hate messages by telecommunication or electronic means, including through the Internet;

and harassing a person or retaliating against a person who filed a complaint for a discriminatory practice. The Act specifies that affirmative action measures for groups disadvantaged on the basis of the prohibited grounds are not discriminatory practices.

There is a Commission and a Tribunal to enforce the Act. The Commission receives and investigates complaints about discriminatory practices and refers those, which it considers founded, to the Human Rights Tribunal. The Commission's mandate also includes promoting information on the Act and the Commission, and research relating to the Commission duties and the principle of equality.

Section 40 of the Act provides that those who have reasonable grounds to believe that a person is engaging in a discriminatory practice may file a complaint with the Human Rights Commission. It should be noted that the complaint may be filed by anyone who is aware of the practice, not only by the victim. However, when a complaint is made by a person other than the victim, the Commission may require the consent of the alleged victim to deal with the complaint. The Commission can also initiate a complaint on its own.

The Commission must deal with complaints which are within its jurisdiction, unless a complaint can be more appropriately dealt with by other procedure, or is frivolous, or made in bad faith (section 41). The Commission assigns an investigator to the complaint. The investigator may apply to a judge to obtain a warrant to search specific premises, and the warrant will be granted if there are reasonable grounds to believe that there is evidence related to the complaint under investigation in the premises (section 43).

At any moment after the filing of a complaint, the Commission may request the Human Rights Tribunal to institute an inquiry into the complaint, if it is satisfied that an inquiry is warranted (section 49). The inquiry is conducted by one member of the Tribunal, or by a panel of three members if the matter is complex. The Tribunal hears the complainant and the person against whom the complaint was made, and any other interested party may be given the opportunity to appear at the inquiry, present evidence, and make representations either in person or through counsel (section 50).

After the inquiry, the Tribunal dismisses the complaint if it is not substantiated. If it is substantiated, the Act provides for a number of remedial orders that the Tribunal can make against the person who engaged in a discriminatory practice (section 53). The Tribunal may order the person to cease and desist from the practice and adopt measures to prevent it from happening again; to make available to the victim the rights or opportunities that have been denied as a result of the practice; to compensate the victim for wages lost or expenses or additional costs incurred as a result of the practice; to compensate the victim for pain and suffering in an amount not exceeding $20,000; and/or to pay a special compensation to the victim, not exceeding $20,000, when the Tribunal finds that the person has engaged wilfully or recklessly in the discriminatory practice. The Tribunal may make any one, or a combination, of these orders.

When the complaint relates to the discriminatory practice of communicating hate messages, there are three orders that the Tribunal may make: order to cease the practice; order a special compensation to the victim; and/or order the person to pay a penalty of no more than $10,000.

Criminal Victimization

While racism, as an opinion or a belief, is not a crime in Canada, inciting genocide and promoting hatred are crimes. In addition, any crime that is motivated by hate is subject to harsher punishment. In the following we will examine the legislation regarding criminal law protection against criminal racial victimization.

Inciting Genocide

Section 318 of the *Criminal Code* prohibits advocating or promoting genocide against an "identifiable group." At the time of its initial adoption, section 318 included in its definition of an identifiable group, any section of the public distinguished by colour, race, religion, or ethnic origin. The definition was amended in 2004 to include "sexual orientation."

Genocide is defined as: "any of the following acts committed with intent to destroy in whole or in part any identifiable group, namely: (a) killing members of the group; or (b) deliberately inflicting on the group conditions of life calculated to bring about its physical destruction." This definition is similar to the definition found in article 2(a) and (c) of the United Nations' *Convention on the Prevention and Punishment of the Crime of Genocide*.

The only Canadian jurisprudence dealing with promoting genocide is the case of *Mugesera v. Canada (Minister of Citizenship and Immigration)* [2005] 2 S.C.R. 91, which was decided by the Supreme Court of Canada in June 2005. In this case, Mr. Leon Mugesera, an ethnic Hutu and former Rwandan politician living in Quebec for over ten years as a permanent resident, was found inadmissible to Canada pursuant to the *Immigration Act* because a speech he had made in Rwanda constituted incitement to genocide. In seeking his deportation, Canada alleged that Mugesera had incited genocide, murder and racial hatred against the Tutsi minority in a 1992 speech, and was therefore inadmissible to Canada due to crimes against humanity and incitement to genocide. Mr. Mugesera was not charged with the criminal offence of promoting genocide in Canada. His case was based on the *Immigration Act* and he was therefore tried under administrative rather than criminal law. As a result, a lesser burden of proof was applied. Nevertheless, the ruling of the Court is instructive and binding as to the essential elements of the offence of promoting genocide.

The Supreme Court of Canada decided, that in the circumstances it was delivered, Mr. Mugesera's speech incited to genocide. In order to arrive at the decision, the Court examined the elements of the offence under section 318. First, the Court stated that it was not necessary to establish a direct causal link between the speech and any acts of murder or violence committed in Rwanda. Because incitement is an inchoate offence, it is punishable by virtue of the criminal act alone, irrespective of the result.

Second, the Court stated that the incitement had to be direct and public. Section 318 does not refer to incitement made in public, but this element can be inferred from the activities of advocating and promoting, which require an audience. Also, the Court noted that this offence was based on Article III of the *UN Genocide Convention*, which requires making punishable "direct and public incitement to commit genocide."

To satisfy the direct element, the incitement must specifically provoke another to engage in a criminal act. The incitement requires more than vague or indirect suggestion. The direct element must be appreciated in light of its cultural content, and of the audience that receives it. The Court did not elaborate on the public element as it was not an issue in the case, the alleged incitement having been made during a public speech in a public place.

The required *mens rea* for advocating and promoting genocide is intent to directly prompt or provoke another to commit genocide. The Court said that the person who incites must also have the specific intent to commit genocide and a desire to cause another to have the state of mind necessary to commit genocide, as defined in section 318 of the *Criminal Code*. Intent can be inferred from circumstances, such as: "systematic perpetration of other culpable acts against the group; the scale of any atrocities that are committed and their general nature in a region or a country; or the fact that victims are deliberately and systematically targeted on account of their membership in a particular group while the members of other groups are left alone" (*Mugesera* at para. 89). The environment in which a statement is made can also be an indicator of the intent, as it will affect the impact of the statement. Inciting genocide is an indictable offence punishable by a maximum penalty of five years of imprisonment.

Inciting or Promoting Hatred

Section 319 of the *Criminal Code* makes it an offence to incite hatred against an identifiable group by communicating statements in a public place where this incitement could result in a breach of the peace (subsection 1) or to wilfully promote hatred against an identifiable group by communicating statements other than in a private conversation (subsection 2).

The word "statement" is defined in subsection (7) to include: "words spoken or written or recorded electronically or electromagnetically or otherwise, and gestures, signs or other visible representations." The *Code* also defines "communicating" to include "communicating by telephone, broadcasting, or other audible or visible means."

In *R. v. Keegstra*, the Supreme Court of Canada examined the meaning of the word: "hatred." The Court said that it is not a word of casual connotation. In the context of these offences, the word "connotes emotion of an intense and extreme nature that is clearly associated with vilification and detestation." It is an emotion that implies that those against whom it is exercised are to be: "despised, scorned, denied respect and made subject to ill-treatment." To promote hatred is to instil detestation, enmity, ill-will and malevolence in another.

The offence of inciting hatred The offence under subsection 319(1) covers situations where a person makes a statement promoting hatred in circumstances where it constitutes a serious risk of bringing about an immediate reaction from the audience. The *actus reus* of the offence consists in a statement, made in a public place, inciting hatred against an identifiable group, and likely to lead to a breach of the peace. A public place is defined in subsection (7) as: "any place to which the public have access as of right or by invitation, express or implied." The statement must be considered objectively, by a reasonable person, in the circumstances and the context in which it was delivered. The tone and manner in which the speech was delivered, and the audience to whom it was addressed, should also be taken into account in determining whether the statement incites hatred. The guilty mind, or mens rea, required for this offence is something less than intentional promotion of hatred (Keegstra).

This offence can be prosecuted as an indictable offence or as a summary conviction offence. When prosecuted by indictment, the offence is punishable by a maximum penalty of two years of imprisonment, and to a maximum penalty of six months of imprisonment and/or a fine of no more than two thousand dollars when prosecuted on summary conviction.

The offence of wilfully promoting hatred The offence of subsection 319(2) applies to a statement wilfully promoting hatred against an identifiable group and communicated other than in a private conversation. This provision does not prohibit views expressed privately. In *R. v. Keegstra*, the Supreme Court of Canada commented that a conversation intended to be private remains private conversation even though: "through accident or negligence an individual's expression of hatred for an identifiable group is made public" (Keegstra, para 107). Therefore, a private conversation conducted in a public place and overheard by individuals not privy to this conversation, would not fall within the purview of the offence.

The word "promotes" indicates active support or instigation. It indicates more than simple encouragement or advancement. Direct and active stimulation of hatred against an identifiable group must be intended or foreseen as substantially certain (Keegstra, para 115). In the *R. v. Keegstra* case, the accused, a high school teacher, was charged with this offence because of anti-semitic statements that he made in his lectures.

The offence also requires the promotion of hatred to be wilfull. The meaning of this word has been examined by the Ontario Court of Appeal in *R. v. Buzzanga and Durocher* ((1979) 49 *Canadian Criminal Code* (2nd) 369) referred to by the Supreme Court of Canada in *R. v. Keegstra* (1990). The Courts concluded that, in the context of subsection 319(2), wilfully meant with the intention of promoting hatred and did not include recklessness.

There are four specific defences to this offence. A person will not be convicted of the offence:

1. if the person establishes that the statement was true;
2. if the person expressed in good faith an opinion on a religious subject or based on a religious text;
3. if the person believed, on reasonable grounds, the statement to be true and the statement was relevant to a subject of public interest discussed for the public benefit; or
4. if the person intended in good faith to point out, for the purpose of removal, matters tending to produce feelings of hatred against an identifiable group.

An offence under subsection 319(2) is either an indictable offence or a summary conviction offence. A person found guilty of an offence is subject to a maximum penalty of two years of imprisonment if the offence is prosecuted by indictment and subject to a maximum penalty of six months of imprisonment and/or a fine of a maximum of $2,000 if the offence is prosecuted as a summary conviction offence.

The offence of wilfully promoting hatred against an identifiable group was challenged on the ground that it was inconsistent with section 2(b) of the *Canadian Charter of Rights and Freedoms*, which guarantees freedom of expression. In the *Keegstra* decision in 1990, the Supreme Court of Canada upheld the provision. The Court found unanimously that the provision interfered with freedom of expression, but held by a 4/3 division that it constituted a reasonable limit in a free and democratic society, as provided for in section 1 of the *Canadian Charter*.

It is worth noting that the communication of hate messages can either be found a discriminatory practice under the *Canadian Human Rights Act (CHRA)* or prosecuted as an offence under the *Criminal Code*. The process and consequences are different whether it is treated as a human rights case or as a criminal case. There are important differences in the initiation of the proceedings, the evidence to be presented, and the decision rendered. The main differences are the following:

1. It is the Human Rights Commission that decides to bring a discriminatory practice before the Human Rights Tribunal, while it is generally the police who lay an information for a prosecution before a court of criminal jurisdiction.
2. The standard of evidence is the balance of probability before the Human Rights Tribunal while it is "beyond reasonable doubt" before a court of criminal jurisdiction.
3. There is no criminal liability attached to the finding that a conduct constitutes a discriminatory practice under the *CHRA*, while a person will be held criminally responsible if found guilty of an offence of hate propaganda.
4. There are four specific defences to the *Criminal Code* offence, which are not available under the *CHRA*.
5. No intent is required under the *CHRA* while the offender must wilfully promote hatred under the *Criminal Code*.
6. Private conversations are excluded from the offence under the *Criminal Code*, but are not excluded for purposes of discriminatory practice.
7. The decision of the Human Rights Tribunal provides a remedy for the victim while the decision of the criminal court punishes the offender.

As a result of these differences, the communication of statements that would not constitute a criminal offence can constitute a discriminatory practice under the *CHRA*. Indeed, the *CHRA* has been so far more frequently used than the *Criminal Code* by victims of hate statements.

Seizure and forfeiture Subsection 319(4) of the *Criminal Code* provides that the judge may order the forfeiture to the Crown of all instruments used in the commission or in relation to the offence.

Section 320 provides for the forfeiture of hate propaganda material kept for sale or distribution, and section 320.1 provides for the deletion from the Internet of hate propaganda material available to the public. Hate propaganda is defined as: "any writing, sign or visible representation that advocates or promotes genocide or the communication of which by any person would constitute an offence under section 319" (subsection 320(8) Cr. Code). The forfeiture provision is an *in rem* procedure that applies independently from charges being laid. The material found in Canada can therefore be destroyed to avoid its distribution even when the communicator of the statement is unknown or, mostly in the case of material on the Internet, when the communicator is outside the jurisdiction of Canadian courts.

Hate Crimes

Apart from the criminal offences of inciting genocide and promoting hatred, any *Criminal Code* offence constitutes a hate crime when it was motivated by: "bias, prejudice or hate based on race, national or ethnic origin, language, colour, religion, sex, age, mental or physical disability, sexual orientation or any other similar factor" (subparagraph 718.2(a)(i)). When there is evidence that an offence was so motivated, section 718.2 provides that it is an aggravating circumstance for sentencing purposes. As a result, the sentence should be increased to take account of this aggravating factor.

A finding that an offence is a hate crime under section 718.2 does not allow the judge to impose a penalty higher than the maximum penalty available for the offence. However, it means that the judge should impose a sentence that will be closer to the maximum available than would have otherwise been imposed if the offence had not constituted a hate crime.

Offences that are more likely to be motivated by racism or other prohibited grounds include: assault (sections 266, 267 and 268 of the *Criminal Code*); mischief (section 430); threatening a person (section 264.1); publication of a defamatory libel (sections 300 and 301); criminal harassment (section 264); or harassment through repeated telephone calls (subsection 372(3)).

It is difficult to measure the impact of this provision on the length of sentences. When evidence of hate motivation is provided by the Crown, judges generally mention that they have taken this element into account in deciding of the sentence, but rarely indicate by how much they have lengthened the sentence because of hate motivation.

The Extent and Nature of Racial Victimization

As noted earlier, racial victimization refers to the violation of the human rights of an individual or group because of their race or ethnicity. This can be criminal (e.g., hate crimes) or non-criminal (e.g., name-calling) as well as by an individual or a group (e.g., institutionalized racism). Important questions are whether racial victimization is common or uncommon and what are the different forms that it takes? In the following, an overview of the available research on the extent and the nature of racial victimization will be presented.

Prevalence

Since the 1990s there have been various efforts to measure and document the extent and nature of hate-motivated crimes. Each study is fraught with limitations, but together they give us some insight into the scope and the nature of racial victimization in Canada.

One of the first comprehensive studies on hate-motivated crime in Canada was conducted by Julian Roberts (1995). Commissioned by the Department of Justice Canada, in the run up to Bill C-41, which allowed stiffer punishment to be given for hate-motivated crimes, the study aimed to establish the incidence of hate crime in Canada. Using available police data and aggregate data from community groups such as B'nai Brith and Gay and Lesbian groups, Roberts estimated that annually, 60,000 hate-motivated crimes were committed in Canada's major centres.

Roberts' study highlighted many of the existing shortcomings with the available data. To begin with, there was little agreement between police forces on the definition of hate crimes. While everyone agreed that victimization based on race or sexual orientation would constitute a hate crime, gender was not always included in their definition (Roberts, 1995; Faulkner, 2003). Consequently, crimes like the 1989 Montreal Massacre, in which Marc Lepine clearly targeted women, would not be considered to be a hate crime by police in Winnipeg, Ottawa or Edmonton (Roberts, 1995). At the time of completing this chapter, there was still no practical definition for police of what constitutes a hate crime and there is no national standard for the collection of hate crime statistics (Silver, et al., 2004).

Nevertheless, since the 1990s there have been continued efforts to encourage the police to keep standardized data on hate crime. The Canadian Centre for Justice Statistics, in collaboration with 12 major police forces[1] launched the Hate Crime Pilot Survey, which is an important step towards the introduction of systematic police data on hate crimes in Canada. However, the data is not representative for Canada and, while each of the police forces was collecting information on hate crime, the information was not gathered in any uniform or standardized format (Silver et al., 2004). These are major limitations and great caution must be used when interpreting the results.

---

1 The 12 police forces that participated in the study are: Calgary, Edmonton, Toronto, Halton Regional, Montreal, Regina, Windsor, Winnipeg, Sudbury, Ottawa, Waterloo and the RCMP.

The Hate Crime Pilot Survey collected data from the participating police forces for the years 2001 and 2002. During this period, 1,119 criminal and non-criminal incidents were reported to police, of which 928 were classified by the police as criminal hate incidents. The remaining 191 incidents were non-criminal incidents such as arguments and insults (Silver et al., 2004). Police data is, however, incomplete. More than half (59 per cent) of all victimizations are never reported to the police (Besserer and Trainor, 2000). Although some studies suggest that hate crimes are underreported to the police (Bowling, 1994; Levin and McDevitt, 1993) the Canadian victimization survey data suggest that hate crimes are reported more often than non hate crimes. In 1999, 37 per cent[2] of all victimizations were reported to police while 45 per cent of all hate crimes were reported to the police (Silver et al., 2004). Research in the UK on racial victimization suggests that police attitudes towards racial harassment and violence may influence victims' reporting of hate motivated crimes (Phillips and Sampson, 1998; also see Webster in this collection). Unless police forces have dedicated units that are sensitized to the issues and receive the necessary ongoing training, they are unlikely to be able to collect the required evidence to support a prosecution (League for Human Rights B'nai Brith, 2005). The inadequacies of the police data make it vital to assess victims' experiences. In 1999, for the first time, hate-motivated victimization was included in Statistics Canada's General Social Survey (GSS), a national victimization survey which was first introduced in the 1980s. The definition of hate crime used in the GSS included *crimes motivated by the offender's hatred of a person's sex, ethnicity, race, religion, sexual orientation, age, disability, culture or language.* By asking victims instead of police, the study revealed that 4 per cent of victimizations were hate motivated and that this translated to 272,732 incidents annually (Janhevich, 2001). The 2004 victimization survey shows similar results: 4 per cent of victimizations were hate motivated (Gannon and Mihorean, 2005).

However, the GSS also has its limitations. While the GSS provides access to victims, the number of respondents in the sample from minority groups is small. Thus, problems that are specific to minority groups may not be well represented in the sample, which may lead to underestimation of their victimization. In order to obtain a sample with sufficient ethnic minorities, Statistics Canada introduced the Ethnic Diversity Survey (EDS) in 2002. Although the study is aimed at understanding the various ethnic and cultural backgrounds of Canada's population rather than victimization, respondents are asked *if in the last five years or since their arrival in Canada, they were a victim of assault, fraud, robbery or vandalism.* Those who report that they have been victimized are then presented a definition of hate crime and asked if they believe that any of their victimizations could be considered a hate crime. The definition for hate crime presented is : "In Canada hate crimes are legally defined as crimes motivated by the offender's bias, prejudice or hatred based on the victim's race, nationality or ethnic origin, language, colour, religion, sex, age, mental or physical disability, sexual orientation or any other similar factor" (Silver, et al., 2004: 5).

---

2 5 per cent of respondents didn't know if the vicitimization had been reported to police or not.

The EDS, which targets ethnic minorities, found a much higher rate of hate-motivated incidents than other studies. No less than 9 per cent of victimizations in the past five years were considered hate crimes. This percentage is twice as high as that found in the 1999 and 2004 GSS (4 per cent). Thus, suggesting that the actual incidence of hate motivated victimization in the general population may be much higher than was previously thought.

However, the GSS, EDS and the police data are limited to criminal victimizations. Incidents such as name calling and racial slurs are not crimes and do not fall under the GSS or the EDS. Data collected by the League for Human Rights of B'nai Brith Canada (2005) on anti-semitic incidents in Canada shows that much racial victimizations is not criminal. To the frustration of many victims, harassment such as name calling, even where there are repeated episodes, does not amount to a crime, unless criminal harassment can be proven. In a similar vein, US data suggest that ethnic harassment in the workplace represents the largest proportion of racial victimizations (Bryant-Davis and Ocampo, 2005a). A study by Schneider et al. (2000) found that between 40 to 67 per cent of Hispanic participants experienced ethnic harassment in the workplace. The most common form of harassment found in this study was verbal ethnic harassment such as racist jokes and insults. While such acts are not criminal, as we will see later, they can be traumatic for the individual. Thus, much racial victimization is not currently being captured in the available surveys because they focus exclusively on criminal victimization.

The B'nai Brith data is also interesting because the League has been keeping a record of anti-semitic incidents in Canada since the mid–1980s. Each year the League publishes an annual *Audit of Anti-semitic Incidents in Canada*. In 2006, 935 incidents were recorded which represents the highest number in the history of the Audit. Since 2000, the total number of incidents recorded by the League has more than tripled (League for Human Rights B'nai Brith Canada, 2005). However, the 1999 and 2004 GSS do not show an increase in hate victimization (Silver et al., 2004). Thus we cannot simply conclude that racial victimization is on the rise.

Another important limitation in the GSS, EDS and police data is that they focus on crimes by citizens against citizens. Systemic racial victimization within social institutions, like the criminal justice system, is excluded from these studies (Faulkner, 2003). Researchers, such as Wortley (2003), argue that Canada's criminal justice system is fraught with racism. In 1992, the Ontario Government established a Commission on Systemic Racism in the Ontario Criminal Justice System. After three years of hearings, the Commission published its report in which it claimed that well-founded concerns about systematic racism in police practices were widespread (Commission on Systemic Racism, 1995). In addition, the Commission found evidence of racial discrimination among private policing organisations (i.e., security guards). While the Commission's report constitutes the most comprehensive examination of issues of systemic discrimination in policing in Canada, many of its recommendations have not been acted upon (Stenning, 2003). Wortley (2003) makes a case that the over-representation of visible minorities in prison may be due to bias at the pre-trial stage. However, police in Canada are not required to report the race of the people they target for field investigations and the absence of data makes it hard to prove police discrimination. Citing British and American research, Wortely argues that visible minorities have a greater probability of being stopped by police, killed or injured, and denied bail. If they are granted bail, then they are given more conditions with it, which makes violation of conditions more likely.

To summarize, while various attempts to measure racial victimization have been made, each study is fraught with limitations. Only a fraction of offences are ever reported to the police, which makes police data an unreliable source of information. The self-report victimization data are not filtered by the police; however, they only focus on certain types of criminal victimization. The B'nai Brith data is not limited to criminal victimization; however, it only looks at anti-semitism. Research on systematic racial victimization in social institutions is excluded from all organized studies. Thus, the actual incidence of racial victimization in Canada is unknown.

The Victimizations

Hate crimes tend to be violent crimes rather than non-violent property offences. The 1999 GSS data revealed that about three-quarters (77 per cent) of hate crimes recorded were personal offences compared to 58 per cent of non-hate related incidents. In addition, almost half (49 per cent) of all hate crimes were assaults (Janhevich, 2001). Similar results are reported in the 2004 GSS survey (Gannon and Mihorean, 2005). The limited police data that is available also shows that most victimizations are crimes against the person (52 per cent), followed by property offences (31 per cent). The remaining hate crimes (17 per cent) were other violations such as hate propaganda (Silver et al., 2004).

However, the data from the League for Human Rights of B'nai Brith Canada (2005) suggest that most racial victimization is not violent crime but non-criminal harassment. In 2004, the League registered 857 incidents, which were classified as follows: 457 (53.3 per cent) harassment; 369 (43.1 per cent) vandalism; and 31 (3.6 per cent) violence. As we will see later, even when it is not considered criminal, the impact of harassment on the victim can be considerable. We will return to racial violence later in our discussion of the impact of racial victimization.

The Victims

Hate crimes often target the victim's race or ethnic origin. The findings from the 2004 GSS show that 65 per cent of hate-motivated victimizations target the victim's race or ethnic origin while one quarter (26 per cent) target the victim's gender, 14 per cent target their religion and 12 per cent are directed at the victim's sexual orientation (Gannon and Milhorean, 2005). The data from the Hate Crime Pilot Survey also show that hate crimes most often target the victim's race. Incidents motivated by race or ethnicity accounted for more than half (57 per cent) of all hate crime recorded by police, followed by those targeting religion (43 per cent) and sexual orientation (10 per cent) (Silver et al., 2004).

Similarly, the EDS data found that visible minorities were over-represented among hate crime victims (Silver et al., 2004). In particular, visible minority men in the EDS study experienced hate crime at more than double the rate of men who are not a visible minority (26 per 1,000 vs. 12 per 1,000).

The EDS also examined whether immigrants or Canadian-born visible minorities are more at risk of hate-motivated victimization. This is interesting from a Cultural-Conflict perspective, which sees crime and victimization as the result of a conflict between cultures (Wortley, 2003). Surprisingly, not immigrants but Canadian-born visible minorities had the highest hate crime victimization rate, at 31 per 1,000 population (Silver et al., 2004). Thus, it is the second generation immigrants, who are familiar both with Canadian culture and that of their parents, who appear to be particularly at risk. It is unclear whether this finding reflects a bias against second generation immigrants or that this group is more sensitive to racial victimization and therefore more likely to perceive an act as racially motivated than new immigrants who are less familiar with Canadian culture.

The Offenders

Relatively little data is available about those who commit racial victimization as most offenders are never identified. The Hate Crime Pilot Survey, which only captures a small, non-representative portion of hate crimes, shows that in 48 per cent of all hate crime incidents recorded by the police there was a chargeable accused identified. Based on the cases solved by the police, we can identify offender characteristics. In the majority of cases (86 per cent) only one perpetrator was involved in the offence. Most of the accused (83 per cent) were strangers to the victim. In 15 per cent of the cases, the accused was a casual acquaintance or a business relationship (Silver et al., 2004). The majority of the accused are male (84 per cent). The average age of the accused was 29.5 years. Most of the accused did not have a prior police record: fewer than one-in-ten had been involved in previous criminal activity.

However, the police data may not be representative for all offenders. The 1999 GSS results indicate that in almost half of all cases (46 per cent) the perpetrator was unknown to the victim (Silver, et al. 2004). This is substantially lower than that found in the police data. Some authors argue that in cases where the perpetrator is known, victims will often not report the crime because they fear retaliation (Weis, 1997). The higher proportion of crimes committed by strangers found in the police data may reflect victims' reluctance to report the crime to the police when the offender is someone they know.

Impact on Victims

Statistics fail to convey a sense of the true harm inflicted upon the individuals and groups that are the target of racial victimization. The harm lies in the consequences for the individual, his or her family as well as the group. While our discussion on the extent and the nature of racial victimization has focused on the Canadian situation, in this section we present international research. This is in part due to the lack of available research on the impact of racial victimization in Canada. In addition, research with crime victims shows great agreement across western cultures with respect to the impact of victimization (UNODCCP, 1999). Thus while we must bear in mind that much of the research that is presented does not focus on Canadian victims, this does not exclude the possibility that the research findings are relevant in Canada.

Impact On The Individual

Physical impact According to police data, hate motivated assaults resulted in greater physical injury than other types of assaults (Levin and McDevitt, 1993; Roberts, 1995). For example, Levin and McDevitt (1993) found that 30 per cent of hate crime assaults require treatment at a hospital while only 7 per cent of assaults in general require hospitalization.

However, these findings may say more about when victims are likely to report hate motivated victimizations to the police than about the nature of racial victimizations. It is possible that victims are more likely to report their experience to the police when this resulted in physical injury than when the violence is uniquely psychological. This example illustrates how important it is that we understand the social processes that generate hate crime statistics. Without an understanding of what leads people to report hate crimes and how their reports are recorded, stored and manipulated by police, summary data on trends and patterns are easily misinterpreted.

Psychological reactions Victims of racial victimization may experience a wide range of emotional reactions including anger, fear, sadness, feelings of powerlessness, vulnerability and suspicion of others (Barnes and Ephross, 1994; Weiss, 1997; Craig-Henderson and Sloan, 2003; Silver et al., 2004;). Victims of racist incidents may exhibit difficulty remembering, difficulty concentrating, self-blame (Morris-Prather et al., 1996) and exhibit psycho-physiological or somatic symptoms (Clark et al., 1999). Survivors of racist incidents may have difficulty trusting and connecting with those who are similar to their perpetrators (Craig-Henderson and Sloan, 2003; Bryant-Davis and Ocampo, 2005a). They may be shocked and overwhelmed by the unexpected violation, which prevents them from speaking up or responding. Being unable to respond because of shock is often a source of shame and self-blame for victims who wish they had been able to defend themselves at the time of the violation (Bryant-Davis and Ocampo, 2005a).

There is some debate as to whether anger constitutes a predominant response to racial victimization. Barnes and Ephross (1994) report that 68 per cent of the victims of hate violence in their sample experienced anger and that this was the predominant emotional reaction reported by victims of hate violence. However, Garofalo (1997) found that victims of hate motivated personal crimes were less likely than other crime victims to report being angry or mad as their predominant response. Instead, he found that victims of hate motivated personal crimes were more likely than other crime victims to report being frightened or scared as their predominant response.

Fear is another common reaction among victims of racial victimization. The data from the EDS shows that people who reported having previously experienced a hate crime were four times more likely to be worried about suffering subsequent hate crime victimizations than those who had not been victimized (19 per cent vs. 4 per cent respectively) (Silver et al., 2004). However, it is important to realize that victims' increased fear pertains not only to themselves but also to their family

(Weiss, 2005). Barnes and Ephross (1994) found that 51 per cent of the victims of hate violence in their sample experienced fear that their family or they personally would be injured.

Like victims of crime, some victims of racial victimization report behavioural changes. One-third of the victims in Barnes and Ephross' (1994) study reported moving, reducing social interactions, taking security measures, or purchasing guns for increased safety and in preparation for retaliation if attacked again.

While some researchers argue that the predominant emotional responses and behavioural coping responses of hate violence victims are similar to those of victims of other types of personal crime (Barnes and Ephross, 1994), others argue that victims' reactions to hate motivated crimes are different (Craig-Henderson and Sloan, 2003). Racial victimization is considered by some authors to be more debilitating than other types of victimization. Racism has been found to be a risk factor in the development of Post Traumatic Stress Disorder (PTSD) (Schneider et al., 2000; Loo, et al, 2001). There is some evidence that, compared to other crime victims, victims of hate crimes are more likely to rate their crimes as very serious (Garofalo, 1997). A survey conducted by the National Institute Against Prejudice and Violence (cited in Weiss, 1997) found that victims of racial violence experienced a greater number of negative psychophysiological symptoms than victims of random violence. These included feeling depressed or sad, feeling more nervous than usual, having trouble sleeping and feeling very angry. Victims of racial violence also reported a greater number of social and behavioural changes than victims of random violence, such as moving to another neighbourhood, buying or carrying a gun, taking a self-defence class.

The differential impact of racial victimization that is found in some studies may be due to the finding that, according to police data, hate crime tends to be more violent than non-racially motivated assaults. Levin and McDevitt (1993) find that because hate crimes tend to be more violent, the victims experience two to three times more negative psychological and behavioural consequences than victims of violence not motivated by racial or ethnic hatred. However, as was pointed out earlier, this may be an artefact of how police data are collected. Much of the racial victimization that is non-criminal (e.g., harassment) and non-violent is not reported to or recorded by police. However, psychological violence such as harassment and insults can equally be traumatizing (Wemmers, 2003).

Although criminal victimization may impact one's social relations, racial victimization will also affect inter-group relations. This is unique to attacks upon one's group identity. According to Craig-Henderson and Sloan (2003), victims of hate crimes may be especially likely to attribute their victimization to harmful motives that they believe are harboured by all members of the perpetrator's social group. Thus, they may be more likely to generalize the risk of victimization to others. Also, believing that one is being attacked for how one looks, or for one's identity, can create an ongoing level of fear that one is forever at risk (Weiss, 1997).

While many researchers recognize that racism may exacerbate the impact of criminal victimization (Roberts, 1995), few researchers conceptualize racism as a form of trauma. Bryant-Davis and Ocampo (2005) argue that racism, in and of itself, is a form of trauma. In other words, independent of whether the victim suffered a criminal victimization, the fact that he/she suffered racism is viewed as potentially traumatizing. They contend that even not physical or physically threatening racist incidents (i.e. non-criminal) can result in trauma symptoms. Although the current definition of PTSD is limited to acts that threaten the physical integrity of the victim and therefore excludes racism, Bryant-Davis and Ocampo (2005a) argue that the Diagnostics and Statistics Manual of the American Association of Psychiatrists should be changed to include racism. Further research in this area is needed in order to understand whether racism alone can trigger PTSD.

Racial victimization may not be a single event (Barnes and Ephross, 1994; Phillips and Sampson, 1998). The impact of multiple victimization is cumulative (Shaw, 2001). Before the victim has time to recover from the initial victimization, a new victimization occurs. The victim essentially suffers trauma on top of trauma. Even if one incident alone is not traumatizing, multiple micro-aggressions can build to create an intense traumatic impact (Bryant-Davis and Ocampo, 2005b). Because racism is so prevalent and often re-occuring, some authors talk about "internalized racism" to refer to lasting feelings of inferiority experienced by members of racial minorities. Williams and Williams-Morris (2000) found a positive association among internalized racism and alcohol consumption, lower self-esteem, lack of socio-emotional development in children of mothers in whom racism is highly internalized, symptoms of depression and chronic health problems.

It is important to realize that racial victimization, not only affects the individual victim but also his or her family. In particular, fear can be contagious. Victims may worry about the safety of their family members (Bowling, 1994; Barnes and Ephross, 1994) and family members may worry as well. While family members are affected by criminal victimization as well (Baril, 1984), the impact of racial victimization on family members may be particularly acute due to their shared social identity.

Impact on the Group

The harm of racial victimization is not restricted to just the victims involved and their families. Hate crimes convey a message of fear to all members of the community to which the specific individual belongs. Being a member of a target group may result in symptoms caused by awareness of potential victimization and the necessity of guarding against it. This has been identified as *vicarious traumatization effect* (Craig-Henderson and Sloan, 2003). Witnessing, experiencing second-hand, or hearing about racist crimes that victimize others may cause secondary traumatic stress, causing denial, anger, sadness and grief (Bryant-Davis and Ocampo, 2005a). The trauma of extreme racial victimization, such as the Holocaust, can be transmitted from one generation to the next (Danieli, 1998; Barankowsky et al., 1998). Much of the research on the impact of racial victimization on the group looks at fear of victimization. Visible minorities are more likely to be fearful of racial victimization than non-visible minorities (Silver, et al., 2004). This would seem logical, given that visible minorities have a greater risk of racial victimization (Silver et al., 2004).

However, as with victimization in general, fear of victimization is not necessarily related to one's risk of victimization. For example, women tend to be more fearful of racial victimization than men, while men are at a higher risk of racial victimization

(Bowling, 1994; Silver, et al., 2004). Bowling (1994) found that Asian women were particularly fearful while their risk of victimization was not particularly high. Of course these survey data fail to capture the full range of possible ways in which racial victimization can affect the community. An underestimated aspect of racial victimization is how the ripple effects of racial victimization manifest themselves. Weiss (1997) gives an example of how community members socially isolated a victim in the hope that by not associating with the victim they would reduce their own risk of victimization. Such reactions augment the victims' suffering while entrenching fear in the community.

Social and Judicial Responses to Racial Victimization

In Canada, as most other parts of the world, we still know little about what happens to the victim after the incident or after the incident was reported to the police. What limited available research there is gives us no information on how criminal and civil justice action (or inaction) affect the victim, the offender or the wider community (see Bowling, 1994).

US research suggest that racial and ethnic minorities have less access to mental health services, receive poorer quality mental health care, and are underrepresented in mental health research compared with European Americans (Williams and Williams-Morris, 2000). While it is not clear whether or not these gaps are due to racism, sexism or socio-economic discrimination (Bryant-Davis and Ocampo, 2005), it is clear that lack of access to services will augment impact of victimization. The extent to which such processes may be at work in Canada, where national health care is available, is unclear. Victimological research shows that victims of crime are often faced with secondary victimization (Wemmers, 1996; 2003). Secondary victimization refers to the finding that insensitive reactions by (criminal justice) professionals, such as the police, can exacerbate the victim's suffering (Symonds, 1980). While no research to date systematically studies secondary victimization among victims of racial victimization, this group may be particularly vulnerable to its negative effects. For example, victims who find that the police are reluctant to register their victimization as a hate crime will not only *not* find the recognition and respect in the criminal justice system that victims typically seek, they may also perceive the justice system as racially biased. Frequently, victims of racial victimization harbour anger toward the police (Weiss, 1997). Like most crimes, most hate crimes are not solved (Roberts, 2000; Silver et al., 2004). Victims' frustration regarding the lack of resolution is often directed at the police and other aspects of the criminal justice system (Weiss, 1997).

Discussion/Conclusion

In Canada, it is not illegal to have racist opinions or beliefs. However, manifestations of racism are prohibited by human rights legislation and, for some extreme forms, by the criminal law. Anti-discriminatory legislation is relatively recent in Canada. It was not until the 1970s that Canada adopted its first binding legislation against racial victimization. Today discrimination is prohibited by the *Canadian Human Rights Act*, which covers organizations under federal jurisdiction. For all other organizations, provincial human rights legislation applies and today all provinces in Canada have their own human rights act. Equality before the law is guaranteed under the *Canadian Charter of Rights and Freedoms*. In addition, the *Canadian Multiculturalism Act* protects against institutional racism, ensuring that the police carry on their activities in a manner that is sensitive and responsive to ethnic diversity.

With respect to criminal victimization, the Canadian legislation was conceived in the wake of the Holocaust. Consequently, inciting genocide and promoting hatred are crimes found in the *Canadian Criminal Code*. In addition, since 1995, any crime that is motivated by bias, prejudice or hatred, is considered a hate crime and, as such, is liable to receive a harsher punishment. However, the judge is not allowed to impose a penalty higher than the maximum penalty available for the offence. The impact of this provision on the length of sentences is not known.

It is difficult to know the extent to which racial victimization occurs. This despite the fact that the Canadian government has funded several studies (Roberts, 1995; Janhovich, 2001; Silver et al., 2005) and invested in the development of the Hate Crime Pilot Survey. All of these studies have focussed on hate crimes. That is, they focus exclusively on hate motivated criminal offences committed by fellow citizens. For this type of crime the data suggest that as much as 9 per cent of criminal victimizations are hate motivated (Silver, et al., 2004). We know much less, however, about non-criminal and institutional racial victimization. Yet, the limited data that is available suggest that non-criminal and institutional racial victimization may be much more common than hate crimes (Schneider et al., 2000; Wortley, 2002).

Statistics fail to convey the sense of harm inflicted upon the individuals and groups that are the target of racial victimization. Victims' reactions include anger, fear, Post-traumatic Stress Disorder (PTSD) as well as behavioural changes such as avoidance. These reactions resemble those found in the victimological literature on crime victims. It is unclear whether and how racial vicitimization impacts victims differently than other forms of victimization. Many researchers agree, however, that racially motivated crimes have an added impact on victims. Victims of racial victimization cannot simply attribute their victimization to bad luck and are forced to accept that their social identity was targeted. Some researchers argue that racism alone can be traumatizing and argue for greater awareness of the profound impact of racism on victims (Bryant-Davis and Ocampo, 2005a).

Because racial victimization targets the person's social group, its impact is not limited to the individual victim but also has important social consequences. Racial victimization affects victims and their families as well as their communities. Victims may feel fearful for other members of their family. The family members of victims may become fearful too. In extreme cases, vicarious traumatization is possible (Barankowsky, et al., 1998). Inter-group relations can be adversely affected by racial victimization as victims generalize their lack of trust to other members of the offender's group (Craig-Henderson and Sloan, 2003).

Much of the available research on racial victimization focuses on the crimes. There is relatively little empirical research available on the impact of racial victimization on victims and we know even less about the impact of racial victimization on communities (Bowling, 1994; Garofalo, 1997; Kelly and Maghan, 1998; Loo et al., 2001). Is too much attention being directed at the wrong question? From a victimological perspective, the answer to this question has to be "yes." Victims are being forgotten. The end result is a narrow definition of racial victimization that focuses on hate crimes and excludes certain groups (i.e., women) as well as non-criminal victimization and provides little insight into the consequences of racial victimization and the social and judicial responses to it.

References

Adachi, K. (1976). *The Enemy That Never Was: A History of the Japanese Canadians*. Toronto: McClelland and Stewart.

Backhouse, C. (1999). *Colour-Coded: A Legal History of Racism in Canada, 1900–1950*. Toronto, ON: University of Toronto Press.

Barankowsky, A., Young, M., Johnson-Douglas, S., Williams-Keeler, L. and McCarrey, M., (1998). PTSD Transmission: A Review of Secondary Traumatization in Holocaust Survivor Families. *Canadian Psychology*, 39, 4, 247–256.

Baril, M. (1984). L'envers du crime. Cahier no. 2, Montréal, Centre international de criminology comparée, Université de Montréal.

Barnes, A. and Ephross, P. (1994). The Impact of Hate Violence on Victims: Emotional and Behavioral Responses to Attacks. *Social Work*, 39, 3, 247–251.

Berk, R., (1994). 'Foreward,' in Mark Hamm (ed.), *Hate Crime: International Perspectives on Causes and Control* (v–ix). Cincinnati, OH: Anderson Publishing Company.

Besserer, S. and Trainor, C. (2000). La victimisation criminelle au Canada, 1999. *Juristat*. Centre Canadien de la statistique juridique, 20, 10.

Bnai Brith Canada (2007). 2006 Audit of Antisemitic Incidents. Available at : http://www.bnaibrith.ca/audit2006.html. Accessed 14 July 2007.

Bowling, B. (1994). Racial Harassment in East London, in Mark Hamm (ed.), *Hate Crime: International Perspectives on Causes and Control* (2–36). Cincinnati, OH: Anderson Publishing Company.

Bryant-Davis, T. and Ocampo, C. (2005a). Racist Incident-Based Trauma. *The Counseling Psychologist*, 33, 4, 479–500.

Bryant-Davis, T and Ocampo, C. (2005b). The Trauma of Racism: Implications for Counseling, Research and Education. *The Counseling Psychologist*, 33, 4, 574–578.

Clarke, R., Anderson, N., Clark, V. and Williams, D.R. (1999). Racism as a Stressor for African Americans: A Biospyschosocial Model. *American Psychologist*, 54, 805–816.

Cohen, M. (1966). Report of the Special Committee on Hate Propaganda in Canada, [aka the Cohen Report], Ottawa, Queen's Printer, 455 pages.

Commission on Systemic Racism. (1995). *Report of the Commission on Systemic Racism in the Ontario Criminal Justice System*. Toronto: Queen's Printer for Ontario.

Craig-Henderson, K. and Sloan, R. (2003). After the Hate: Helping Psychologists Help Victims of Racist Hate Crime. *Clinical Psychology: Science and Practice*. 10, 4, 481–490.

Danieli, Y. (1998). *International Handbook of Multigenerational Legacies of Trauma*. New York: Plenum Press.

Faulkner, E. (2003). Comment: Hate Crime in Canada: An Overview of Issues and Data Sources. *International Journal of Comparative Criminology*. 2, 2, 239–260.

Gannon, M. and Mihorean, K. (2005). La victimisation criminelle au Canada, 2004. *Juristat*, Centre canadien de la statistique juridique, 25, 7.

Garofalo, J. (1997). Hate Crime Victimization in the United States, in R. Davis, A. Lurigio and W. Skogan (eds.) *Victims of Crime Second Edition* (134–145). Sage Publications: Thousand Oaks CA.

Iacovetta, F., Perin, R. and Principe, A. (2000). *Enemies Within: Italian and Other Internees in Canada and Abroad*. Toronto: University of Toronto Press.

Janhevich, D. (2001). *Hate Crime in Canada: An Overview of Issues and Data Sources*. Statistics Canada. Catalogue no. 85-551-XIE (January).

Kaplan, W. (1993). Maxwell Cohen and the Report of the Special Committee on Hate Propaganda, in William Kaplan and Donald McRae, (eds.) *Law, Policy and International Justice: Essays in Honour of Maxwell Cohen* (243–274). Montreal: Mc-Gill-Queen's University Press.

Kelly, R. and Maghan J. (1998). *Hate Crime: The Global Politics of Polarization*. Carbondale: Southern Illinois University Press.

League for Human Rights B'nai Brith. (2005). 2004 Audit of Antisemitic Incidents in Canada.

Levin, B. (1992–93). Bias Crimes: A Theoretical and Practical Overview. *Stanford Law and Policy Review*, 4, 165–169.

Levin, B. and McDevitt, J. (1993). *Hate Crimes: The Rising Tide of Bigotry and Bloodshed*. New York: Plenum Press.

Loo, C., Fairbank, J., Scurfield, R., Ruch, L., King, D. and Adams, L., (2001). Measuring Exposure to Racism: Development and Validation of a Race-Related Stressor Scale (RRSS) for Asian American Vietnam Veterans. *Psychological Assessment*, 13, 4, 503–520.

Maghan, J. (1998). An Annotated Bibliography of Hate Crime Literature, in R. Kelly and J. Maghan (eds.) *Hate Crime: The Global Politics of Polarization* (239–252). Carbondale: Southern Illinois University Press.

Morris-Prather, C, Harrell, J, Collins, R., Jeffries-Leonard, K, Boss, M. and Lee, J. (1996). Gender Differences in Mood and Cardiovascular Responses to Socially Stressful Stimuli. *Journal of Ethnicity and Disease*, 6, 109–122.

Phillips, C. and Sampson, A. (1998). Preventing Repeated Racial Victimization: An Action Research Project. *British Journal of Criminology*, 38 ,1 ,124–144.

Roberts, J. (1995). *Disproportionate Harm: Hate Crime in Canada - An Analysis of Recent Statistics*. Working Document WD 1995-11e. Ottawa: Department of Justice, Canada.

Roberts, J. and Hastings, A. (2001). Sentencing in Cases of Hate-motivated Crime: an Analysis of Subparagraph 718.2(a)(i) of the Criminal Code. *Queen's Law Journal* 93, 27.

Schneider, K., Hitlan, R.and Radhakrishnan, P. (2000). An Examination of the Nature and Correlates of Ethnic Harassment Experiences in Multiple Contexts. *Journal of Applied Psychology*, 85, 1, 3–13.

Shaw, M. (2001). Time Heals All Wounds? in G. Farrell and K. Pease (eds.) *Repeat Victimization. Crime Prevention Studies*, volume 12, (218–233). Monsey NY, Criminal Justice Press.

Silver, W., Mihorean, K. and Taylor-Butts, A. (2004). Hate Crime in Canada. *Juristat*, Canadian Centre for Criminal Justice Statistics. 24, 4.

Stenning, P. (2003). Policing the Cultural Kaleidoscope: Recent Canadian Experience. *Police and Society*, 7, 13–47.

Symonds, M. (1980). The Second Injury. *Evaluation and Change*, Special Issue, 36–38.

UNODCCP. (1999). *Handbook on Justice for Victims*. New York: United Nations Office for Drug Control and Crime Prevention.

Weiss, J. (1997). Working with Victims of Ethnoviolence, in G. Greif and E. Ephross (eds.) *Group Work with Populations at Risk*. (121–133). New York, NY : Oxford University Press.

Weiss, J. (2005). Working with Victims of Hate Crimes, in G. Greif and P. Ephross (eds.) *Group Work with Populations at Risk*, Second Edition (197–211). New York, NY: Oxford University Press.

Wemmers, J. (1996). *Victims in the Criminal Justice System*. Amsterdam: Kugler.

Wemmers, J. (2003). *Introduction à la victimologie*. Montréal: Les presses de l'Université de Montréal.

Williams, D. and Williams-Morris, R. (2000). Racism and Mental Health: The African American Experience. *Ethnicity and Health*, 5, 3/4, 243–268.

Wortley, S. (2003). Hidden Intersections: Research on Race, Crime and Criminal Justice in Canada. *Canadian Ethnic Studies*, 35 ,3 , 99–118.

Jurisprudence

Mugesera v. Canada (Minister of Citizenship and Immigration), [2005] 2 S.C.R. 91.
R. v. Buzzanga and Durocher, (1997) 49 C.C.C. (2nd) 369 (C.A. Ont.).
R. v. Keegstra, [1990] 3 S.C.R. 697.
Little Sisters Book and Art Emporium v. *Canada (Minister of Justice)*, [2000] 2 S.C.R. 1120.

Helpful Websites

www.pch.gc.ca/multi/plan_action_plan/index_e.cfm – Multiculturalism – A Canada for All
www.narcc.ca – National Anti-Racism Council of Canada
http://www.chrc-ccdp.ca – Canadian Human Rights Commission
http://www.statcan.ca/Daily/English/051124/d051124b.htm – The general site for the Canadian victimization data as obtained through the General Social Survey

Chapter 3

England and Wales

Colin Webster

Introduction

Any discussion of racist victimisation in Britain is overshadowed by Sir William Macpherson's inquiry (begun in 1997) into the failed police investigation of the racist murder of Stephen Lawrence, a young black man, in South London in 1993. The inquiry report (Macpherson, 1999) received widespread publicity and support – its recommendations being endorsed by the British government and the police – and succeeded in bringing the issue of racist violence from the periphery to the centre of law and order policy in Britain.

The inquiry arose from a longstanding campaign by the victim's parents, Doreen and Neville Lawrence, to seek justice, yet no one has been convicted of the murder. Announcing a string of initiatives and changes in policy and the law since the inquiry, the UK government both reflected and led changes in the ways that racist violence came to be popularly perceived. It had been helped in this task by the support of the *Daily Mail* newspaper, which led a campaign supporting the Lawrence's fight for justice. This was a key development since this traditionally right wing newspaper's readership includes that constituency of 'respectable', 'middle class' and 'middle England' voters crucial to the outcome of British general elections (see Cook, 2006 for a discussion about this elusive demographic). This influential, mostly white group – traditionally aloof, indifferent and sometimes hostile to the plight of Britain's black and minority ethnic urban population – seemed persuaded of the injustice and seriousness of racist violence directed towards Britain's black and minority ethnic population.

These wider implications are seen in the ways that the Macpherson report subsequently:

> ... set the tone and the content of the British government's commitments to ethnic minority communities on issues of crime and community safety. These commitments were unprecedented in that not only were they explicit and high profile but they were also attached to a wide-ranging programme of action (Fitzgerald, 2001: 145).

This chapter begins by presenting a brief ethnic profile of Britain before going on to recount the processes and events surrounding the racist murder of Stephen Lawrence and the findings of the inquiry into the failure of the (London) Metropolitan Police to successfully apprehend his killers. Some implications of the inquiry are noted and there is a critical discussion of these implications and assessment of the subsequent effects in respect of policing racist victimisation and changes in the law. Next, racist victimisation and crime are understood in their historical and geographical context showing that their processes, patterns and meaning change within and between localities over time. Racist victimisation involves a social and power relationship between the police, victim and perpetrator and this relationship changes (e.g., better policing, rises in racism, and the ability of victims to defend themselves) and outcomes are unpredictable (also see the Introduction to this text for further discussion). It is though important to inquire about perpetrators as well as victims. Third, the extent of racist victimisation in England and Wales is outlined to show trends and changes in self-reported victimisation, victimisation reported to and recorded by the police, and in the prosecution of perpetrators by the Crown prosecution Service and the Courts. After considering what theoretical framework might best explain racist victimisation, the chapter ends with a prognosis of changes in racist victimisation and of police effectiveness.

Britain's Ethnic Profile

Changes in Britain's ethnic makeup are complicated by much diversity of origin, educational and occupational status and geography within and between ethnic groups. Arguably Britain is distinctive compared to America, Europe and Australia in that immigrants from the New Commonwealth had a right to full British citizenship as embodied in the *British Nationality Act 1948*. Although small numbers of minority ethnic groups have lived in Britain for centuries, their populations increased dramatically as a result of high rates of immigration in the 1950s and 1960s, reinforced by high birth rates. Mass immigration from the 'New' Commonwealth and Pakistan occurred from the 1950s to the mid–1970s. However, this took place in the context of successively more restrictive legislation that had the paradoxical effect of increasing immigration as groups entered Britain before these restrictions disqualified immigrants from entering. The minority ethnic population of England and Wales increased from 103,000 in 1951 to 4.6 million (7 per cent of the population) in the UK today (Owen, 2003).

Minority ethnic groups are overwhelmingly concentrated in the large urban areas of London, Birmingham, Leeds, Leicester and Manchester, and smaller industrial towns in the Midlands and the North of England. As would be expected this geographical concentration is reflected in the geographical concentration of racist victimisation.

South Asian ethnic groups (British Indian, Pakistani and Bangladeshi) comprise 3.2 per cent of the total UK population, and black ethnic groups comprise 2.1 per cent with the African-Caribbean group now the third largest group after Indians and Pakistanis (Owen, 2003). These groups – especially South Asian – are very significantly more youthful than the white population which in part accounts for their greater racist victimisation. Almost half of the minority ethnic population live in Greater London and it has been suggested that there has been a growing residential segregation of some minority ethnic groups within cities and towns (Cantle, 2002; Ouseley 2001; Owen 2003) but this has been challenged by others (Dorling and

Thomas, 2004; Simpson, 2004; Webster 2004). Growing ethnic residential and social segregation has been seen by some (Webster, 2003; Dench et al., 2006) as an important cause of racist hostility and victimisation.

Multiple deprivation among Britain's minority and some members of the white majority ethnic group – when these groups live in contiguous neighbourhoods – has been blamed for high levels of racist violence in these places (see below, and Webster, 2003). However, among ethnic minority groups there has been growing polarisation both between and within groups, and for some, deprivation and disadvantage has declined or disappeared while in others it has increased (Kalra, 2000; Mason, 2003; Pilkington, 2003). British Pakistan and Bangladeshi young people in particular belong to the poorest ethnic groups in British society while they have suffered the highest rates of racist victimisation (Mason, 2003; Modood, 2003; Owen, 2003; Pilkington, 2003; Webster, 2003, 2006).

Case Study: The Racist Murder of Stephen Lawrence

Stephen Lawrence, accompanied by another young black man – his friend Duwayne Brooks – was racially abused and surrounded by a group of five or six young white men while waiting at a bus stop. Despite being stabbed twice by his assailants he ran over 100 yards with his friend to escape his attackers, whereupon he collapsed and later died as he was taken into hospital. His attackers ran off. The Macpherson inquiry subsequently uncovered a litany of police actions and attitudes towards the victim, his friend, the victim's parents and in the conduct of the murder investigation that revealed – perhaps unwitting – racist assumptions among the investigating officers. From the very beginning – the arrival of police officers at the murder scene – insensitive, unsympathetic, suspicious and stereotyping assumptions, attitudes and actions were conveyed by police officers.

The police seemed more interested in questioning Duwayne Brooks than tending to the victim before the ambulance arrived, stereotyping him as unpleasantly hostile and agitated rather than traumatised. The police took a line of questioning that assumed Stephen Lawrence had been in a fight rather than that he'd been the victim of an unprovoked racist murder. There was a lack of urgency in pursuing suspects early in the investigation. The underlying message of Macpherson was that because the victim was black this disqualified him from being considered an 'ideal victim' (Goodey, 2005) by the police (i.e., someone wholly innocent and deserving of an urgent, dedicated, determined and professional police investigation to catch his killers).

Macpherson (1999: 317) concluded that the investigation of Stephen Lawrence's racist murder was "marred by a combination of professional incompetence, institutional racism and a failure of leadership by senior officers". The victim was not given first aid by police officers; officers did not take any immediate proper steps to pursue the suspects; the parents of the victim were treated with insensitivity and lack of sympathy; the investigating officers misjudged and delayed, and did not take responsibility, for their failure to arrest suspects; and the course of the investigation was marked by "a series of errors, failures, and lack of direction and control" (ibid:

320). For Macpherson (1999: 321), the overall explanation for these failures was the existence of institutional racism in the police, defined by him as:

> ... the collective failure of an organisation to provide an appropriate and professional service to people because of their colour, culture or ethnic origin. It can be seen or detected in processes, attitudes and behaviour which amount to discrimination through unwitting prejudice, ignorance, thoughtlessness, and racist stereotyping which disadvantage minority ethnic people.

Macpherson has been criticised on a number of counts, not least because of the methodological difficulty of grounding the concept of institutional racism in an investigation of a single incident of a failed murder inquiry (Lea, 2000).

Macpherson and its Aftermath: Policing Racist Victimisation and the Law

Fitzgerald (2001) assessed what had been achieved post-Macpherson with regard to the handling of racist incidents. One of the central thrusts of Macpherson was that the failure of the police to adequately deal with racist incidents had resulted in a lack of trust in the police among minority ethnic groups. Fitzgerald (2001) argues that government commitments to ethnic minorities arising from Macpherson are in tension with other government priorities, particularly in respect of disproportionate stops and searches of black people.

Historically, the recording of racist incidents required police officers to identify racial motivation. In response to criticism the police adopted a wider definition of what constituted a 'racial' incident and officers were not to have the last say whether an incident was racially motivated or not. Finally, Macpherson offered a wholly victim-centred definition whether there was actual independent evidence of racial motivation or not. According to Fitzgerald (2001), the main effect of Macpherson was to have greatly increased the willingness of the police to record incidents as racist thus closing the gap between what the self-report British Crime Survey (BCS) had revealed about the number of racist incidents and what the police recorded – the gap between under reported and under recorded incidents and actual incidents. Further, that this was a particularly London rather than a national effect on police recording practices. Police forces, however, were still not addressing 'low level harassment' – as demonstrated by the London figures during and after the Macpherson inquiry. Perhaps of most significance is that following the publication of the Macpherson report and the embracing of a definition of racist incidents irrespective of the ethnicity of the victim or perpetrator, the proportion of recorded incidents involving white victims has increased and the proportion of victims from visible ethnic minorities has declined, and although whites were still the main perpetrators, a higher proportion of suspects were recorded as black than previously.

Fitzgerald (2001) concluded that the Macpherson effect was to have greatly increased reporting of racist incidents during 1998–1999 – a sustained period of sympathetic media coverage and senior police commitment – but that this increase seemed mostly based in the London Metropolitan Police area rather than elsewhere. At the same time, in some police circles and amongst some whites, there was a backlash against the perceived privileged treatment of ethnic minorities which may have encouraged the reporting by and recording of white victims. Fitzgerald reserved her most telling criticism of Macpherson towards the label of 'institutional racism'. The implications of this concept are that accusations of racism may be inadvertently widened and extended in unwarranted ways serving to exacerbate rather than resolve underlying racial tensions. Furthermore, it is tautological in that it merely describes what requires to be explained in the first place – police racism. It is unhelpful because abstract, denies personal responsibility and 'may generate a sense of impotence at best and resentment at worst' (Fitzgerald, 2001: 162). John Lea (2000, 1986) and others (see Marlow and Loveday, 2000; Rowe, 2004) have made similar arguments adding that the concept of 'institutional racism' fails to locate the causes of racism within the structure of operational policing and the relationship between police and minority communities. If, as Macpherson insists, racism in the UK is generated by the way institutions function, intentionally or otherwise, rather than by the individual attitudes of their members, then we still need to know *which* institutional processes, dynamics and unintended consequences of the working of institutions, encourage racism. Although Macpherson blames a restrictive UK police occupational culture – lack of contact between white officers and black people outside a policing context – Lea (2000) suggests that policies that flow from this explanation have a long history of failure. For Lea (2000) the problem lies elsewhere, in power and community relations between the police and economically and politically powerless groups, including those within the white population – groups towards whom the police have little incentive to respond to their demands, who are most likely to be disproportionately stopped and searched and who are as likely to be discriminated against because of their social class and area of residence as because of their ethnicity – a crucial factor ignored by Macpherson.

Nevertheless, Macpherson's contribution in drawing attention to the unintended consequences of the workings of institutions, and linking the handling of racist victimisation and disproportionate stop and search, both engendering distrust of the police, were important if undeveloped advances on previous official views. The chapter now turns to Macpherson's effect on changes in the law in respect of racist victimisation.

The *Crime and Disorder Act* of 1998 introduced into law the concept of specific racially aggravated offences in relation to violence, harassment, public order and criminal damage. The *Anti-terrorism, Crime and Security Act* of 2001, extended this concept to include religiously aggravated offences. Whereas previously police forces recorded racist incidents on the basis of a definition that relied at least in part on police officer's interpretation of the presence of racial motivation or an allegation of racial motivation by any person (ACPO, 1985), in 1999 the police adopted Macpherson's (1999) definition that any incident which is perceived to be racist by the victim or any other person is racially motivated.

In respect of racially or religiously aggravated offences however, the offender must demonstrate hostility towards the victim around the time of the offence, or that the offence is motivated (wholly or partly) by such hostility, based on the victim's presumed membership of a racial or religious group (Home Office, 2005). This shift from an earlier organisational definition for purposes of recording, to a legal definition, that includes hostility to the victim's presumed membership of a racial or religious group marks a very significant change in how the police and criminal justice system have come to perceive racist incidents and racial motivation.

Recorded aggravated offences increased 3 per cent between 2001/2 and 2002/3, and 13 per cent between 2002/3 and 2003/4 – more than was the case with recorded racist incidents. For both recorded racist incidents and aggravated offences, police forces vary widely in the number and type of offences recorded, cleared-up, prosecuted, convicted, cautioned, not tried or acquitted. In 2002/3 the Crown Prosecution Service (CPS) saw a 12 per cent increase in defendants for prosecution of a racist incident from the previous year of whom 74 per cent were prosecuted. Overall, about one-third of both racially and non-racially aggravated offences were cleared up by the police. There was a 17 per cent increase of persons cautioned or prosecuted by the courts for aggravated offences in 2003 compared to 2002 (Home Office, 2005).

This growing formalisation of the offence of racist victimisation in law and the recognition that such offences have a basis in hostility to the victim's membership of a group reflects wider changes in Britain's cultural values and how these changes have influenced English law. This shift from laws and a criminal justice system that assumed a culturally and ethnically homogenous society to a system that increasingly recognises cultural and ethnic heterogeneity risks two distinct and opposed possibilities: either the law and criminal justice system become inconsistent, confused and contradictory or fairer (Smith, 1994). As David Smith (1994) notes the fundamental ideal of liberal democratic justice is that everyone is equal under the law after specific case characteristics have been taken into account. On the other hand, in practice, justice may discriminate on grounds of ethnicity or race (Hood, 1992; Feilzer and Hood, 2004) and generate a disproportionate attention to the arrest, prosecution and punishment of one social or ethnic group than of another (Hudson, 1993). This raises parallel issues not just for the treatment of offenders, but for the recognition of victims of racial and religious crimes too. In February 2006, the English parliament debated a controversial Bill to make incitement to religious hatred a criminal offence, with uncertain outcomes as to how it will be enforced, whether the offence mistakenly confounds and confuses religious and racial hatred (see Spalek, 2002) and with unforeseeable implications for free speech.

The legal and criminal justice implications of changes since Macpherson are a fundamental and novel tension between a tradition which concentrates on securing fairness for the individual and more recent developments that recognise and seek fairness for groups. As Smith (1994: 1045) has previously argued, from one point of view:

> equal treatment does not mean the same treatment. Hence there is room for different treatment of groups according to their specific needs: for example, for the police and other agencies to take special action to meet the needs of ethnic minorities as victims of racial attacks.

This takes us back full circle to our earlier discussion of balancing an encouraging and increasing recognition among whites that black and minority ethnic populations are disproportionately racially victimised whilst discouraging any white backlash –

especially among poor whites – that may perceive BME (Black and Minority Ethnic) groups as receiving preferential treatment. As the next two sections will show, surveying the historical background to racist victimisation and the recent trends and extent of racist victimisation in England and Wales, reveals a complex but clear story of disproportionate racist victimisation of black and minority ethnic people.

Historical Background to Racist Victimisation

The pattern of development of racist victimisation in Britain is from an earlier period of larger scale white 'race' riots that attacked black people and the places they lived to a more recent, smaller scale, 'routine', lower level harassment. Often hidden in the recent period are occasional outbursts of usually unreported street skirmishes between groups of black and minority ethnic and white young people (Husband, 1989; Webster, 1996). Although large-scale immigration from the Indian sub-continent and the Caribbean began in the post–1945 period, earlier settlement of black and minority ethnic residents had occurred in Britain's ports (see, for example, Hiro, 1991). Thus the white 'race' riots of 1919, which occurred in nine British ports, are seen as having most significance in the history of English racist violence. However, it is important to emphasise that the victims of white violence were not passive as black people reacted to, and resisted, racist attacks through organised forms of self-defence, and on occasion, with equal violence (Jenkinson, 1993; Hiro, 1991). For example, widespread violence against black people and property in the Notting Hill area of London in August 1958 resulted in black people forming vigilante groups which patrolled the area in cars.

Histories of racist violence point to the importance of local factors and specific events that precipitate and join with underlying racist hostility and anti-immigration feelings, based in a wider background of nationalist and post-colonial anxieties about social change and economic insecurity (Pearson, 1976; Layton-Henry, 1984; Panayi, 1993; Solomos, 1993; Holmes, 1988; Colley, 1992). For example, Pearson (1976) pointed to racial hostility as a response to the decline of the cotton industry and the culture that went with it in NW England. Here local perceptions find expression in forms of 'racial anxiety' rooted in a local lore of economic decline and depression of wages associated with the arrival of Pakistani migrants.

Violence against Asians reached a climax and became national news during the 1970s, particularly as a result of skinhead attacks, culminating in two murders of Asians in the latter part of the decade (see Hiro, 1991). The response to these kinds of attacks became increasingly politicised through the organisation of the Asian Youth Movement and its complaints that the police were unwilling to protect Asian areas (Hiro, 1991; CARF/Southall Rights, 1981). Racist victimisation became entrenched in certain areas because of their histories of immigration and other peculiarities such as insularity and traditions of extreme right-wing political behaviour in London's East End (Husband, 1982) and a defensive economic logic in NW England's cotton manufacturing areas (Pearson, 1976). An important aspect of this entrenchment was the contesting of territory between majority and minority groups of young people (Hesse et al., 1992; Webster, 1995). In this sense racial hostility and resentment takes different although linked forms among young people and adults. Among adults hostility tends to be focused on perceived competition for access to welfare entitlements and public services, including education and crucially, housing (Foster, 1999; Collins, 2004; Dench et al., 2006). Among young people hostility focuses on struggle over public space because of their closer proximity to street culture (Webster, 1995, 1996, 2003). Young people's and adult's hostility however, are linked, because in localities where white hostility towards black and Asian people are common and widely accepted, perpetrators of racist violence – usually young people and young adults – draw support from the broader adult 'perpetrator community', who although they may not carry out racist acts themselves, tacitly condone them by their expression of racist attitudes (Sibbit, 1997).

Despite the historical longevity and entrenchment of racist violence in British localities, and plentiful evidence of the scale and seriousness of attacks against British Asians in particular in the 1960s and 1970s (see London, 1973; Hiro, 1991; Pearson, 1976; Layton-Henry, 1984), official recognition of the problem only began in 1981 with the publication of a Home Office report on racial violence (Home Office, 1981). This official endorsement began to spawn surveys and monitoring exercises, which counted the prevalence of racial attacks and pointed to the inadequacy of police statistics, reporting practices and police responses to racial incidents (Bowling, 1993), to the extent of highlighting racial harassment by the police against black people (GLC, 1984). The Home Office report on racial attacks in 1981 was followed by the Home Affairs Select Committee report on racial attacks in the following year (Home Affairs Committee, 1982). The subsequent Home Office report, *Racial Attacks* (Layton-Henry, 1984) provided an initial policy impetus to change in statutory agencies' attitudes to racial harassment. It revealed that Asian people were fifty times more likely to be attacked on racial grounds than white people, and black people were thirty six times more likely to be attacked.

Controversies surrounding the definition, reporting and recording of racist victimisation, and responses amongst policy makers have continued (Bowling, 1998; see below). For example, the House of Commons Home Affairs Committee in its report in 1986 defined racial harassment as criminal or offensive behaviour motivated wholly or partly by racial hostility (Home Affairs Committee, 1986), and the Greater London Council's Race and Housing Action team concluded in 1985 that harassment includes:

> Racial name-calling, rubbish, rotten eggs, rotten tomatoes, excreta, etc. dumped in front of victims' doors, urinating through the letterbox, door-knocking, cutting telephone wires, kicking, punching and spitting at victims, serious physical assault, damage to property, e.g. windows being broken, doors smashed, racist graffiti daubed on door or wall (GLC, 1985, cited in Bowling 1998: 134).

Smith's (1994: 1106) definition perhaps best captured the nature of racist victimisation as:

> … victims of a pattern of repeated incidents motivated by racial hostility, where many of these events on their own do not constitute crimes, although some crimes may occur in

the sequence, so that the cumulative effect is alarming and imposes severe constraints on a person's freedom and ability to live a full life.

A common thread throughout the history of racist victimisation in England and Wales are complaints by black and minority ethnic communities that they are over-policed and under-protected (see Bowling, 1998; Webster 2004). There is clear evidence that in respect of the earlier white 'race' riots mentioned previously, the police not only did not protect victims or their property and blamed the presence of minority ethnic communities for the disorders, but they colluded or offered tacit support to the white rioters (see Hiro, 1991; Panayi, 1993). Here, as later, there was a marked distrust between the police and minority ethnic communities. Whitfield (2004) has shown how deterioration in relations between the police and London's Caribbean community went unnoticed or was treated with indifference during the crucial early years of immigration. This downward spiral, which began in the 1950s, continued in the following decade because of a series of factors affecting London's Metropolitan Police (Met) including: a lack of genuine political accountability to the representatives of the Caribbean community; arrogance and complacency on the part of senior officers towards this deterioration, blaming it on the West Indian community, rather than police race relations policies; rising crime rates and housing shortages created a climate of racial discrimination and racist attacks that the Met perceived as a burden and a problem associated with the presence of immigrants; a fear on the part of the Met that white society might accuse them of showing bias towards black people, while unable to see that its own policy of not taking sides in racist incidents would inevitably erode black confidence in the police still further.

Bowling (1998) has argued that despite senior police managers in the recent years prioritising racial attacks on members of minority ethnic groups, the police continue to be ineffective in the prevention of incidents, protection of victims, and prosecution of perpetrators. The explanation, according to Bowling (1998), lies in police discretion towards racist incidents and the lack of importance they are accorded in officer's hierarchy of the 'police relevance' of crime events. Rank-and-file police work is dominated by a working common sense understanding of the law and the more discretionary and ambiguous the legal matter, the greater the opportunity for occupational, common sense values to enter operational matters. Because racist incidents are not taken seriously, even assaults occasioning injury, this makes a strenuous law-enforcement response less likely.[1]

Bowling (1998) goes on to suggest that racist incidents are seen as legally ambiguous – indeed officers consistently question or deny the importance or relevance of racism or racial motivation to crimes. They are seen more as 'neighbourhood disputes', 'anti-social acts' or 'disturbances' rather than serious crimes. Victims and perpetrators tend

---

1 Despite numerous campaigns to recruit more police officers from minority ethnic groups these groups are considerably under-represented in the police service. Just under 3 per cent of police officers were from minority ethnic groups in 2002/3 although under-representation seems to be reducing. Mixed ethnicity police officers were 1.3 per 1,000 population, black officers 0.5 and Asian officers 1.2 compared to 2.6 white police officers per 1,000 population (ICPR, 2004). The main barrier would appear to be a perception among minority groups that the police are a racist organisation (Holdaway, 1996).

to be people of low social status so the police perceive there to be a low likelihood of detection or arrest, or the victim might withdraw the allegation at a later point (see Bowling 1998). Police officers identify and have sympathy with the viewpoint of the 'white community', seeing its resentment and its expression in violence as 'natural' and understandable. Perpetrators are perceived as indistinguishable from ordinary 'yobs'[2] and victims as inherently or naturally vulnerable.

Summarising the history of racist victimisation in England and Wales, the longevity of and resistance to racist victimisation can really be said to have reached a climax in the 1970s and 1980s. Of particular note, this period saw an increase in organised forms of 'self-defence' by black and minority ethnic young people claiming to be defending the Asian community from threats by far right organisations to march through Asian areas (Race Today Collective 1986; Independent Black Collective 1986). Meanwhile, the 1990s saw a marked increase in the reporting by whites and/or recording by the police of racist incidents involving Asian on white attacks (Webster, 1995, 1996; FitzGerald, 2001). This period saw the development of an increasing perception that whites rather than blacks could be the victim of racist violence although in reality visible ethnic minorities continued to be far more at risk of being victimised than whites. What is notable is that throughout these periods faith in the police to tackle racist victimisation remained low.

It is relatively recently that racist victimisation has once again come to have an explicit and direct relationship to serious public disorder (see Cantle, 2002; Kundnani, 2001; Lea, 2003; Young 2003; Webster, 2003, 2004). The immediate events leading to the wide scale public disorders that took place in Northern English towns in 2001 appeared to be a confused series of well publicised violent 'racist' clashes and attacks against people and property involving Asian and white young people. The context was a climate of fear and rumour within Asian communities that extreme right-wing racist political parties were going to march into Asian areas in the context of local elections, despite banning orders authorised by the Home Secretary. The British National Party (BNP) had visited the area to demonstrate their support of the white population against racist attacks, and the relative electoral success of the BNP in some local council elections seemed to affirm significant support for ideological racism (Oldham MBC and GMP, 2001; Clarke 2001). The overall effect were disorders and attacks against the police by Asian and white young people. As had happened in the past, long-term economic decline in the areas affected, high levels of fear, crime and violence, supposed increasing ethnic residential and school segregation and declining housing markets, all conspired to create a situation of racist hostility and violence. Against these usual explanations there is a strong argument that ethnic segregation is declining in both Britain and the areas affected, but that polarisation between poor – both Asian and white – and affluent areas has increased (Simpson 2004; Dorling and Thomas 2004).

---

2 'Yobs' can be defined as a sub-group of young white working class males who are generally characterised as being foul-mouthed, irresponsible, and generally unemployed and exhibit a propensity for violence (Coward, R. 1994:32 from the *Guardian Weekend – September 2*).

Of late – increasingly reflected in legislation outlawing 'incitement to religious hatred' – 'racial' victimisation has been linked to attacks on religious groups, particularly Muslims. In Britain as elsewhere there is considerable congruence of ethnicity and religion because most British Muslims belong to visible minority groups. The next section spells out what was argued at the beginning of this chapter. That racist victimisation cannot be understood without close scrutiny of perpetrators – a requirement that has often gone unheeded in studies of racist victimisation.

Perpetrators: The Missing Link in Understanding Racist Victimisation

The simple condemning of perpetrators adds much to a perhaps justified self righteousness but adds little to our understanding of the causes and dynamics of racist victimisation. An early local study of perpetrators of racist victimisation over five years (Webster, 1994, 1995, 1996, 1997, 1998) found that the power relationship of perpetrators and victims changed over time such that an initial high level of white on Asian victimisation was very significantly reduced.

The explanation for this reduction in victimisation was the increasing ability of Asian young people to defend themselves from attack and harassment through designating and defending 'safe' territory – various parks and areas deemed to 'belong' to Asians, while avoiding 'white' areas. What had begun among Asian young men as a defensive form of street masculinity altered local power relations – reducing perpetrator's opportunities, creating and winning 'safe havens' from attack in Asian-only youth centres, gaining more co-operation from some sections of the local police and schools, and successfully competing for scarce urban resources – at the expense of less powerful and less well organised young white men.

The study also found that perpetrator and victim communities were highly differentiated according to white young people's involvement in racist harassment and perpetrator's commitment to violence, and according to the degree of risk faced by potential victims, their different responses to racist victimisation – passive or active – and in their commitment to different forms of self defence. Thus within the wider perpetrator community (Sibbit, 1997) of white young people – the majority living in the area – was found a pervasive common sense racism that condoned attacks on Asians in circumstances of fighting but drew back from condoning racially targeted violence. These, the normal racists, differentiated themselves from potential and actual perpetrators of racist victimisation, the aggressive and violent racists. This apparent difference between 'respectable' and violent racism introduced considerable ambiguity in young people's – both white and Asian – accounts about what constituted racist victimisation. It was found however, that violent racists were also invariably engaged in other (non-racial) forms of violence and criminality.

More recently, Larry Ray and colleagues studied young adult and adult racist offenders under the supervision of the Probation Service and in prison in Greater Manchester in the north of England (Ray et al., 2003, 2004; Ray and Smith, 2004). They argue that on the one hand a single focus on the individual motives and intentions of racist offenders ignores the grounding of such offences in wider cultural and social contexts of violence, exclusions and marginalisation. On the other hand, the "dominant images of the racially violent offender are one-dimensional and exaggerate the degree to which such people are politically conscious 'haters'" (Ray and Smith, 2004: 682). As white working-class communities displace "resentment at economic decline and social decay onto apparent representatives of a 'cosmopolitan' culture" (ibid: 695), encouraged in this by local media representations and far-right political parties, these wider crises of deindustrialisation and neighbourhood destabilisation become displaced onto the biographies and structures of feelings of individuals, including racist offenders. These processes involve the transformation of offender's unacknowledged shame rooted in multiple disadvantages and perceptions that Asians are illegitimately given preferential treatment and are more successful than them. Shame turns to fury and rage directed against Asians within a cultural context in which violence and racism are taken for granted (Ray et al., 2003, 2004, also see Dench, 2006).

Extent of Racist Victimisation: Patterns and Trends

The police have recorded racist incidents since 1986. There is some evidence that the number recorded rose steadily to a peak in 1986/7 then declined until the early 1990s (Home Office, 1981, 1989; Webster, 1995; Bowling, 1998) but this whole period is marked by the problem of severe under reporting, especially among black and minority ethnic groups compared to whites, and under recording by the police (Hesse et al., 1992; Bowling, 1998; Brown, 1994; Home Office, 1989; Fitzgerald and Hale, 1996). FitzGerald and Hale (1996) compared racist incidents reported to the 1988 and 1992 British Crime Surveys and established that ethnic minorities are more likely to be victims of crimes and serious threats than whites, because of their younger age structure, their socio-economic characteristics and the type of area they live in, as well as because of their ethnicity. Significantly, in areas where racial attacks are *perceived* as a problem, both minority and white respondents tend to have higher levels of fear of crime. Most importantly, the BCS provided no evidence of the large rise in racist incidents between 1988 and 1992 suggested by police reported crime figures, but shows a large gap between racist incidents reported to the police and those actually recorded over that period (Fitzgerald and Hale, 1996) (see Graph 3.1).

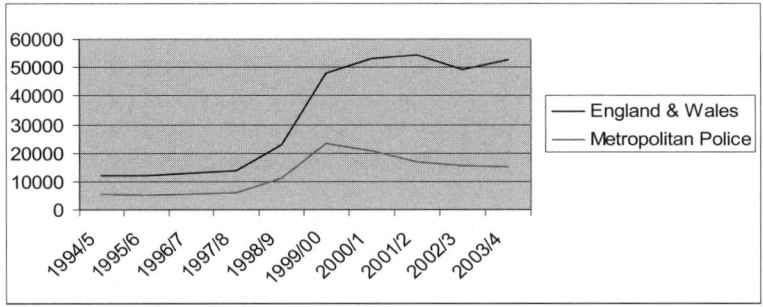

**Graph 3.1 Ten year trend in reported racist incidents
(England, Wales and London)**
Source: Home Office (2004, 2005); Nicholas et al. (2005)

As the graph shows, dramatic rises in reported racist incidents from 1998/9 can almost certainly be accounted for by a greater willingness to report and changed police recording practices – especially in London – directly as a result of the Macpherson inquiry and changes in the law. This second cycle of rises in recorded racist incidents from 1996/7 to a peak of 54,370 in 2001/2 then saw a fall until 2002/3. Importantly, the increase until 2001/2 set beside the BCS finding of a decline over this period suggests a progressively fuller recording on the part of the police and possibly increased confidence in reporting to the police (Home Office, 2004). There were however, wide variations in whether recorded incidents rose or declined between police force areas over time. Although the number of racist incidents recorded by the police rose by 7 per cent between 2002/3 and 2003/4 (following a 10 per cent fall the previous year), the Metropolitan Police showed a slight decline, and the BCS showed little change over the period. Overall, the BCS has shown that the number of racially motivated incidents has fallen since the mid–1990s (see Clancy et al., 2001) but may have recently begun to rise again.

According to the BCS 2002/3 and 2003/4, Asians appear to be far more at risk of crime than other ethnic groups and whites all of whom experience comparable risks. However, Black and Minority Ethnic (BME) groups, and Asians in particular, face significantly higher risks of personal crime than whites. The striking exception to this overall pattern is that blacks face dramatically greater risks of homicide and are much more likely to be shot than any other group. These findings require caution because after allowing for age, Asian people face only slightly higher risks of crime than others.

Young people are generally more at risk of crime than others, and the Asian population is younger than average. What is striking are the experiences of people of mixed origin[3] who faced higher risks for burglary, robbery and vehicle crime than any other group. The BCS 2003/4 found that over the previous twelve months 26 per cent of whites and blacks, 31 per cent of Asians and 39 per cent of people of mixed origin were victimised. Most of the greater risks of crime faced by BME groups can be attributed to demographic factors such as area of residence, age, social class and income. The same cannot be said for the mixed group whose higher risks do not disappear even after allowing for age, and the type of area (affluent/deprived) in which the person lived. The BCS 2004/5 found a 10 per cent increase for both recorded less serious racially-aggravated wounding and racially-aggravated harassment, and reductions of from an 8 to 5 per cent in racially-aggravated common assault and damage to a dwelling, between 2003/4 and 2005/5.[4] In both years the detection rate for racially-aggravated violence and harassment increased by 40 per cent compared to less serious offences such as racially-aggravated damage to dwellings and vehicles. Two per cent of all common assaults in 2004/5 were racially or religiously aggravated (Nicholas et al., 2005). These – the most recent findings – found a narrowing of the gap between ethnic groups in crime risks compared with

---

3 For the first time the 2002/3 BCS used the new 2001 Census classification of ethnicity that includes a 'Mixed' category.

4 There is a discontinuity in the police recorded trend for violence (including racially-aggravated violence) in 1998 and 2002 when new offence categories were added.

earlier sweeps of the BCS, but also the emergence of a mixed origin group especially vulnerable to crime.

As argued elsewhere groups living in relatively high crime, deprived areas – disproportionately BME groups and poor whites – tend also to be more at risk of racist crime (Webster, 2003). The BCS asks all crime victims whether they thought that the incident was racially motivated. Risks of racially motivated victimisation were higher for people from all the BME groups than for white people and highest for those from a mixed background.

As numerous studies have shown the majority of racist incidents recorded are either damage to property or verbal harassment, regardless of jurisdiction in the United Kingdom (Home Office, 2005; Maynard and Read, 1997; Clark and Moody, 2002; Jarman, 2002), although an early local self-report survey found much higher levels of violent compared to damage to property incidents (Webster, 1995). These and other findings again should counsel caution in how we interpret overall statistics given local and temporal variation.

The 2002/3 BCS – consistent with previous sweeps – found that risks of racially motivated victimisation were higher for people from all the BME groups than for white people. However, just as we saw the emergence of the mixed origin group as having the highest victimisation rates in respect of crime, so they also have the highest rates of racially motivated victimisation. Results from the 2002/3 BCS showed that less than 1 per cent of white people had experienced a crime that they thought was racially motivated compared to 2 per cent of black people, 2 per cent of Chinese and 'other' minority ethnic group, 3 per cent of Asian people and 4 per cent of mixed origin people. People of mixed origin were least likely to report crimes (31 per cent) and Asians were most likely to report (42 per cent). Between BME groups, Asian people had higher levels of worry about violent crime compared to people from other groups (Home Office, 2005).

To summarise from the data presented thus far, the larger BME groups face crime risks that overall are similar to those faced by white people, although Asian people have slightly higher victimisation rates, but this is likely to be because of the relative youth of the Asian population and where they live.

There remain considerable problems with survey data. Risks of racist victimisation between groups take into account the age profile of the group, social class and area of residence to see whether these comparisons hold. According to the Home Office (2004) and the BCS there appears to have been some convergence of crime risks over the last few years, except for those who are of mixed ethnic origin – whose risks are significantly higher than others. White people reported the lowest rates of racially motivated offences, but again although this picture is unlikely to change dramatically, a somewhat different picture may emerge if groups are disaggregated according to age (e.g. the BCS does not ask under-16s about their victimisation), area of residence (e.g. whether affluent or deprived, ethnically mixed or not) and social class and income.

If the apparent greater but declining risks faced by Asians in respect of racist victimisation can be explained by the younger profile of this population, and where they live, compared to some other BME groups and whites in particular, there remain some unanswered questions. They include:

- The statistical patterns and trends are unable to account for local conditions and smaller area risks influenced by events and the entrenchment of racist attitudes and victimisation in some areas and not others.
- Comparing victimisation rates and risks with the demographic characteristics of the group – that it is younger and young people are more likely to be victimised – also needs to take into account the extent to which the victim population are available not just their age profile. For example, young Bangladeshi men in particular tend to reside in overcrowded housing pushing them to spend their leisure time on the street where they are more available and vulnerable.
- To what extent does an area accommodate motivated racist offenders because of the peculiarities of the area and whether local influences encourage or discourage resentment and hostility?
- Guardianship may, or may not, be available depending on whether potential victims are able to defend themselves or use avoidance strategies, or whether the police are able to police racist victimisation effectively. For example, there may be an interaction effect insofar as perpetrators perceive that victims are vulnerable and available in a context they perceive will have few consequences and little redress against them.
- We still know far too little about racist victimisation among children and in early teenage.
- The emergence of a hitherto ignored group – people of mixed origin – who by far suffer the highest risks of both criminal and racist victimisation compared to other BME groups and whites is still to be explained.
- There are important grounds for identifying white ethnic victimisation in respect of poor British white, Irish and Jewish groups (Stenson, 1996; Stenson and Watt, 1998), although this does not take away from the fact that visible minority ethnic groups have and are likely to continue to experience heightened, intensive, repeated and prolonged risks of racist incidents compared to other groups – a quite different qualitative experience to most whites (Sampson and Phillips, 1992).

If we ignore these contextual factors of reporting – to the police or the BCS or, a local survey – then we ignore the particular social context in which information, experience and knowledge is influenced, given and received. National and aggregate statistics about racist victimisation tell us an important part of the general picture about *whether* incidents are increasing or not for certain groups, but they do not tell us *why* what they describe is happening, nor do they tell us where or to whom, or to what, we should look too for an explanation (Webster, 1996).

Responses to Racist Victimisation in England and Wales

As seen above, the long history of racist victimisation in Britain from its origins in the late nineteenth and early twentieth century found in 'anti-alienist' and 'anti-immigration' feelings, particularly towards Jewish and Irish people (Cesarani,

1990; Husband, 1983, 1989; Holmes, 1988; Panayi, 1993) and white 'race riots' against small long-standing black communities, to the growth in racist victimisation accompanying large scale immigration from the 1950s, official responses took the form of blaming victims. It wasn't until the 1980s that racist victimisation came to be seen as a legitimate area of official concern. Since then and particularly in the late 1990s there has been a growing trend and awareness of racial victimisation as a concern in the context of a growing political influence of minority ethnic groups. Britain's expanded social, cultural and ethnic diversity has seen a growing confidence and success in challenging racist victimisation, first by minority ethnic groups themselves, and eventually by the government and the police. Although welcome, these responses and challenges should not lead to complacency. Changes and improvements in the prevalence of race thinking and racist victimisation, government legislation and police reform towards tackling racist victimisation, are all contingent on cultural, political and policing climates that are subject to unforeseen events that can easily reverse earlier gains (Chan, 1997) as the period since 11 September 2001 has demonstrated. In the UK as elsewhere (for example see Poynting et al., 2004) criminal justice and police responses and cycles towards racist victimisation are such that on the one hand the protection of victims vies with the criminalisation of minority ethnic groups on the other.

The final section provides a brief 'audit' of what has been achieved with the proviso that policy towards racist victimisation also needs to address wider racist victimisation found in the criminalisation of minority ethnic groups.

Conclusion: Has Understanding and Policy towards Racist Victimisation Improved?

What longer-term evidence is there of improvement in the policing, handling, reporting, recording, prevention and understanding of racist victimisation since the Macpherson inquiry? In particular, have changes in police and other agency codes and practice and the law been more consistent and effective in increasing victim satisfaction with the handling of racist incidents? These questions can begin to be answered from the review presented here. A recent Home Office assessment of progress (Docking and Tuffin, 2005) has concluded – through surveys of all police forces and local authorities in England and Wales, and in-depth studies of attitudes and practices of individuals in three areas – that police and other agencies' policies and practice have improved. As would be expected there was regional variation in this improvement but overall, both reporting and recording has increased although some officers continued to see most incidents as minor and not worth bothering about or failed to understand why something may be interpreted as racist. There remained major problems in schools and Local Education Authorities (LEAs) in monitoring and recording racist incidents.

Overall, police and agencies' treatment of victims and witnesses had very significantly improved compared to the era prior to the Lawrence Inquiry, in terms of increased sensitivity and understanding of the issues, and greater willingness to deal with racist incidents, particularly among specialist rather than operational officers.

Officers criticised the CPS for not taking racist offences more seriously. Despite some promising Probation Service work, relatively little work was being carried out to tackle perpetrators' views or prevent potential perpetrators from committing racist offences or holding racist views. The main conclusion, however, from Docking and Tuffin's (2005) assessment, is that although trust and confidence in the police and agencies handling of racist incidents has improved, the recording of incidents perceived by victims to be less serious, but which might have a cumulative impact, continues to be neglected.

As fitting, given earlier arguments, the chapter concludes with Ray and Smith's (2004: 693) focused study of racist offenders in which they argue, "the figures on racist incidents have been produced by a greater readiness on the part of whites than of Asians to report incidents they believe to be racially motivated, and willingness to believe this has itself been encouraged by the police and the media accounts of the problem since the mid–1990s". Meanwhile, "white residents of areas close to neighbourhoods with a large Asian population feel threatened and at risk, and become more likely to report to the police incidents that might have gone unreported in a less fearful environment" (ibid: 694). This is perhaps, one of the most significant unintended consequences of changes since Macpherson and the accompanying recent improvements in reporting and greater trust of the police in handling racist victimisation.

Despite its limitations, the Macpherson inquiry is a watershed in understanding and policy toward racist victimisation in England and Wales. On this basis alone, it is to be welcomed. In the post-colonial and post-Lawrence policing climate found in Britain however, improvements and gains in the policing of racist victimisation can be overtaken by events. Chan's (1997) study has shown in a different national context how police reform is fraught with difficulties and how easily events can be overtaken. For example, disproportionate stop and search continues to be of concern, particularly in respect of Terrorism legislation and policy, although recent studies have questioned whether BME groups are disproportionately targeted (Waddington et al., 2004; Hallsworth and Maguire, 2004). Others have argued that negative attitudes to poorer minority ethnic areas, can lead to aggressive and antagonistic policing strategies that discipline particular segments of the population legitimised in terms of the maintenance of public order (Choongh, 1997). In Britain as elsewhere, the key to understanding racist victimisation is to recognise how different forms of racism and the groups targeted by racism change over time and according to context, and policies aimed at ameliorating racist victimisation need to respond accordingly.

References

ACPO (Association of Chief Police Officers) (1985) *Guiding Principles Concerning Racial Attacks*, London: ACPO.

Bowling, B. (1993) *Policing Violent Racism: Policy and Practice in an East London Locality*, D. Phil Dissertation, London: London School of Economics and Political Science.

Bowling, B. (1998) *Violent Racism: Victimisation, Policing and Social Context*, Oxford: Clarendon Press.

Brown, C. (1984) *Black and White Britain: The Third PSI Report*, London: Heinemann.

Cantle, T. (2002) *Community Cohesion: A Report of the Independent Review Team*, London: Home Office.

CARF/Southall Rights (1981) *Southall: The Birth of a Black Community*, London: Institute of Race Relations.

Cesarani, D. (1990) *The Making of Modern Anglo-Jewry*, Oxford: Basil Blackwell.

Chan, J. (1997) *Changing Police Culture: Policing in a Multicultural Society*, Cambridge: Cambridge University Press.

Choongh, S. (1997) *Policing as Social Discipline*, Oxford: Oxford University Press.

Clancy, A., Hough, M., Aust, R. and Kershaw, C. (2001) *Crime, Policing and Justice: The Experience of Ethnic Minorities: Findings from the 2000 British Crime Survey*, Home Office Research Study No. 223, London: Home Office.

Clark, I. and Moody, S. (2002) *Racist Crime and Victimisation in Scotland*, Crime and Criminal Justice Research Findings No. 58, Edinburgh: Scottish Executive Central Research Unit.

Clark, T. (2001) *Burnley Task Force*, Burnley: Burnley Borough Council.

Colley, L. (1992) *Britons: Forging the Nation 1707–1837*, London: Yale University Press.

Collins, M. (2004) *The Likes of Us: A Biography of the White Working Class*, London: Granta Books.

Cook, D. (2006) *Criminal and Social Justice*, London: Sage.

Dench, G., Gavron, K. and Young, M. (2006) *The New East End: Kinship, Race and Conflict*, London: Profile Books.

Docking, M. and Tuffin, R. (2005) *Racist Incidents: Progress Since the Lawrence Inquiry*, Home Office Online Report No. 42, London: Home Office.

Dorling, D. and Thomas, B. (2004) *People and Places: A 2001 Census Atlas of the UK*, Bristol: Policy Press.

Feilzer, M. and Hood, R. (2004) *Differences or Discrimination? Minority Ethnic People in the Youth Justice System*. London: Youth Justice Board.

FitzGerald, M. (2001) 'Ethnic Minorities and Community Safety', Matthews, R. and Pitts, J. (eds.) *Crime, Disorder and Community Disorder: A New Agenda*, pp. 145–166, London: Routledge.

FitzGerald, M. and Hale, C. (1996) *Ethnic Minorities, Victimisation and Racial Harassment*, Research Findings No. 39, London: Home Office.

Foster, J. (1999) *Docklands: Cultures in Conflict, Worlds in Collision*, London: UCL Press.

GLC (Greater London Council) (1984) *Racial Harassment in London: Report of a Panel of Inquiry Set Up by the GLC Police Committee*, London: GLC.

GLC (Greater London Council) (1985) *Report by Head of Housing Services*, GLC (TH192), February 1985. London: GLC.

Goodey, J. (2005) *Victims and Victimology: Research, Policy and Practice*, Harlow: Longman.

Hallsworth, S. and Maguire, M. (2004) *Profiling the City of London Exercise of Stop and Search*, London: Report for the City of London Police.

Hesse, B., Rai, D. K., Bennett, C. and McGilchrist, P. (1992) *Beneath the Surface: Racial Harassment*, Aldershot: Avebury.

Hiro, D. (1991) *Black British White British: A History of Race Relations in Britain.* London: Grafton.

Holdaway, S. (1996) *The Racialisation of British Policing*, Basingstoke: Macmillan.

Holmes, C. (1988) *John Bull's Island*, Basingstoke: Macmillan.

Home Affairs Committee (1982) *Racial Attacks: Second Report from Session 1981–82*, London: HMSO.

Home Affairs Committee (1986) *Racial Attacks and Harassment*, London: HMSO.

Home Affairs Committee (1987) *Racial Attacks and Harassment – Second Follow-up to the Home Affairs Committee's Report in 1986*, London: HMSO.

Home Affairs Committee (1989) *Third Report from the Home Affairs Committee, Session 1986-88: Racial Attacks and Harassment*, London: HMSO.

Home Office (1981) *Racial Attacks*, London: Home Office.

Home Office (1986) *Home Office Good Practice Guide for the Police: The Response to Racial Attacks*, London: Home Office.

Home Office (1989) *The Response to Racial Attacks and Harassment: Guidance for the Statutory Agencies*, London: Home Office.

Home Office (2000) *Statistics on Race and the Criminal Justice System*, London: Home Office.

Home Office (2004) *Race and the Criminal Justice System: An Overview to the Complete Statistics 2002–2003*, London: Home Office.

Home Office (2005) *Statistics on Race and the Criminal Justice System*, London: Home Office.

Hood, R. (1992) *Race and Sentencing*, Oxford: Clarendon Press.

Hudson, B. (1993) *Penal Policy and Social Justice*, London: Sage.

Husband, C. (1982) 'The East End Racism 1900–1980: Geographical Continuities in Vigilantist and Extreme Right-wing Political Behaviour', *London Journal*, 8(1): 3–26.

Husband, C. (1983) *Racial Exclusionism and the City: The Urban Support of the National Front*, London: Allen & Unwin.

Husband, C. (1989) 'Racial Attacks: the Persistence of Racial Harassment in British Cities', Kushner, T. and Lunn, K. (eds.) *Traditions of Intolerance: Historical Perspectives on Facism and Race Discourse in Britain*, pp. 63–87, Manchester: Manchester University Press.

Independent Black Collective (1986) *Bradford Black*, July/August.

Institute for Criminal Policy Research (2004) *Race and the Criminal Justice System: An Overview to the Complete Statistics 2002–2003*, London: Home Office.

Jarman, N. (2002) *Overview Analysis of Racist Incidents Recorded in Northern Ireland by the RUC 1996–1999*, Belfast: The Office of the First Minister and Deputy First Minister, Research Branch.

Jenkinson, J. (1993) 'The 1919 Riots', Panayi, P. (ed.) *Racial Violence in Britain 1840–1950*, Leicester: Leicester University Press, pp. 92–111.

Kundnani, A. (2001) *From Oldham to Bradford: The violence of the violated* (http://www.irr.org.uk/2001/october/ak000003.htm1), accessed 15 April 2006.

Layton-Henry, Z. (1984) *The Politics of Race in Britain*, London: Allen & Unwin.

Lea, J. (1986) 'Police Racism: Some Theories and their Policy Implications', Matthews, R. and Young, J. (eds.) (1986) *Confronting Crime*, pp. 145–165, London: Sage.

Lea, J. (2000) 'The Macpherson Report and Question of Institutional Racism', *The Howard Journal of Criminal Justice*, 39(3): 219–233.

Lea, J. (2003) *From Brixton to Bradford: Ideology and Discourse on Race and Urban Violence in the United Kingdom* (http://www.bunkers8.pwp.blueyonder.co.uk/misc/riots.htm), accessed 15 April 2006.

London, L. (1973) 'The East End of London: Paki-bashing in 1970', *Race Today*, 5: 337–341.

Macpherson, W. (1999) *The Stephen Lawrence Inquiry*, London: The Stationery Office.

Marlow, A. and Loveday, B. (2000) *After McPherson: Policing After the Stephen Lawrence Inquiry*, Lyme Regis: Russell House.

Mason, D. (ed.) (2003) *Explaining Ethnic Differences: Changing Patterns of Disadvantage in Britain*, Bristol: The Policy Press.

Maynard, W. and Read, T. (1997) *Policing Racially Motivated Incidents*, Crime Reduction and Prevention Series Paper 84, Police research Group, London: Home Office.

Modood, T. (2003) 'Ethnic Differentials in Educational Performance', in Mason, D. (ed.) *Explaining Ethnic Differences: Changing Patterns of Disadvantage in Britain*, Bristol: The Policy Press, pp. 53–67.

Nicholas, S., Povey, D., Walker, A. and Kershaw, C. (2005) *Crime in England and Wales 2004/2005*, London: Home Office.

Oldham MBC and GMP (Greater Manchester Police) (2001) *Building a shared future for Oldham: Interim Report to the Home Secretary*, Oldham: Oldham Partnership Board.

Ouseley, Sir Herman (2001) *Community Pride Not Prejudice: Making Diversity Work in Bradford*, Bradford: Bradford Vision.

Owen, D. (2003) 'The Demographic Characteristics of People from Minority Ethnic Groups in Britain', Mason, D. (ed.) *Explaining Ethnic Differences: Changing Patterns of Disadvantage in Britain*, Bristol: The Policy Press, pp. 21–52.

Panayi, P. (ed.) (1993) *Racial Violence in Britain 1840–1950*, Leicester: Leicester University Press.

Pearson, G. (1976) '"Paki-Bashing" in a North-East Lancashire Cotton Town: A Case Study and its History', in Mungham, G. and Pearson, G. (eds.) *Working Class Youth Culture*, pp. 48–81, London: Routledge.

Pilkington, A. (2003) *Racial Disadvantage and Ethnic Diversity in Britain*, Basingstoke: Palgrave Macmillan.

Poynting, S., Noble, G., Tabar, P. and Collins, J. (2004) *Bin Laden in The Suburbs: Criminalising the Arab Other*, Sydney: Sydney Institute of Criminology.

Race Today Collective (1986) *The Struggles of Asian Workers in Britain*, London: Race Today.

Ray, L. and Smith, D. (2004) 'Racist Offending, Policing and community Conflict', *Sociology*, 38(4): 681–699.
Ray, L., Smith, D. and Wastell, L. (2003) 'Understanding Racist Violence' in Stanko B. (ed.) *The Meanings of Violence*, London: Routledge.
Ray, L., Smith, D. and Wastell, L. (2004) 'Shame, Rage and Racist Violence', *British Journal of Criminology*, 44(3): 350–368.
Rowe, M. (2004) *Policing, Race and Racism*, Cullompton: Willan Publishing.
Salisbury, H. and Upson, A. (2004) *Ethnicity, Victimisation and Worry About Crime: Findings from the 2001/2 and 2002/3 British Crime Survey*, Home Office Research Findings No. 237, London: Home office.
Sampson, A., and Phillips, C. (1992) *Multiple Victimisation: Racial Attacks on an East London Estate*, Police Research Group, Crime Prevention Unit Series, Paper no. 36. London: Home Office.
Sibbit, R. (1997) *The Perpetrators of Racial Harassment and Violence*, Home Office Research Study 176, London: Home Office.
Simpson, L. (2004) 'Statistics of Racial Segregation: Measures, Evidence and Policy', *Urban Studies*, 41(3): 661–681.
Smith, D.J. (1994) 'Race, Crime, and Criminal Justice', in Maguire, M., Morgan, R. and Reiner, R. (eds.) (1994) *The Oxford Handbook of Criminology*, Oxford Clarendon Press, pp. 1041–1117.
Solomos, J. (1993) *Race and Racism in Britain*, 2nd Edition, London: Macmillan.
Spalek, B. (ed.) (2002) *Islam, Crime and Criminal Justice*, Cullompton: Willan Publishing.
Stenson, K. (1996) *Young People, Race and Crime*, Occasional Paper 1, Social Policy Research Group. High Wycombe: Buckinghamshire College.
Stenson, K. and Watt, P. (1998) 'The Street: "It's A Bit Dodgy Around There", Safety, Danger, Ethnicity and Young People's Use of Public Space', Skelton, T. and Valentine, G. (eds.) *Cool Places, Geographies of Youth Cultures*, London: Routledge, pp. 249–265.
Waddington, P.A.J., Stenson, K. and Don, D. (2004) 'In Proportion: Race, and Police Stop and Search', *British Journal of Criminology*, 44: 1–26.
Webster, C. (1994) 'Racial Harassment, Space and Localism', *Criminal Justice Matters*, No. 16: 18–20.
Webster, C. (1995) *Youth Crime, Victimisation and Racial Harassment: The Keighley Crime Survey*, Centre for Research in Applied Community Studies, Bradford: Bradford & Ilkley Community College Corporation.
Webster, C. (1996) 'Local Heroes: Violent Racism, Spacism and Localism Among White and Asian Young People', *Youth & Policy*, No 53: 15–27.
Webster, C. (1997) 'The Construction of British "Asian" Criminality', *International Journal of the Sociology of Law*, 25: 65–86.
Webster, C. (1998) 'Researching Racial Violence: A Scientific Realist Approach', Vagg, J., and Newburn, T. (eds.) *Emerging Themes in British Criminology: Selected papers from the 1995 British Criminology Conference*. Available online at: http://www.britsoccrim.org/volume1/004.pdf, accessed on 30 November 2006.

Webster, C. (2003) 'Race, Space and Fear: Imagined Geographies of Racism, Crime, Violence and Disorder in Northern England', *Capital & Class*, No. 80, May, pp. 95–122.

Webster, C. (2004) 'Policing British Asian Communities', Hopkins Burke, R. (ed.) *Hard Cop/Soft Cop: Dilemmas and Debates in Contemporary Policing*, pp. 69–84, Cullompton: Willan Publishing.

Whitfield, J. (2004) *Unhappy Dialogue: The Metropolitan Police and Black Londoners in Post-war Britain*, Cullompton: Willan Publishing.

Young, J. (2003) *The Riots in Bradford and Oldham* (http://www.malcolmread.co.uk/JockYoung/bradford.htm), accessed 15 April 2006.

Helpful websites

http://www.homeoffice.gov.uk – Home Office.
http://www.runnymedetrust.org – Runnymede Trust.
http://www.irr.org.uk – Institute of Race Relations.
http://www.kickitout.org/ – Let's Kick Racism Out of Football.
http://eumc.eu.int/eumc/index.php – European Monitoring Centre on Racism and Xenophobia.
http://www.statewatch.org/ – Statewatch: Monitoring the State and Civil Liberties in the European Union.

Chapter 4

France

Sophie Body-Gendrot

Introduction

In February of 2006, a 23-year-old mobile phone seller named Ilan Halimi was kidnapped. He was brutally tortured for three weeks and left to die near a railway station by a multiethnic gang calling itself 'Barbarians.' The gang's leader, Youssouf Fofana, had immigrated with his parents from the Ivory Coast to France as a child. Fofana claimed that the crime was merely for money extortion and not racially motivated. The fact that Halimi was Jewish and that the gang shared the stereotypical view that 'Jews have money' raised the question of whether the attack was in fact motivated by anti-Semitic sentiment. The incident ignited considerable public reaction as tens of thousands of people and most political leaders marched against racism and anti-Semitism. Even some of France's major politicians spoke out against the incident. Unfortunately such acts are neither new nor infrequent. France has had a long history of racially based violence and victimization.

Although extreme, the Fofana story can serve as an example for examining racial victimization in France because it displays some of the features of current racially based violence in France, especially that of *banlieue* neighbourhoods (i.e., the disadvantaged urban areas that contain high concentrations of minority ethnic population). Interethnic antagonism between youth of post-colonial origin (Algeria, Morocco, Tunisia, Francophone Africa) and young Jews have plagued specific marginalized neighbourhoods and their schools, in particular since the second Intifada (i.e., the Palestinian campaign directed at ending the Israeli military occupation which started in September 2000). The potential for problems is further increased by the fact that France has the largest Jewish and Arab-Muslim communities in Europe. The Jewish community is composed of around 600,000 people while those of Arab-Muslim heritage add up to about 5 million. However, unlike other European multicultural countries, French authorities and the media have tried to downplay interethnic tensions, instead emphasizing forms of opposition to state agents from male youth in these areas. But in recent years, minorities have been involved in a game of competitive victimhood, each group trying to outbid the other for sympathy. A first issue is that relatives of Arab-Muslim victims in particular openly express their resentment, because they feel that Jewish people tend to be treated more sympathetically by the middle classes and their political representatives than they are whenever victimization occurs.

Secondly, the Jewish community, for its part, says that old forms of anti-Semitism are still very evident and that they have been revived by the Middle East issue. In

Sarcelles, a locality in the Parisian region, where some 15 000 Jews live, there was a notable exodus of families who moved back to Israel in 2005. Emigration increased by 27 per cent in comparison with the previous year. The major reason given for this was anti-Semitic attitudes towards them. The radicalization of the Jewish Defence League, which brings together a lot of youngsters eager to defend themselves with arms and violence, cannot be denied. One might recall that in 2004, Ariel Sharon (1928-2006), then Prime Minister of Israel, invited French Jews to move back to Israel because of the "wildest anti-Semitism" in France.

Thirdly, the status of violence marking youth street culture in marginalized urban areas and reflecting, in general, harsher social relations in France was pushed to its extreme with the Halimi episode. Is this a crime of the times, a form of magnifying glass on the real state of French society? It cannot be denied that disenfranchised young people, who are unable to diffuse their frustrations with words, frequently resort to physical assaults against weaker ones and that more young people are victimized in these areas than elsewhere. A recent report by the National Observatory of Delinquency showed that the younger they are, the more they are at risk. The 14-19 age group represents 12.2 per cent of the victims, while 20-29 10.7 per cent. 10 per cent of public housing project residents state that they have been assaulted at least once (Thieffry, 2006).

In the Halimi case, the gang was of immigrant and French descent and included Islamic radicals; these youth felt alienated (i.e., they were in a state of anomie) and violence against individuals, social groups and mainstream institutions was part of their repertoire. Youssouf Fofana garnered considerable attention among youth from his neighbourhood because of the intimidation that, as a gang leader, he exerted upon others.

Fourthly, the Left first looked at this type of crime with suspicion, which reveals the reluctance it generally feels at targeting criminals of immigrant origin in order to avoid any confusion with the position of the far right. Similar attitudes were observed during the three-week disorders in November of 2005 which disrupted some three hundred neighbourhoods throughout France.

This reluctance can also be seen in the political treatment of the Marie L. case. In the Spring of 2004, Ms. L called the police claiming that she had been assaulted by "four North Africans and two blacks" on a regional train near Paris. Her attackers, she asserted, had said that "in district 16, there are only Jews" (District 16 is an affluent area in Paris). Soon after, the French Prime Minister denounced this odious crime through the media, and the Anti-Racist League described the offenders as "Nazis from the banlieues." Most of the French public, along with various government officials and major television and media outlets, came to the defence of Ms. L's case. She, and other young French women, were considered as potential victims of Arabs and Blacks "who do not bring anything to the national life of a country where they just happen to have been born by chance" (Ténisien, 2004). Unfortunately, it turns out that the whole story was fabricated by a young woman desperate for attention. Ironically, Marie L. was never accused of racism and no apologies were offered to the two insulted communities by any of those who spoke out against the alleged offenders.

In this chapter, I propose to examine racial victimization in France. I will first place the concept of 'racism' within a French context before examining the historical background of racial victimization in the country. Various significant events will be presented so as to offer a conceptual framework by which one can understand the subject matter. Then the chapter will analyze racist crimes and the law as well as the nature and extent of racist victimization in France. It will end with various types of reactions to these phenomena.

Defining Racism in France

'Racism' in France is generally understood as "any form of violence exerted against another human group from prejudice and/or contempt to discrimination; from segregation to random or organized murder." In addition, within a more abstract context, the term racism is currently understood as any form of hostility towards a designated group (e.g., anti-youth, anti-cops, etc.) (Guillaumin, 1994: 67-68). The term 'polysemic' characterizes French racism. Polysemic racism is premised on the idea that human groups have specific, physical and transmitted features, which are superior or inferior to each other (Guillaumin, 2002). Countries such as the United States and the United Kingdom give recognition to institutional racism, which only serves to amplify ideological and political racism in rules related to housing, work, school, health and police work. By contrast, France is silent on this type of racism and strongly resists debates on racism in general. As Poli (2001: 198) observed: "the first reaction to questions related to racism is silence." In fact, in 1992, French social scientists met in order to suppress the term *race* from their vocabulary (Mots, 1992). The social scientists also attempted to persuade politicians to remove the term from the French Constitution. They argued that the term was devoid of substance. They claimed that if racism was real, the concept of race was unscientific. In their discourse the scientists referred to a popular French mode of thinking that was summarized by President Pompidou: "Sometimes, the mere fact of mentioning the term calls for the idea and unfortunately, frequently, reality follows the idea" (*Le Monde*, 1 September 1973). This French attitude is also well exemplified by Alain Terrenoire, the *rapporteur* of the 1972 law against racism: "Speaking of races is always a delicate matter, for we run the risk of giving credibility to the idea that there are different distinctions (qualitative) within the human species. That is why we must separate the justified and necessary struggle against racism and its misdeeds from the factual recognition of differences between people according to their origins, their religion, and the colour of their skin" (quoted by Bleich, 2000: 58).

In essence, any debate between the nature and culture of racism was solved by a denial of the phenomenon. Currently, however, there is an agreement that the concept needs to be qualified; French racism is differentialist and cultural, "a racism without races" (Taguieff, 1993). In France, racism is not *based on nature and on skin color*; rather it finds its roots in the decay of the working-class, in the shrinking of the labour market, and in the loss of bearings of vulnerable middle classes (Guillaumin, 2002).

Ever since the two United Nations declarations of 1950 and 1951, taken up by UNESCO in 1952, the institutional construction of racism has been based on three types of situations: anti-Semitism, colonialism, and apartheid. In France, it is a "political object referring to boundaries between social inclusion and exclusion" (Balibar, 2005, 14-15). The danger for scientific analysis is that racism then has no limits. That is, based on the UN definition, the scope of racism can symbolically range from violence to acts of discrimination. Therefore, for the purpose of this chapter, I will limit the discussion of racial victimization in France to incidents involving quantifiable acts of victimization.

The reader should be aware, however, that French officials repeatedly claim that France is not a racist or an anti-Semitic country (see Chebel d'Appolonia, 2005: 6). Yet, the apparent increase in racist and anti-Semitic incidents in the recent years beg the question of whether racist, anti-Semitic and xenophobic acts are real or generated by better reporting and recording or simply an aberrant expression of distorted media attention (Mayer and Michelat, 2005).

Is there a new islamophobia and/or is there a new judeophobia which would be distinct from traditional racism and xenophobia? Are the neo-racist groups different in nature from the 'ordinary racists' who are usually found in the low-income social strata, who have ethnocentric and authoritarian attitudes and are usually close to right and extreme-right parties? We will attempt to address these questions in the rest of this talk.

Historical Background of Racist Victimization in France

Racism against ethnic minorities in France is nothing new. France has a long history of internal and external migrations, first from neighbouring countries (Belgium, Italy, Spain, Germany or Switzerland), then after the First World War, from Czechoslovakia and Poland. That refugees also rushed to France and sought asylum explains why in 1931, France had a rate of foreigners exceeding that of the United States (6.58 per cent). (Weil, 2005: 14). After 1947, citizenship given to Muslims in colonies allowed them free circulation between France and their residence. This free circulation only ended in 1974. According to the census of 1974, 758 000 Portuguese and 710 000 Algerians constitute the largest immigrant groups, followed by Spaniards (479 000), Italians (462 000), Moroccans (260 000) and Tunisians (139 000). Immigrants make up 6.2 per cent of the population (Weil, op.cit. 16). Currently, legal immigrants make up 7.4 per cent of the population (including 1 600 000 from the European Union and 1 300 000 from North Africa). 170 000 foreigners a year settle legally in the country either through marriage (44 000), naturalization or as students (out of 200 000 foreign students in French universities, 54 per cent come from Africa) or via labour contracts (Tabet, 2005: 8; Corroler, 2006: 4).

The difficulty in documenting the rate of racial victimization in France is compounded by the fact that statistically, racial and ethnic based crimes do not exist. French political and philosophical principles make it against the law to record a person's race or ethnicity, implying that, once French, everyone will benefit from equal protection under the law. The only distinction is between French citizens and foreigners. In practice, the country is experiencing a 'pas de deux' with race. On the one hand, access to identifying the nationality of inhabitants in France has always been rather easy by comparison with other countries (Weil and Crowley, 1994). On the other hand, all along the history of the country since the Revolution of 1789, moments of race-awareness have revealed contradictions with the principles of colour-blindness.

This general trend is steeped in France's colonial past. While there was no mass slavery in France, slavery did exist in the French Caribbean islands. Slavery was abolished in 1794, re-instated for almost fifty years under Napoleon's regime before being permanently abolished in 1848 by the Second Republic. Today, some French of African descent organize and revive the collective memory of slavery. A date of commemoration has officially been set on the calendar.

The status of Arab-Muslims in North African departments (counties) during colonization also revealed the contradictions between principles and practices. Although formally recognized as French citizens, they were in fact treated as second-class citizens and some of them consider themselves to be victims of a social-cultural conflict that seems ever present. These views are supported in an article by Sayad (1991) who asked: "How to be French without being French yet being supposedly French by law?"

Although throughout French history acts of racially motivated crimes have been largely based on socio-economic conditions, Noirel (1988) has observed that racially motivated offences were committed against Belgians, Poles and Italians during the 19th and 20th centuries. He studied several generations of Immigrants in Longwy, a mining area of Lorraine and showed that during the first half of the 20th century, foreign miners of Polish and Italian origins who were part of the proletariat were not immune from xenophobic acts but that later on, having moved into lower middle classes, they exerted similar forms of xenophobia and racism against newcomers from the former colonies moving into working-class jobs, thus hampering the latter's ethnic upward mobility.

The Alfred Dreyfus Affair, in the late 1800s, and the responsibility of the Vichy regime in the tragic historical persecution of Jews and other visible minorities, which are well-known French historical dramas, come to mind in this brief retrospective. In addition, the round up of Jews in 1942, known as "Vel d'Hiv roundup," officially condemned by President Jacques Chirac in 1995, may explain why anti-racist organizations have been more mobilized in cases of anti-Semitism than in those of post-colonial racism which has never been fully addressed.

That the nature and extent of racial victimization in France in earlier times is not well-documented is also explained by the French principles which officially minimize ethnic and racial differences in order to cement a "One and Indivisible nation." Consequently, state responses to racial violence stem from sources other than the racist violence itself. Until recently, collective conflicts, especially local conflicts, were analyzed in terms of class, and historians and researchers documenting the working class or the malaises of French society would do it via socio-economic analyses. In situations in which racist violence was not perceived as constituting a major problem by the public and the political situation at large, responses were taken at the local level by councillors, police officers and mayors and the issue was minimized. Because "the racism of French society" was not constructed theoretically, it was not propelled on the political agenda (Witte, 1996:

7). Consequently, the perception that ethnic lobbying would lead to a blind alley did not incite the victims of racist violence to claim that their ethnic or racial identity was a cause for victimization, least they would lose social ground or be stigmatized as "other." This situation changed with the episode of the Algerian war.

The Trauma of the Algerian War

The historian Benjamin Stora (2002) explains why the trauma of the Algerian war of 1954, still impacts today's French society in terms of racism and exclusion. The 1950s and the 1960s were years of decolonization and the process had an effect on the ex-colonies as well as on France. Opposition to decolonization was led by activists belonging to the far right, to extreme nationalistic, anti-Gaullist and anti-communist supporters such as the *Union de Défense des Commerçants et Artisans* which was led by Pierre Poujade (1920-2002) who supported French Algeria. In 1962 some one million French referred to as *pieds noirs* (i.e., white colons from North Africa and especially from Algeria) suffered from the independence given to Algeria, where they had always lived. Many could not gain access to their birth or marriage certificates after Algerian independence. Hence some couldn't provide proof that they were French. These French felt betrayed by their home country and some of them sided with the *Organisation de l'armée secrète* (OAS), which conducted terrorist activities in Algeria and in France after 1961. The OAS was responsible for the death of thousands of Algerians and French of European origin during the *ratonnades* (literally rat hunts). Witte (1996) notes that these killings received nominal attention from the police and were essentially tolerated by some of the major security forces in France. The more the Algerian war recedes into the past, the more this repressed history haunts French society (Stora, 2002). In addition, some Harkis – Algerians who sided with France and were tortured and massacred by the Liberation Front in Algeria – managed to escape and settle in France. They were then ignored by the French government and by a society eager to forget the war. Many of the Harkis were placed in hastily established army camps for decades (see Body-Gendrot, 1995: 573; 2004: 154). The plight of these two groups, along with that of the immigrés and their children, tends to keep the painful issue of colonization alive. For instance, a police-led attack on Algerian demonstrators on October 17, 1961 against a curfew imposed by the Paris Chief of Police, Maurice Papon (also a former member of the French Vichy government who was later charged for his involvement in the deportation of Jews during World War II) played a key role in the death of an estimated 30-50 peaceful protestors from the Algerian National Liberation Front. For a long time, this event was met with amnesia and racist violence was simply not an issue for the government. "The specific victimization of Algerian communities in France did not enter the dominant discourse" (Witte, 1996: 84). When the consequences of the 1961 demonstration finally received an official recognition from the current mayor of Paris, not only could few people attend the ceremony due to the large police presence surrounding the site, but the plate placed on the wall facing the Paris Prefecture of Police has been removed several times since then by anonymous hands.

Fuelled by the state of social, political and economic turmoil in the 1970s, Algerians were increasingly targeted by members of extreme-right paramilitary groups as well as subjected to racist attacks by unorganized people. And while the acts subsided with time, it was difficult for the French to ignore such a wide cataclysm. With its refusal to analyze the war and draw consequences from it, Stora observes, the Republic was unable to fight the extreme right which interpreted the colonial war within a racial paradigm and therefore violently rejected multiculturalism (Stora 2002: 20). In Algeria, colonization was indeed based on a hierarchical ranking, with the French colonists being at the top and the 'unmeltable' Arabs at the bottom of the social order. The same differentialist racism was spread by far right groups such as *Ordre Nouveau* (sometimes using the slogan "neither right nor left") led by the likes of Alexandre Marc, and it has also been referred to as "the communitarian third way," which prevailed in the 1970s.

With immigration becoming a more visible issue after the country had closed its doors to immigrants in 1973, France was confronted with a dramatic wave of racist violence. An incident in Marseille in which a mentally disturbed Algerian youth stabbed a bus driver triggered a series of racist killings. Soon after, three Algerians were separately killed in that city and another one in the Parisian region. The editor of a Marseille newspaper wrote that "racism is Arabic; after all, there is no European racism, since we have accepted the abuses of the Arab world for a long time... We have had enough! Enough of the Algerian thieves, enough of the Algerian rowdies, enough of the Algerian braggarts, enough of the Algerian agitators, enough of the Algerian syphilis carriers, enough of the Algerian rapists, enough of the Algerian pimps, enough of the Algerian lunatics, enough of the Algerian killers" (Tahar Ben Jelloun, 1984: 68). This sense of indignation reflected the prevailing theme of racist-based thinking. Hostility towards the 'Dangerous Other' grew and over the next few years an estimated 52 Algerians (with or without French citizenship) were either killed or badly wounded, frequently during hunts for Arabs in their places of work or residence (Guidice, 1992). Ironically, there was little response from the government. The government was reluctant to recognize the racist character of violence except for the banning of *Ordre nouveau*.

As pointed out by Schain, municipalities governed by the Left in the 1970s and early 1980s took action against the disproportionate number of immigrant families who had settled in their locality. For instance, in Vénissieux, a suburb of Lyon, the exclusion of immigrant families from a public housing project was supported by authorities at various levels on the basis of the tipping point. Immigrant children were excluded from summer camp programs and from winter ski schools sponsored by the mayors. Interestingly, the term immigrant also included French born in overseas départements (Body-Gendrot and Schain, 1992). Another striking political move came from the communist mayor of Vitry sur Seine in the Paris region. On Christmas Eve 1980, he led a demonstration against the transfer of 300 Mali workers to a hostel in his locality. In the meantime, a bulldozer was driven into the hostel. Then another well-known communist mayor (later to become a Minister) publicly accused a Moroccan family of trading drugs and organized a hate demonstration in front of this family's house. These and other hostile actions by the French militant groups did not spare the second generation of North African immigrants, especially those between the ages of 15-24 who numbered some 700, 000 in 1983 (Jazouli, 1986). Their problems were due to their visibility and their poverty as well as the reluctance of their parents to return to their native country. The situation was further compounded by the fact that these groups were caught in a vacuum of social isolation which left them even more vulnerable when attacked by racist individuals or groups.

It was particularly alarming that a disproportionate number of racially motivated victims were youths. For example, during the summer of 1982 a young person by the name of A. Boutelja was killed in the suburbs of Lyon. A month later, A. Guemiah was murdered in a segregated and ghettoized area of Nanterre at the periphery of Paris, and that same month, A. Haouette and W. Hachichi were also shot. These incidents marked the beginning of a series of racist crimes committed by French 'sheriffs' and by racist policemen, still influenced by colonial ideas. In 1983, xenophobic propaganda reached unprecedented heights when the extreme right party, led by Jean-Marie Le Pen, accused North Africans of being responsible for the rising rates of unemployment and crime throughout France. Le Pen, President of the far-right *Front National* Party, used the general social unrest in major French cities, such as Dreux, Roubaix, Lyon, Marseille, Mulhouse, Toulon, Grenoble and the Paris region, to support his ideological point of view. Given the deep roots of racism and anti-Semitism among the French public there was a general consensus of support that even the media expressed.

These episodes were followed by additional incidents such as the deaths of M. Merzogh, 19 years old, shot in a mall by a security guard in Livry Gargan, A. Zioch shot by a neighbor in Argenteuil and K. Lettad, seriously wounded with a pruning knife by racist vigilantes. In July, there was the death of T. Ouanes, 9 years old, shot by a depressed neighbor at La Courneuve, a massive public housing project in the Parisian region, then M. Rabahi, 11 years old, died from a head injury in a public housing project of Nancy, and A. Amouri died after an assault in Cergy. This continued in July with two more attacks of North African youths in Saint Denis and this followed with more deaths in August and in September, making a total of twenty that summer (Jazouli, 2002). The bullets generally came from isolated snipers, sometimes from racist posses, but the series of crimes indicates that a sort of epidemic had taken place (Wieviorka, 1998).

The incident rate of racial victimization and the interest it generates appear to ebb and flow in France. Racially motivated acts are closely linked to the social, economic and political climate of the time. While such acts diminished in the late 1980s, there was a series of racially motivated attacks that received international attention in October 2005 with the violent riots north-east of Paris, followed by riots in two other major centres in France. The 2005 riots occurred after two youths of North African origin were accidentally electrocuted after attempting to run away from the police.

While these acts continue to take their toll, Arab-Muslim groups and their supporters have not remained passive and their efforts should be mentioned.

Racism, Racist Crime and the Law in France

The 1972 Law against Racism and Anti-Semitism

France was one of the earliest countries in Europe to pass a comprehensive anti-racist legislation. In response to the French ratification of the (UN) International Convention on the Elimination of All Forms of Racial Discrimination (New York, 1965), the 1 July 1972 anti-discrimination legislation was passed. It included three elements:

1. It targeted incitement to racial hatred,
2. It outlawed racial discrimination, and
3. It gave powers to the state to ban racist groups (Freeman, 1979).

Eric Bleich (2000) has offered a relevant explanation of what an Anti-racist law could be like in a country which is race-blind in his analysis of this foundational law of 1972. In sharp contrast with the corresponding British legislation, Bleich (2000) observes that the law generated very little controversy at the time it was passed and was adopted with a unanimous vote in both Chambers. Previous vain attempts to pass anti-discrimination bills had taken place in 1959, 1962, 1967 and 1969. The popular reason for rejection was that, everyone being equal under the law, there was no need for specific protection to be offered to one group over another (Freeman, 1979). The impetus for the anti-racial legislation came from the Human Rights interest group, *Mouvement Contre le Racisme et pour l'Amitié entre les Peuples* (MRAP), sympathetic to the Communist Party, and opposed to the Vichy regime and its anti-Semitism. Paradoxically, the term *race* was added at the last moment without much consideration for its implication. The MRAP was fighting against the rebirth of anti-Semitic elements and neo-Nazism in films and in the press, while fighting for the legal right of associations to participate as civil parties in court cases. Unlike most of France's neighbouring countries, French laws against racism did not include provisions for counting, protecting or aiding groups defined by race or ethnicity.

Policy experts viewed antidiscrimination procedures as 'complicated and expensive' and thought that the mere threat of them would be effective. Affirmative action against racism was perceived as 'Anglo-Saxon' and was then rejected as dangerous – and to a large extent, it still is today. Compared with other countries such as the UK, France has only dealt with the source of racist violence since the early 2000s – much later than its neighbours (Britain did it in the early 1980s and Germany in the early 1990s). As noted earlier, France's response was triggered by the dramatic increase in racist and anti-Semitic incidents which forced the government to adopt new measures. In other words, unlike differentialist countries which passed anti-racist legislation early under the pressure of minority groups, the French anti-racist law of 1972 was passed without such pressure, to align France with other countries. In the end, the 1972 law against racism was mostly used by Jewish organizations to combat anti-Semitism, while new immigrant groups, who were only granted the freedom to organize in 1981, mobilized much later.

The 1990 Law Against Racism (the Gayssot Law)

After the Juppe government came into power, it introduced a proposal to draft an anti-racial law. This law was also intended to address anti-Semitism. For example, those who denied the existence of the Holocaust were to be punished by law. New legislation was provided to punish individuals guilty of racist crimes. Offenders could be stripped of their civil rights (Le Pen was obviously someone legislators had in mind because in a 1987 speech he had referred to the Holocaust as a mere 'detail' of history). Annual reports on racism and xenophobia were mandated by law. However, unlike the 1972 law, this law was hotly contested. It was argued that the law could harm newspaper editors, civil rights groups (some defended Le Pen's right to exist) and revisionists (the historians' lobby was fearful of an 'official history'). Hence, many legal experts did not consider the Gayssot Law to be very efficient.

From 1990 to 1994, there were 44 convictions for discrimination, which makes an average of nine a year, a very small number in comparison with neighbouring countries. The 1990 law was finally strengthened in February 2002. Tougher penalties were established for racist, anti-Semitic or xenophobic offences. The year before, under pressure from the European community, non-intentional discrimination was banned in Labour laws (art. L. 122-45). This was the first time such measures had been introduced into French law.

Laws Passed in 2003 and 2004

In 2003, a law (the Lellouche Law 2003-88) was passed against crimes of a "racist, anti-Semitic, or xenophobic" nature. "The new law classifies racist motivations for violent acts as aggravating circumstances and mandates harsher punishment for these crimes" (France, 2006: 3). In March of 2004, legislation also increased punishment for 'hate' crimes which is now regularly applied in the prosecution of those found committing anti-Semitic crimes.

In-spite of the various government initiatives to curb anti-Semitic crimes, the number of convictions has remained notably low: one in 1997, one in 1998, three in 1999, and seven in 2000 (Lanquetin, 2000: 79-81). Even in matters of anti-Semitism, the CNCDH remarks that judicial commitment remains weak (2004: 12). Moreover, as noted previously with the Lellouche law, some measures are merely symbolic and: are "likely to just gather dust in criminal law books" (Bleich, 2004: 17). No convictions had been made by the end of 2003 (in contrast with the 4, 000 charges the first year the equivalent law was passed in Britain) (Ibid). A book entitled *Les territoires perdus de la République*, published in 2002, has been circulated in schools to increase children's awareness of the necessity to oppose racism and anti-Semitism. But it remains to be seen whether these acts of socialization have an impact or not in high schools.

Finally, about 1200 police officers and 15 million Euros have been dedicated to security in 'sensitive sites' such as synagogues and other Jewish institutions as well as mosques. Furthermore, in June of 2005, a Paris court ordered French internet service providers to block websites that promoted hatred and were associated with 'false' stories of the Holocaust (e.g., the Association of Former Connoisseurs of War and Holocaust Stories) (France, 2006).

Measures Against Discrimination

In 1998, the struggle against discrimination became a dominant theme in the anti-racist rhetoric. But as far as victims were concerned, very few changes took place until 2005. In 2003, a study was led by the present author of this chapter and Wihtol de Wenden on police discrimination in France (Body-Gendrot and Wihtol de Wenden, 2003) based on a survey of trainers in police academies, on a toll-free number registering victims' grievances and on numerous interviews. This study concluded that there was general denial on the part of the French administration that there could be widespread abuse regarding a differential treatment according to age, gender and ethnic origin. Institutional racism was simply not recognized. Although France was condemned several times on the topic of police force abuse by the European Committee for the Prevention of Torture and Inhumane or Degrading Treatment or Punishment (CPT), the French State has always challenged such 'allegations,' claiming that there was no 'evidence' (Body-Gendrot, 2006). Similar patterns were observed in the army and in district courts (de Wenden and Bergossi, 2006; Jobard, 2005). In its 2004 report, the National Commission on the Ethics of Security (Commission nationale de déontologie de la sécurité, 2005: 495-496) pointed out police bias in respect to the *banlieues*, and it also revealed numerous instances of abuse during police search and control procedures. Finally, it denounced racial profiling (ibid). Most of the time, as observed in my previous work (Body-Gendrot, 2006), no institutional redress is given to police acts of violence and discrimination; grievances are ignored and judges side with policemen when there is no clear proof.

In 2005 however, in the aftermath of the shock of the 2002 Presidential elections when the run off opposed Le Pen and Chirac in the second round, and due to the pressures of the European community (see below), various administrative bodies decided to coordinate their anti-discrimination efforts. The Ministry of Labour and Social Cohesion and the Ministry of Justice took the lead. The bureau dealing with migrant populations added an anti-discrimination approach to its social actions of social integration (*Fonds d'action et de soutien pour l'intégration et la lutte contre les discriminations* – FASILD), and promoted the training of executives in the public sector. Four trade unions signed a chart promoting equal treatment, non-discrimination, and diversity.

Fighting Discrimination in the Workplace

The law passed on 6 January 1978 and modified on 6 August 2004 provides a legal framework regarding data collected for the purpose of fighting workplace discrimination. It forbids the gathering and treatment of data that directly or indirectly reveals ethnic origins, but exceptions are made for programs designed to fight specific cases of discrimination. The Commission Nationale Informatique et Libertés (CNIL) set up a working group in 2005, and asserted that in cases of discrimination, the ethnic origin of a person could not be deducted from the name or the address. However, an employee can give his or her consent to a firm that would want to establish an anti-discrimination program and use such personal data. But this data should remain confidential and secure, and if put on a computer, it should be deleted after its specific use.

The question of documenting ethnic and racial origin in order to fight discrimination remains controversial. How can one measure the ethno-racial composition of a firm's employees in order to promote diversity? Due to the collective guilt resulting from the treatment of Jews by the Vichy regime, there has been a colossal resistance to ethnic self-definitions; researchers disagree over methods and over who should be in charge of establishing statistical categories. Should they be instantaneous or continuous? Should they be used for the hiring or the evaluation of the whole staff? Should the methods of the census-takers be the same as those used by the employers? Demographers have made three attempts to bypass interdictions. In 2001, in the context of a study on how youths were faring when they left school, the Centre d'Etudes et de Recherche sur l'Emploi et les Qualifications (CEREQ), asked a question about the father's origin. In 2003, the National Institute of Statistics (INSEE) inserted, for the first time, a question on the ethnic origin of 35,000 people in their survey regarding training and occupational categories. In 2005, they also included this question in their job profile survey. A question on the parents' origin was also added to the 1999 national census. (This questionnaire can be found on the website of the National institute of demography (www.ined.fr) under the heading 'Mobilité intergénérationnelle et persistance des inégalités'.)

Extent and Nature of Racist Victimization in France

According to the 2004 report of the National Advisory Commission on Human Rights (CNCDH, 2005), racist and anti-Semitic acts and threats have globally increased by 132.5 per cent since 2003, from 858 to 1565 incidents, hitting a higher peak than that of 2002. Five features characterize these threats and acts:

1. Violence against people and property almost doubled in 2004 compared with 2003 (369 incidents vs. 189) and resulted in 56 individuals being injured in 2004. Threats and intimidation also doubled in 2004 (1196 incidents). However, we should be aware of the limitations of these figures. Because of underreporting and discrimination in the workplace, housing, and services, they do not reveal the real picture of the phenomenon of victimization.
2. Acts of anti-Semitism surpass other forms of racism. 62 per cent of racist acts were committed against Jews, who constitute 1 per cent of the total population in France. 970 acts were committed, a 61.4 per cent increase compared with the year before. Threats to Jews almost doubled from 474 in 2003 to 750 in 2004. There were 65 incidents of Jewish synagogue and cemetery vandalism in 2004 as compared to 44 incidents in 2003. The region of Alsace has been a hotspot for such acts, where Jewish locations are frequently marked with neo-Nazi graffiti.

3. In 2004 there was an unprecedented upsurge of racist and xenophobic acts against North Africans. Such acts increased by 250 per cent compared to 2003, from 232 to 595 (Graph 4.1). They resulted in 20 injured people (there had been 11 in 2003; 21 in 2002 and one death; 33 in 1994 and three deaths). Threats and acts of intimidation also increased by 204 per cent.

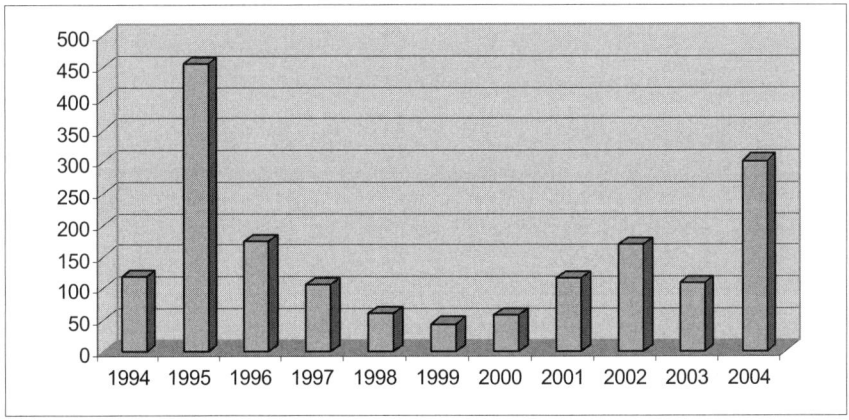

Graph 4.1 Evolution of racist and xenophobic 'threats' against North Africans in France since 1994
Source: CNCDH (2005)

4. 12 per cent of crimes committed in schools in 2004 were violent racist threats or acts, again showing a 20 per cent increase compared to 2003. There were 1275 incidents recorded and 75 per cent of these incidents were punished. However the specialist E. Debarbieux claims that under-reporting characterizes institutional data. Taking bullying as an example, he found that the rate of victimization in the investigations led by his team was 210 times more than that claimed by institutional statistics. While the rate of victims of insults was officially 0.23 per cent of the cohort, he found a 73.2 per cent rate, and as for racism, the contrast is 0.01 vs. 16.7 per cent, which is 1670 times higher (Debarbieux, 2006: 75).
5. Corsica stands out as the region with the largest number of racist actions in 2004, followed by Ile de France, Rhone-Alpes, Marseille and Alsace (Graph 4.2).

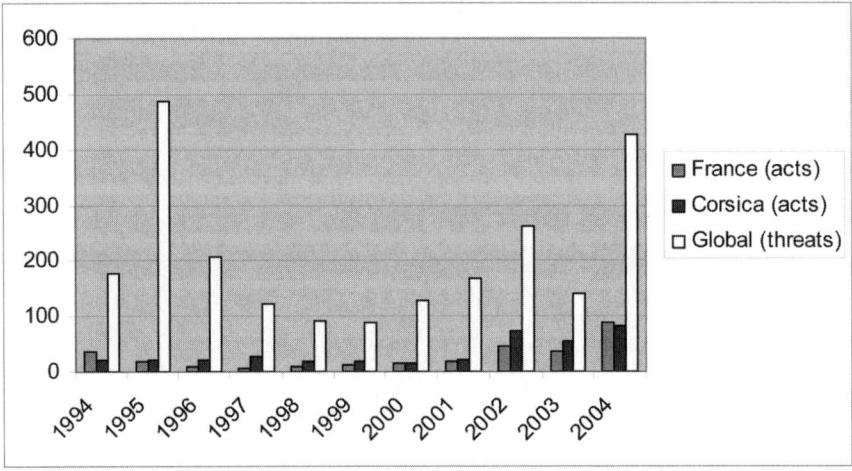

Graph 4.2 Evolution of racial violence since 1994 – racist acts in France – racist acts in Corsica – global threats
Source: CNCDH 2005

Who are the Perpetrators?

59 per cent of the perpetrators belong to the extreme right parties. But a new phenomenon has taken place due to the confusion between immigrés, Maghrebians, Muslims, and Islamists, in other words between culture and religion. Such confusion is partly responsible for the hostility towards Arabs and Muslims. The paradox in France comes from the growing ethnicization of social relations in a country that officially ignores racial and ethnic categories. As noted earlier, young and poor male Maghrebians living in the *banlieues*, with few prospects of upward social mobility, have been criminalized as a group by the media and even by some politicians. As Wistrich, 1992: 12) notes, to some extent, the North Africans have replaced the Jews as the feared 'Other' in a multicultural Europe.

According to some researchers, and as noted earlier, perpetrators of racist crimes live at the periphery of large cities (i.e., *banlieues*) and they say that they are themselves the victims of anti-Arab or anti-Muslim racism (Trigano, 2002). Furthermore, two political scientists point out that one third of the 'new' French, that is, those of African and Turkish origin, can be characterized as anti-Semitic, and 5 per cent of these approve resorting to material damages as a type of political expression (Brouard and Tiberj (2005: 16). Many young Arab-Muslim French see similarities in their own marginalization where they live in France and the fate of Palestinians under Israeli domination. A small minority of them may verbally attack Jews out of resentment for the latter's supposed wealth (i.e., the culture of poverty syndrome) or because of the Palestinian cause which helps them transcend their own marginalization. To quote a police officer, the perpetrators of anti-Semitic acts are "predominantly delinquents without ideology, motivated by a diffuse hostility to Israel, exacerbated by the media representation of the Middle East conflict, a conflict which, for them reproduces the picture of exclusion and failure of which they feel they are victims in France" (cf. Chebel d'Appolonia, 2005: 2). However, the good news is that with each new generation born in France, the incidence of prejudicial interactions is abating. The 'new' French become less and less prejudiced (Brouard and Tiberj, 2005).

Who are the Victims?

Before elaborating further, it is noteworthy to point out that victimization due to judeophobia or islamophobia is still relatively infrequent in France. Besides the emphasis on the inclusiveness of the culture already noted, the fact that 36 per cent of the French population have foreign parents or grand parents (Trigano, 2002) could be part of the explanation. Attacks against Jewish people and Jewish institutions were relatively limited among various forms of racism prior to 2000, except for the infamous attack on the Jewish cemetery in Carpentras, in the south of France. But in 2000, Jewish victims outnumbered those from the 'immigré' community of North African/African origin.

Jews constituted 80 per cent of the victims of hate crimes recorded in 2000, 45 per cent of the victims in 2001 and 62 per cent of the victims in 2002. In 2004, anti-Semitic acts resulting in 36 injured victims marked a new increase from 2003. After the decrease in the number of hate crimes in 2005, the 2006 Halimi case stunned the country. What puzzles analysts is the upsurge of anti-Semitic acts, combined with a decrease of anti-Semitic feelings in the French opinion, including that of North African origin youths. For Chebel d'Appolonia (2005: 1), "the coexistence of these two parallel and contrasting phenomena illustrates the specificity of the French case."

The intent of discrimination is hard to prove. Different factors (education, personal features) may also explain why certain individuals or groups are held back. Yet, according to D. Fougère and J. Puget, two statisticians, the likelihood for the son of two parents born abroad to become a civil servant is five times lower than that of an 'old-stock' French person. By contrast, almost one third (32.5 per cent) of executives in the public sector are civil servants' children (Reverchon, 2005: 11). Discrimination can be observed at the work-place (21 per cent), in housing (15 per cent), in services (8 per cent) and in daily life (3 per cent). Racist insults are the most frequent type of discrimination (33 per cent). The other types of discrimination are lower than 10 per cent each.

According to an official report for the commission on women's rights at the National Assembly, M.J. Simmermann, a Parliament member who commented on this report observes that immigrant women, who make up 50.3 per cent of immigrants in France, suffer disproportionately from discrimination in the workplace. Their rate of employment is lower, and they occupy seven out of eight unskilled occupations as opposed to three out of eight for French women. Finally, only 8.8 per cent of them are executives (Roger, 2005: iii)

The Reactions to Racist Victimization in France

State Reactions

As already stated, several laws (1972, 1990, 2002, 2003, 2004) have been passed to combat racism and anti-Semitism in France and to impose penalties for offences. But convictions have remained low when compared with other countries. It must nevertheless be emphasized that France has undergone some significant changes in recent years in an effort to both acknowledge and address issues related to racial victimization. While the process might be described as evolving slowly, it has required a dramatic shift of ideological and political ways of thinking.

Since 2005, under pressure from the European Union, France has set up an independent administrative authority to combat all types of discrimination and promote equality (HALDE- Haute Autorité de lutte contre les discriminations et pour l'Egalité). This authority has investigative powers and employs more than twenty lawyers to examine files and provide legal assistance. Although it can impose fines and use testing methods, it has nevertheless gained much less legitimacy thus far than the British Commission on Racial Equality. Its budget (around 11 million euros in 2006) is far too limited.

Other sources of knowledge have been created. For instance, an investigation report on anti-racism and anti-Semitism was commissioned from a well-known doctor, J.C. Rufin (CNCDH, 2005) as well as an evaluation of public information relative to anti-racism and anti-Semitism, from the High Council on Integration.

As recently as 2005, President Jacques Chirac addressed the French public on television and called for a new type of national voluntary service which would enable youths from the *banlieues* and students from elite schools to work together; it would provide job opportunities and initiatives against discrimination. But so far, governmental calls for a more inclusive, fair and open society have not been balanced against the growing social, economic and cultural rift that appears to be dividing France.

Police Reactions

That functional racism is part of police culture and of a reactive character applies to numerous countries, but what is specifically French is the lack of sessions on this issue in the initial and continuous training that policemen receive and the fact that the police are not accountable to anyone but the central administration. Accountability to citizens in the French public sector is just not being discussed. This is one of the reasons why community policing did not last long and why evaluation of public policies remains so unusual (Body-Gendrot, 2006).

Although the Council of Europe has required since 1994 that the police develop a more accurate, respectful, and sensitive vision of various ethnic and racial groups (Conseil de l'Europe 1994: 15, 19) and in spite of the injunction of the French Ministry of Interior in 1999 that the composition of police forces should be more reflective of the populations they serve, the institution has proven resistant to change. One of the reasons is that, whereas in other decentralized countries, change is frequently triggered by pressures exerted by organized minority groups acting from the bottom up and by legitimized anti-discriminatory organizations which, under favourable circumstances, find political allies in the system of decision-making, in comparison, the French national police is insulated from third party pressures which receive no back up from the mainstream political parties. Since there is no political recognition of the problem, the status quo persists.

Another major difference concerns the weak intervention of French justice to redress institutional discriminations and its lack of involvement in promoting minorities' constitutional rights. Judges are reluctant to condemn policemen for their misconduct and acts of discrimination.

When internal sanctions do occur (between two hundred fifty and three hundred fifty each year), the public – and victims particularly – are not informed, which confirms the lack of transparency. In 2002, only 2 per cent of French policemen were sanctioned by police inspectors (and most of them only received summons) while police violence has been on the increase in the past several years (more than 6 per cent in 2003), according to official reports of Inspection Generale des Services-IGS).

The same anomaly of unsanctioned ethnic discrimination is found in the administrative review boards or other commissions on infringements from security corps. Whereas in other countries (Canada, the US, and the UK, for instance), citizens' grievances about police misbehaviours are recorded, the National Commission of Ethics in France can only be summoned by citizens via a parliamentary member. In the first year (2001), only 13 cases of requests against the police were examined, and the second year, around 100. While the commission makes no judgement and no decision, it has investigation and hearing powers and issues recommendations, thus giving visibility to cases of misconduct. However, the strategy of the current government (in 2005) is to deprive the commission of the most elementary material resources to conduct its investigations.

Timid steps indicate that isolated initiatives in some police academies as well as experiments launched by localities to improve interactions between the police and citizen organizations have succeeded in creating efficient partnerships. But as long as society remains in demand of more police protection, institutions are unlikely to embrace vigorous reforms (Body-Gendrot, 2006).

Anti-racist Organizations

Anti-racist organizations have existed in France for a long time, such as the League of Human Rights, MRAP (already mentioned) and the *Ligue Internationale Contre le Racisme et l'Antisémitisme* (LICRA). But in the 1980s, after confrontations between immigrant youths and the police in the *banlieue* of Lyon and legal action was taken to deport some of them, local defence committees were set up. A hunger strike was launched in March 1983 by a priest named C. Delorme along with a protestant clergyman called J. Costil, and an Algerian man whose name was Hamid. Very diverse networks including *Jeunes Arabes de Lyon et sa banlieue* (JALB) were formed to support the threatened youths. The first March for Equality and Against

Racism took place from October to December 1983; it started in Marseille with thirty participants and attracted hundreds while it circulated around France, finally finishing in Paris where the marchers were welcomed by François Mitterand (see Halgreaves 1991: 356-361; Lloyd 1993: 218).

The march took place in a contradictory social context of openness and hostility. Reported incidents of racist violence increased. The march was followed by two others in the next two years to protest against the racist murders of the previous years, the racist and 'colonial' police behaviour and the lack of equal treatment minorities received at the workplace and in their neighbourhoods. But soon divisions arose among activists on the issue of racism. In October 1984, a political takeover of these local initiatives took place, when the organization *SOS Racism* was set up with the support of the Socialist party then in power. It asserted the right to be different, and the popularity of its badge, with the slogan "don't touch my buddy," symbolized the success of this organization among youth in general. An anti-racist concert in August 1985 gathered 400 000 on Place de la Concorde in Paris. Another national organization, *France Plus*, aimed at getting citizenship and registering immigrants on political lists so that they could vote like anyone else (Witte, 1996).

Influenced by the racist propaganda of the far right, these anti-racist movements suffered from a lack of legitimacy. Their harsh rhetoric is said to mirror that of racists. The groups also experienced deep divisions due to Middle-East tensions which after 1990 transformed anti-immigrant racism into islamophobia. While in the UK, in 1999-2000, 280 000 racist incidents were reported to the police followed by 4178 warnings and indictments, according to the Home Office, nothing of the kind occurred in France (Bleich, 2004). Anti-racist organizations continue to work within a fragmented paradigm, for instance, in conducting testing experiments in discotheques and the housing sector.

Labor

Notable changes have occurred in the business world. In 2005, forty large firms under the leadership of the Axa surveillance committee signed a chart promoting diversity. In November 2004, Axa's head Claude Bebear, suggested the creation of units to build bridges between firms and low-income neighbourhoods, and between public and private actors. The aim was to coordinate socio-economic insertion programs and to combat discrimination. (Indeed, the rate of unemployment among male second or third generation immigrants in problem areas sometimes reaches 40 per cent and it is one of the sources of violent outbursts.) According to R. Fauroux, a former businessman and director of the National school of Administration (2005), two experiments which attempt to measure diversity with the help of demographers have already taken place. One was led by the hypermarket chain Casino, in four of its stores and the other in four other firms. Audits may help such firms identify internal obstacles to the development of diversity. They may be launched after a *testing* experiment that establishes the assumption that discrimination does exist in the hiring process.

In small and mid-size firms, however, the recruitment of minority employees requires an enormous will to change established practices (via family and friend networks), and this will for change has not been observed so far. Interim agencies in charge of providing employees to firms obviously have a role to play.

Civil Society

The good news comes from elsewhere. In 1990, when the first opinion poll for the French National Consultative Commission on Human Rights (CNCDH) took place, the perception of racism as 'rather' or 'very' widespread in France averaged 90 per cent. In November 2004, a survey carried out by the pollster BVA (Bureau de Verification des Annonces) among a national sample of 1036 individuals representative of the total population of France over 18 years of age revealed that in recent years the share of "very widespread" opinions had decreased from 38 per cent-25 per cent to the benefit of the "rather widespread" opinions. According to that poll, The French are more aware of the consequences of racism, and their prejudices have diminished. The proportion of respondents who said that there are too many immigrés in France went down from 51 per cent in 2002 to 44 per cent in 2004, while those who said that there are too many foreigners decreased from 42 per cent in 2002 to 38 per cent in 2004. The respondents say that they are enriched by the presence of other nationalities (40 per cent), by others of foreign origin (36 per cent) or of another religion (29 per cent).

Nevertheless the image of Islam is constantly deteriorating in public opinion. Only 22 per cent of the French see it positively (28 per cent of the French see the Jewish religion positively) but let it be remembered that the term religion is itself ambiguous in France. (Only 35 per cent of the French have a positive correlation to the word.) 57 per cent of the French see Muslims as the most distant group in their society, perceiving that groups which are targeted by racist and anti-Semitic acts are those which are distant. Attitudes of intolerance are more widespread among men and older generations. Not surprisingly, higher education, leftist ideology, and the presence of foreigners in the family (71 per cent of whom come from another European country) reduce ethnocentrism and intolerance. These dimensions could explain why immigrants are on the whole better accepted year after year in France. The poll shows that 77 per cent of the French think that Muslim French are "French like the others." In addition, 87 per cent of French youths consider anti-Semitic acts to be shameful (UEJF, poll 2000). Finally, 85 per cent of the French say they have friendly feelings towards Jews (CSA *Le Figaro*, 2003) (as opposed to 72 per cent of the French public ten years earlier) and 99 per cent of them assert that "defacing synagogues is a very serious crime."

Conclusion

In brief, it cannot be denied that racist victimization is a serious phenomenon in French society. But the non-recognition of collective rights for any group defined by a community of origin, language and belief and the presence of a large xenophobic party do not allow for any serious debate on the production of racism at a time when society is experiencing macro-changes and is losing its bearings. The older leaders of anti-racist movements are aware of these shortcomings but they know that the French system is only receptive to individual claims and also that statistical tools necessary to redress the harms done to victims are insufficient. On the whole, it is not in the French tradition to mobilize for ethnic and racial rights and those who did so in the marches of the early 1980s have learnt their lesson and have changed their motto "respect my difference" into "respect my indifference" (Body-Gendrot, 1995). As for the leftist parties, they had too little to gain in fighting for ethnic and racial constituencies which are mainly concentrated in the regions of Paris, Lyon and Marseille and which are not numerous enough for their vote to make a difference.

However, in 2006 the French public appears to be more mobilized against racism and discrimination than before, and even if rhetoric does not mean that practices are about to change, 60 per cent of the French say that personally, they are ready to sign petitions, boycott a store or a firm guilty of racism, signal racist behaviour to authorities, demonstrate, wear badges, financially help anti-racist organizations and involve themselves in such organizations (BVA, poll, *op.cit.*).

No one will deny that Europe has been instrumental in defending the victims of racism and discrimination, and influencing national legislations. In studying the construction of a European paradigm of antidiscrimination effort, Andrew Geddes and Virginie Guiraudon (see Arnaud, 2005), have shown how, surprisingly, article 13 of the Amsterdam Treaty had been adopted by France. This article defines the principle of an equal treatment of people, without distinction of race and ethnicity, and allows for affirmative action even in the housing sector, which is not within European jurisdiction. Geddes and Guiraudon explain that between 1997 and 2000, some people who were eager to have this legislation passed, made use of new European competences and of para-legal norms to promote this 'race directive.' The reluctance of France towards the concepts of visible minorities, race and ethnicity was lifted when, with the arrival of Jorg Haider in the governing coalition in Austria, it became obvious that strong tools would be needed at the European community level to fight xenophobic political parties as rapidly as possible. Because Europe had already proved its efficiency on the issue of gender equality (article 119), the French felt secure that article 13 would be the appropriate tool for this new orientation. With this adoption, measures modifying national processes are to be expected, and hopefully, they will gradually change mentalities.

References

Arnaud, L. (ed.) (2005), *Les minorités ethniques dans l'Union européenne* (Paris: a Découverte).
Balibar, E. (2005), "La construction du racisme," *Actuel Marx*, 38: 11-28.
Bebear (2004), "Rien de plus raciste que le communautarisme," *Le Figaro*, June 13: 14.
Ben Jalloun, T. (1984), *Hospitalité Française: Racisme et Immigration Maghrébine* (Paris: Le Seuil).

Bleich, E. (2004), "Making It Hard to Hate: Responses to Racist Violence in Britain, Germany and France." Paper presented at the annual meeting of the American Political Science Association, Chicago, IL, 2 September.

Bleich, E. (2000), "Antiracism Without Races: Politics and Policy in a 'Color-Blind State,'" *French Politics, Culture and Society*, 18(3) Fall, 48-74.

Body-Gendrot, S. (2006), "Safe Neighborhoods", in J. Duyvendak, Knijin and Kramer (eds), *Professionals between People and Policy* (London: Sage).

Body-Gendrot, S. (1995), "Models of Immigrant Integration in France and the United States," in M.P. Smith and J. Feagin (eds), *The Bubbling Cauldron: Race, Ethnicity and the Urban Crisis* (Minneapolis: University of Minnesota Press), 243-262.

Body-Gendrot, S. and Schain, M. (1992), "National and Local Politics and the Development of Immigration Policy in the U.S. and in France: A Comparative Analysis," in D. Horowitz and G. Noiriel (eds), *Immigration in Two Democracies: French and American Experience* (New York: NYU Press), 411-438.

Body-Gendrot, S. and Wihtol de Wenden, C. (2003), *Police et Discriminations Raciales: Le Tabou Français* (Paris: Editions de l'atelier).

Brouard, S. and Tiberj, V. (2005), "Anti-Semitism in an Ethnically Diverse France: Questioning and Explaining the Specificities of African-Turkish and Maghrebian-French." Paper presented at the conference on the politics of anti-semitism in France and Europe (New York University), November.

Chebel d'Appolonia, A. (2005), "We Can't be Antisemitic, We Are All French: History, Legacy and Sustainability of the French Model of Integration." Paper presented at New York University, November.

CNCDH (Commission Nationale Consultative des Droits de l'Homme) (2005), *2004. La Lutte contre le racisme et la xénophobie*. Paris: La Documentation Française.

Coroller, C. (2006), "France cherche étrangers", *Libération*, January 16: 4-6.

CRIF (Conseil Représentatif des Institutions Juives de France) (2003), "Dossier: Le Rapport non publié rur l'Antisémitisme en Europe", www.crif.org/dossiers, December.

De Rudder, V. (1991), "Le racisme dans les relations interethniques," *L'homme et la société*, n°102, 75-92.

France. (2006), "International Relgious Freedom Report 2005." *U.S. Department of State*. Retrieved April 02/06 www.state.gov.g/drl/rls/irf/2005/51552.htm.

Freeman, G. (1979), *Immigrant Labor and Racial Conflict in Industrial Societies* (Princeton: Princeton University Press).

Guidice, F. (1992), *Arabicides, Une Chronique Française 1970-1991* (Paris: La Découverte).

Guillaumin, C. (2002), *L'Idéologie Raciste : Genèse et Langage Actuel* (Réédition. Paris: Essai-Folio).

Guillaumin, C. (1994), "Racism," *Vocabulaire historique et critique des relations inter-ethniques*, Pluriel recherches, L'Harmattan, cahier 2, 67-70.

Halgreaves, A. (1991), "Political Mobilization Among North Africans," *Ethnic and Racial Studies*, 14(3), 350-67.

Hirschman, A. (1970), *Exit, Voice, and Loyalty. Responses to Decline in Firms, Organizations and States* (Cambridge, Ma, Harvard University Press).

Jazouli, A. (1986), *L'Action Collective des Jeunes Maghrébins de France* (Paris: L'Harmattan/Ciemi).
Jazouli, A. (2002), *Les Années Banlieue* (Paris : Le Seuil).
Lanquetin, M.T., (ed.) (2000), *Le Recours au Droit Dans la Lutte Contre les Discriminations. La Question de la Preuve*. Paris: Editions GELD (Groupe d'études et de lutte contre les discriminations), Booklet No.2.
Lloyd, C. (1993), "Racist Violence and Anti-Racist Reactions: a View of France," in T. Bjorgo and R. Witte (eds) *Racist Violence in Europe* (London: Macmillan), 207-220.
Mayer, N., and Michelat, G. (2005), "Analyse du Racisme et de L'Antisémitisme en France en 2004," in CNCDH (Commission Nationale Consultative des Droits de L'Homme) *La Lutte Contre le Racisme et la Xénophobie* (Paris: La Documentation Française), 128-142.
Mots (1992), "Sans Distinction de Race," *Fondation Nationale des Sciences Politiques*, 33 (December) special issue.
Noiriel, G. (1988), *Le Creuset Français* (Paris: Le Seuil).
Poli, A. (2001) "Les Jeunes face au racisme dans les quartiers populaires," in M. Wieviorka and J. Ohanna (eds), *La Différence Culturelle* (Paris: Balland), 198-205
Reverchon, A. (2005), "Devenir Fonctionnaire ? Dans tes Rêves...", *Le Monde*, November 15: 11.
Roger, P. (2005), "Un Rapport Accablant sur les Discriminations Subies par les Femmes Issues de L'Immigration", *Le Monde*, December 8: 10.
Sayad, A. (1991), *L'Immigration ou les Paradoxes de L'Altérité* (Bruxelle: de Boeck).
Tabet, M.C. (2005), "Immigration: Villepin dévoile son plan," *Le Figaro*, November 29: 8.
Taguieff, P.A. (ed.) (1993), *Face Au Racisme* (Paris: La Découverte).
Taguieff, P.A. (2002), *La Nouvelle Judéophobie*. Paris: Mille et Une Nuits.
Ténisien, X. (2004), "Sortir du Petit Monde de Marie L.," *Le Monde*, 9 August.
Thieffry, C. (2006), "Les faits d'insécurité dans l'habitat social en 2004," Paris, Institut national des hautes études sur la sécurité, March report.
Trigano S. (2002), *Actualités Juives*, 25 April.
Unesco (1952) *The Race Concept* (Paris: Unesco Press).
Weil, P. and Crowley, J. (1994), 'Integration in Theory and Practice: A Comparison of France and Britain', *West European Politics*, 17(2): 110-126.
Weil, P. (2005), *La République et sa diversité*, Paris, La république des idées/Le Seuil.
Wieviorka, M. (1998), *Le Racisme, Une Introduction* (Paris: La Découverte).
Wistrich, R. (1999), "The Devil, the Jews and Hatred of the 'Other'," in R. Wistrich (ed.) *Demonizing the Other: Antisemitism, Racism and Xenophobia* (Amsterdam: Harwood Academic Publishers).
Witte, R. (1996), *Racist Violence and the State: A Comparative Analysis of Britain, France and the Netherlands* (London: Longman).

Helpful Websites

www.crif.org – Conseil Représentatif des Institutions Juives de France.
http://eumc.eu.int/eumc/index.php European Monitoring Centre on Racism and Xenophobia.
http://www.statewatch.org/ – Statewatch: Monitoring the State and Civil Liberties in the European Union.

Chapter 5

Germany

Hans-Jörg Albrecht

Introduction: Historical Overview of Racial Victimization in Germany

Germany has a well-known and thoroughly studied history of racial victimization (Cernyak-Spatz, 1985; Arad, 1987; Bauman, 1992; Goldhagen, 1996). However, contrary to perhaps popular opinion, the subject of racial victimization is relatively recent. The holocaust provides for a unique case of racially motivated genocide that victimized Jewish minorities in Europe during the period of German fascism and in particular in the early 1940s. Documentation of these atrocities is also found in the Nuremberg war crime trials (1945–1949) and in the ensuing long process of investigating and prosecuting war crimes and crimes against humanity through a special unit of public prosecution established to investigate German war crimes in Europe (Albrecht, 2004). With the holocaust, racist policies and feelings of anti-semitism climaxed which had raged through Europe for centuries (Weiss, 1997). Jewish minorities were not the only victims of racist policies and racist violence. Various other ethnicities were targeted by racist policies as being inferior and ultimately also subject to extermination practices during the fascist rule (see Aly, 1988).

Particular sensitivities towards right wing extremism, anti-semitism, xenophobia and racially motivated violence in Germany are rooted in this past. The relationship between racist violence in its most extreme form of genocide and the political movement of fascism and related organizations then led in the post second World War period to the emergence of particular legislation aimed at repression and prevention of fascist (or national-socialist) organizations and political parties. The decades after World War II were rather calm as regards visible signs of racism and open racist violence. But, the annual reports of internal intelligence agencies demonstrate that throughout the post war decades anti-semitism continued to express itself in desecration of Jewish cemeteries and Nazi-propaganda. Anti-semitism is found also in surveys on attitudes and perceptions (Bergmann, 2004); however, there is a significant decline in anti-semitist attitudes over the second half of the 20th century with younger generations expressing far less anti-semitism (Bergmann, 2004, p. 27).

Due to the holocaust and the uniqueness of atrocities committed during the rule of German fascism racist violence remains an issue far more sensitively and also differently perceived compared to other European countries. Yet, as a result of the recent past and recent influx of many non-European immigrants (Germany has taken in more refugees than all other EU members states together) and the then pending

World Cup soccer tournament held throughout Germany in summer of 2006, the German publication *Der Spiegel* asked whether Germany was still racist or not? The German public however – according to comparative surveys – does not differ from the European average when looking at hostility and resistance to immigrants, asylum seekers as well as attitudes toward ethnic diversity (Coenders et al., 2004, pp. 3, 4, 5).

Racist Crime and the Legal Context

In 2001 a proposal for a European framework decision was presented that seeks among other things to introduce the concept of hate crimes (COM(2001) 664 final 2001/0270 (CNS), Proposal for a Council Framework Decision on combating racism and xenophobia). According to this proposal (which has not yet been adopted as a binding law), in the response to crimes committed against visible minorities and other vulnerable groups the racist and xenophobic motives should be made aggravating factors and enhance criminal penalties. This would correspond to the creation of explicit hate crime statutes. Hate crime statutes provide for a new genre of crime categories or, as Jacobs has put it: hate crime statutes provide for "a new family of specialized hate crimes" (Jacobs, 1993, p. 113). Here, it is essentially the use of the offenders' motive which defines either the (hate) offence or serves as an aggravating factor enhancing the penalty provided for the generic crime (Fletcher, 1994). This approach has triggered criticism pointing towards possible infringements of the basic right of "free speech" but also to serious conflicts with a harm based theory of criminal punishment (Seehafer, 2003). Besides this move towards introducing uniform hate crime legislation, the European Union has issued four anti-discrimination directives which have to be implemented in the member states. These directives aim at outlawing discrimination on the basis of race, ethnicity, gender, age and seek to protect vulnerable groups from disadvantages rooted solely in their belonging to a certain group. These directives apply in various areas, but in particular in the labour market. After extended debates the German Federal Parliament recently enacted a law that implements these directives (Gesetz zur Umsetzung europäischer Richtlinien zur Verwirklichung des Grundsatzes der Gleichbehandlung, 14 August 2006).

In Germany, explicit hate crime legislation which enhances punishment on the basis of bias motives and which could be compared to North-American legislation, has not yet been brought to parliaments nor does it seem probable that such legislation will be drafted in the near future. But, other concepts are used in the attempt to provide for better protection of minorities from racist violence and other racist crime by means of criminal law and justice.

As regards criminal law, a range of offence statutes addresses the issue of racist crime. A group of criminal offence statutes is linked to activities around banned political parties and groups as well as propaganda activities. However, the rationale of such offence statutes has been to counter communist and neo-Nazi political movements – perceived to be particular dangerous in face of the processes leading up to the fascist rule in Germany from 1933 to 1945. Section 84 of the *German criminal code* threatens criminal penalties (up to five years imprisonment) for anybody who continues to organize a political party or being a member of such party which has been declared unconstitutional by the Federal Constitutional Court or an organization which has been banned by order of ministries of the interior (federal or state). Section 85 addresses the creation and maintenance of substitutes for prohibited organizations or parties. Dissemination of propaganda for prohibited organizations and parties is also criminalized (section 86). Dissemination of propaganda is prohibited, too, if such propaganda comes from a government, organization or institution based outside the territory of the Federal Republic of Germany and pursuing the same objectives as the ones pursued by prohibited organizations or parties. Dissemination of propaganda which is intended to further the aims of former National Socialist organizations is punishable, too (imprisonment of up to three years or a fine). Section 86 II restricts the meaning of propaganda to such written material which is directed against a free and democratic order (as protected by the constitution) or against the peace of nations. Section 86a penalizes the (domestic) distribution or public use/display of symbols of prohibited organizations or parties, their production, import or export.

Denial of the holocaust, incitement to hatred, dissemination of instructions on how to commit crimes and dissemination of graphic descriptions of violence/ glorification of violence point to another group of offence statutes associated with the suppression of racist violence. These offence statutes deal with incitement and propaganda activities. Denial of the holocaust has been penalized (i.e., section 130) in order to respond to right wing extremism and neo-Nazi groups/political parties. In 2005, the offence of denial of the holocaust has been expanded. Glorification, justification or approving the national-socialist (Nazi) terror regime when done in public and in a way which is disrupting public peace and infringing on the dignity of victims (of the Nazi regime) is punishable with imprisonment of up to three years or a fine.

According to section 130 a criminal offence is established if somebody incites publicly hatred or calls for violence against social groups or segments of the population or assaults human dignity through insulting or defaming segments of the population and if such acts may disrupt the public peace. Dissemination or the display of written material that pursues incitement of hatred, calls for violence or assault human dignity establish evenly a criminal offence (section 130 II). Dissemination or the public display of instructions how to commit certain crimes when intended to encourage others to commit such crimes is penalized by section 130a. Finally, dissemination, publicly displaying graphic descriptions of cruel or inhuman acts against humans in a way which glorifies such violence, or downplays the harm of such violence or emphasizes the cruel and inhuman aspects of such violence provided that he way of presentation infringes on human dignity establishes a criminal offence (carrying a maximum of one year imprisonment). Journalist accounts on historical or current acts of violence are exempted from section 131 (section 131 III).

Sections 130, 131 explicitly refer to racial and other discrimination (Krone, 1980). These provisions are meant to protect public peace. Section 130 G.C.C. prohibits infringements on human dignity causing disturbance of the public peace through attempts to incite violence against others or using hate speech (see BayObLG, 1994). Section 131 makes it an offence to provoke racial hatred through the production, distribution, etc. of print or other media that contain messages of hate against groups. These penal provisions have been a response to right wing extremist activities peaking at the beginning of the 1960s and at the beginning of the 1970s. On the other hand, production and display of fascist symbols are prohibited as are prohibited such symbols which refer to political parties which have been declared to pursue unconstitutional goals by the constitutional courts and thus are prohibited or to organizations which have been dissolved by order (e.g., the national-socialist party and left wing extremist parties organizations) of the Ministry of the Interior. Membership in a political party prohibited by the constitutional court as well as membership in an organisation dissolved by the ministry of the interior establish criminal offences as are all activities aimed at re-establishing such parties or organizations.

Besides these criminal statutes hate or racist attitudes (in terms of motives to commit any crime) can be considered in the sentencing decision as the general statute on sentencing (section 46) demands for taking into account the motive of the offender, too. German Criminal law doctrine relies heavily on the idea that both, the act itself and subjective elements (in terms of motives and other psychological factors) should determine the outcome of sentencing. However, motives in general are not made offence characteristics due to the presumption that punishment should be grounded in the criminal harm done and not in mere thoughts (motives). There is but one important exception in the German *criminal code*. This is the murder statute where subjective elements (in terms of specific motives) are introduced to establish 1st degree murder (with the consequence of being eligible for life term imprisonment). Besides sexual motives and the motive of material profit a "catch all" category of "low motives" (niedrige Beweggründe) has been introduced to cover all those motives which are deemed to represent completely unacceptable motives. A "low" motive according to rulings of the Supreme Court is established if a person was killed out of racial hatred (Bundesgerichtshof 5 StR 410/03, 30.3.2004) a low motive is also established if the motive to kill lies in the conviction that the victim is inferior and deserves therefore to die (see Bundesgerichtshof, 1971).

The history of the criminal provisions that criminalize incitement of racial hatred (sections 130, 131) goes back to the 19th century when first Prussia and then some other German states enacted statutes similar to provisions adopted by the French Parliament. Prussia and other German states joined in with adopting legislation which was then also introduced in the first criminal code book for the German Reich in 1871. In section 130 of the *Criminal Code Book of the German Reich* it was stated that "whoever attempts to publicly instigate violence between different social classes of the population in a way which endangers public order and peace in society will be punished by a fine or by imprisonment of not more than two years". This provision was called an "anti-class-struggle" criminal law and continued throughout the 19th century and during the 20th century to be used as an instrument against unions as well as social democrat and communist political parties and organizations. That the latter had been the main target of this provision is underlined by an attempt on the side of the German government in 1975 to amend §130 in a way that would have penalized also instigation of hatred against family, marriage and property. However, this attempt proved to be unsuccessful as was another attempt to criminalize insults against religion, monarchy, marriage, family and property in 1895.

Description of the Extent, Nature and Development of Racist Victimization

Definition of Concepts

As noted in the Introduction, statements on incidence and prevalence of and trends in racist violence are dependent on the definition of racist violence and with that in particular on the definition of violence. The definition of violence has always been an issue of extensive and controversial debates as can be seen in the fields of sexual violence, political violence (in particular terrorism) and state organized repression (Bjorgo, 1997, p. 17). The question of whether it is useful to extend the definition of violence to phenomenon which have been called institutional or structural violence has been debated also extensively and represents a major concern within German politics and German law. But, it seems reasonable to differentiate between physically harming violence on the one hand and social and political structures that confine individuals or groups to conditions that are repressive, discriminating or disadvantageous at large on the other hand.

Experiences of group or individual discrimination or disadvantages coming as a consequence of having the status of a foreign national or being otherwise marginalized are of course important when analyzing and assessing the situation of minority groups as well as for identifying strategies of relief. With using a wide understanding of violence neither meaningful description nor the test of theoretical assumptions would be possible as ultimately the definition of a minority status already would correspond to violent victimization. In particular, international comparative research must rely on narrowly and precisely defined variables. Moreover, possible precursors of violence in terms of incitement to racial hatred or propaganda crimes should be separated from actual violence as should be separated acts that condone or welcome violence or contain graphic or other demonstrations of actual violence. Strategies of prevention, however, should be based also on a thorough analysis of assumed precursors of violence as should be strategies of constructing a legal and comprehensive framework which provides for a fair and just response to offenders, victims and society.

Therefore a clear distinction between violent crime on the one hand and precursors (or facilitators) of violence on the other hand must be made. While violent crime is restricted to the core of violent offence statutes (murder, assault, rape, robbery, vandalism, offence statutes that, moreover, display the least differences in terms of offence characteristics when comparing national criminal code books) racist speech, incitement to racial hatred, being a member of a racist (and therefore prohibited) organization, displaying or distributing racist propaganda and the like are to be understood as facilitators of racist violence.

Normative structures as on display in German criminal law reflect such differences with making differences along different protected interests. Offence statutes such as incitement to racial hatred or hate speech, propaganda crimes and criminal organization statutes reflect either public order interests or interests in penalizing risks and dangers. They represent endangering offences with placing emphasis on a significant potential for provoking actual violence or generating a climate of fear and unsafety. Violent offences, in contrast, represent result crimes that lead to damages, injuries or a loss of life.

Racial (or racist) violence refers to a motive or an intent on the side of violent offenders which is characterized through domination, inferiority/superiority and exclusion. Racist motives might comprise various attitudes, perceptions and other feelings such as hate, bias, and prejudice. These concepts also refer to motives and motivations. But, the reference groups are evidently different.

Differences as regards reference groups follow out of differences in social and official recognitions as to what statuses in a society should be given special protection under (in particular) criminal law. While it is clear that within the European Union a broad agreement on the values of equality and tolerance is opposed to all sorts of differential treatment of all kind of different statuses in society, nevertheless historical particulars and variation in the increasing ethnic and social diversity in modern societies may lead to differences in the type of inter-group tensions that arise and in the political choices that are made in creating special protection of certain statuses. However, definitions of racial or hate violence, therefore, contain always social and political choices as to what status in a society (e.g., ethnic, race, gender, homelessness, disabled, etc.) deserves special protection because of particular harm stemming from long standing status differences and their potential for setting groups up as targets of violence (or other forms of discrimination and exclusion).

Of course, racial violence is not restricted to violence directed against minorities. The last decades have seen at various occasions violent riots originating from minority groups and evidently triggered by alleged acts of (police or other) violence or other real or assumed injustice against such minorities. Furthermore, individual acts of racist violence may be directed also against members of majority groups or may occur between members of minority groups (e.g., Muslim and Jewish groups, or Kurdish and Turkish groups).

In order to understand racist violence in Germany, the concept then has to be analyzed also from a perspective of legitimation and justification. Legitimation of violence operates through techniques of neutralizing the stigma normally coming with exerting violence and adopting systems of justification (Heitmeyer and Müller, 1995, p. 16). Neutralization in case of violence against racially or otherwise defined groups seems to be carried in particular through conveying a threatening picture of immigrants and asylum seekers. With that a process of "defensive exclusivity" may be initiated (Crawford, 1999). Fear and angst are pushing to search for a suitable and visible target or – as Christie and Bruun (1991) have put it – for "convenient enemies". Convenient enemies are those where unanimous consent seems to be in reach without any problems as regards their potential of serving as threatening images and of explaining social problems of the kind which create fears and feelings of unsafety, in particular feelings of instability and social unrest. Conceptions of order and norms as well as policies and social forces interact in producing targets of fear and subsequently hate as well as excluded social groups among which today the new immigrants (asylum seekers, refugees or illegally resident migrants) and the old minorities (like Jewish people and Roma) can evidently evenly be top-ranked (Heitmeyer, 2004). It is thus not others who enforce exclusion but the message points to an individual who commits crimes who him- or herself deliberately chooses the way to the margins of society or even out of society.

Racist violence in Germany, as elsewhere, is to be placed in a social, historical and cultural context. This context shapes forms of appearances of racist violence and the social and legal responses to such violence. Part of the context within which racist violence has to be understood is the increasing influence of international affairs on racist sentiments. Following 11 September 2001, an increase of violent and threatening acts against Muslims has been noted as have been noted increases in bias motivated crimes against Jews and Jewish facilities as a consequence of the Israeli- Palestinian conflict (Senatsverwaltung für Inneres, Abteilung Verfassungsschutz, 2004). Islamophobia thus emerges beside long established anti-semitism as are rising ethnic tensions between minority groups. Images of the victims on both sides evoke negative sentiments that further polarize attitudes, not only of the local populations but also of the world at large. The people of different countries may take sides in this conflict based on cultural, religious, ethnic, or political grounds and affiliation. Two other developments that affect racist sentiment and phenomena are satellite television and the Internet (van Donselaar, 2000). If ethnic hostilities arose before due to local or domestic conditions, they are now also fuelled by global and international affairs disseminated through these and other media.

Phenomena and Concepts

Race, as defined in Germany and elsewhere, is a social construct that attributes certain characteristics to various groups that may differ from each other through skin colour, ethnicity, which are not only claimed to have a biological or genetic basis but are also assumed to highlight inferiority or superiority along various dimensions. Comparison of the debates in Germany on race, and its relationship to religion and ethnicity reveals concepts broader than race, with more emphasis on culture, ethnicity, religion, nationality and with the latter on immigration. This emphasis has been fostered by ongoing migration from societies with various differences in social, cultural, and religious values.

The concepts of race and racism – which basically refer to the "old" minorities like Jews and Roma who throughout European and in particular German history had been preyed upon and had been made targets of racist violence (Brustein and King, 2002), pogroms and ultimately the Holocaust – therefore are increasingly replaced by concepts such as xenophobia, fear of or hostility toward strangers and most recently hate. However, it is evident in modern societies that it is essentially the goal of domination and the perception of inferiority, moreover, the construction and rejection of "otherness", which are behind motives of (exclusive) violence. Otherness can be expressed through various characteristics such as sexual preference, ethnicity, skin colour, gender, nationality, religion, immigration status or conditions of disabledness, mental illnesses, etc. However, what issues arise with the definitional elements of hate or racist/racial violence, concern cultural differences, social norms and political interests.

When looking at criminological theory and research it is clear that racial violence until now with rare exceptions did not play a significant role on research agendas in Germany. While research on violence, in particular youth violence, and research on crime committed by immigrants and ethnic minorities are available in abundance, the particulars of racist violence and racial victimization have not been covered. It is only during the last two decades that research slowly is developing (Kubink, 1997).

Modern criminal law as it emerged during the 19th century was focused on the offence and rarely allowed subjective elements such as motives to be adopted as offence characteristics. Insofar it does not come as a surprise that accounts of violence in police information systems that are pre-designed through criminal law categories traditionally do not account for special motives (with the exception of first degree murder and particular sexual crimes, see also European Monitoring Centre, 2005). This is why regular German police statistics today have no provisions to parcel out acts of racist violence simply because there is no criminal law based categories that would identify racial motives.

Sources of Data and Information

Data and information on racist violence available in Germany can be collapsed roughly into five categories. There exist police and judicial information systems into which data on cases of violence are entered. Since the 1990s German police forces started to collect information on xenophobic crime. A xenophobic motive is established when the main reason to commit the crime lies in the offenders' hostility towards immigrants or foreign nationals. Statistics based on these data are published annually by the Federal Internal Intelligence Service (Bundesamt für Verfassungsschutz) as well as state police organizations (see Bundesministerium des Innern, 2006; Senatsverwaltung für Inneres, Abteilung Verfassungsschutz, 2004). A second category of information concerns survey data stemming from social science (e.g., victim (crime) surveys and/or self-report surveys) or criminological research. In addition, there are general surveys on attitudes and perceptions provide data on how the public views certain minorities. Third, NGOs and other organizations may collect information on particular types of crime (and crime control) related events. Fourth, media do cover racial violence and therefore provide information on relevant cases. Fifth, international and European legal mechanisms produce and summarize data on racisms and discrimination (e.g., European Commission against Racism and Intolerance – ECRI).

NGO data collection suffers first of all from the problem of selectivity, which is far greater than the one encountered in police and judicial statistics. In the latter it is well known through what mechanisms selection occurs and, moreover, data are collected consistently and systematically along routine procedures, which is not the case in NGO information collection processes. Then, data and information collected and disseminated by NGOs follow a (legitimate) strategy of scandalization. Insofar, the suggestion made by Bowling and Phillips (2003) that sources like journalistic accounts or records of local monitoring groups could offer richer and more meaningful information is misleading; such information can be used and is used for political campaigning but does not provide for a sound basis for quantitative scientific analysis which aims at description and explanation of incidence, prevalence and trends. Finally, data presented by international bodies entrusted monitoring of racial violence and discrimination make use of the data sources discussed above and do not provide for added value as regards information on racist violence. But, NGO and media may well serve as data sources in qualitative accounts of racist violence and, moreover, may generate information in areas not accessible for research and researchers.

Information that is collected and assessed by institutions such as the European Commission Against Racism and Intolerance or the European Union related Vienna based Monitoring Centre on Racism and Xenophobia (EUMC, 2005) displays the institutional interests that are driving these organizations. So, for example, the latest report of the European Commission Against Racism and Intolerance on Germany contains essentially information on immigration law and asylum related issues and in its conclusions reveals a strong bias toward simply favoring liberal immigration policies (Europäische Kommission gegen Rassismus und Intoleranz, 2004).

The basic problem that must be addressed when assessing crime related data concerns validity. Victimological research has identified the trivial nature of most victimisations as the main reason for non-reporting beside the perception that reporting an incident would not lead anywhere. In the field of racist violence there are other reasons explaining non-reporting. Uncertainty concerning residence status, fear of consequences for asylum application or being an illegal immigrant, perception of police and authorities as being restrictive and discriminating, negative self-assessment of status in society and experiences of societal exclusion, and fear of further victimisation must certainly be considered as motives not to complain about relevant incidents (Albrecht, 2006).

Another problem stems from the obvious failure to account for particulars of racist violence. Although, Germany has developed and implemented devices aimed at counting racist (xenophobic, anti-semitic) crime and providing thus a basis of assessing the extent of racist crime it seems questionable whether such counting procedures in fact produce the kind of information needed to assess threats and impacts of racist violence. While ordinary crime counting in criminal statistics is based on the assumption that theft, robbery or homicide are regularly displaying similar characteristics with such elements that can generate differences or variation (e.g., extent of losses, type of violence) easily accounted for, racist crime certainly refers to a different set of variables. As a consequence, it makes sense to count crimes under the condition that the mere number of recorded criminal offences is telling about the extent of problems established through a certain number of criminal offences (or offenders) and the possible answers to such problems. Racist violence, however, then cannot be assessed on the basis of counting of cases or the number of offenders involved alone. One single pogrom or another act of massive collective racist violence alone can, for example, deliver an impact which outweighs by far a multitude of individual acts of racist violence. Insofar, collection of data on racist violence must include information of the type of context within which the act occurred. Furthermore, it has been suggested to understand racist violence as a process rather than a measurable incident. The process of racist violence connects everyday experiences (of mostly less serious) racist incidents with extreme and rare cases of racist violence.

The Extent of Racist Violence in Germany

In summarizing the available evidence on racist violence, it can be concluded from data collected by German police and intelligence services (Verfassungsschutzämter) that:

a. the general problem of all police registered crime data, namely that they are dependent on reporting by victims and by resources invested in investigating (victimless) crime (e.g., incitement to racial hatred through the internet or other propaganda crime),
b. the general problem of registration procedures which may vary among various police units,
c. the specific problem of establishing a motive when investigating a crime, and
d. problems that are encountered in initial phases when introducing new registration procedures.

The definition is guided by a focus on right wing extremism and national socialist (fascist) organizations. An xenophobic motive regularly is established when an offender is affiliated to a supremacy group or a nationalist/fascist organization or political party. German police statistics, however, do not break down criminal offences along ethnicity, nationality or race of victims. No police data are available at all on racially motivated violence exerted by certain professions such as police themselves or prison/correctional staff (Albrecht, 2002). However, it is clear that data collection in this field is of particular relevance as for example biased police violence regularly marks the onset of large scale rioting (see Jobard, 2001; Busch, 2000) and reports of the Anti-Torture Comittee of the Council of Europe repeatedly pointed to the risk of detained persons to be maltreated and abused during detention due to their belonging to minority groups (Comité de prevention de la torture, 1991). Information in this field stems almost exclusively from NGO as well as media reports (Aktion Courage, 1999; AI Report, 2001). No police data are available on situations of racist violence amounting to pogroms or other forms of collective though not necessarily organized violence.

Police statistics show that the majority of racist offences are made up by propaganda crimes and crimes of harassment respectively threats. The incidence of racist violence measured by police (or other security forces) information systems is low. The proportion of racist violence at police registered violence at large tends to be below 0.5 per cent. In particular racist murder is extremely rare; however, the crime of murder is also subject to definitional problems and therefore not easily assessed in the context of racist violence. For example, fire bombing of homes for asylum seekers or other residential buildings according to a decision of the German Supreme Court of the early 1990s regularly should be prosecuted and judged on the basis of murder statutes as the use of firebombs indicated knowledge and will to kill other persons (Frommel, 1994; Neubacher, 1998). What is visible also from statistics and research is that fire bombing has spread rapidly as a technique of causing a maximum of destruction.

Information on racist violence based on police statistics suffers from the lack of information on reference groups. As it is not possible to make estimates on the size of "racial" groups in Germany (except for foreign nationals registered and settled down) it is also not possible to make estimates on rates of incidence and prevalence as well as the course of development of racist violence. Thorough assessment of the course of racial violence on the basis of police recorded crime data is not possible:

a. as time series are not exceeding more than approximately 15 years, and
b. as numbers of registered cases of racist violence are actually rather small as to be able to apply sophisticated techniques of analysis of longitudinal data.

What is assumed, however, concerns an increase in racist violence

a. which is located at the beginning of the 1990s , and
b. which seems to be related to the rise of extremist political parties and organizations as well as the political discourses on "asylum problems" and immigration.

Statistics on xenophobic crime demonstrate also waves of violence. These waves or ups and downs are tentatively explained (see for example Lüdemann, 1992) by:

a. violent campaigns,
b. copy cat behaviour, and
c. the mobilizing effects of international violent conflicts.

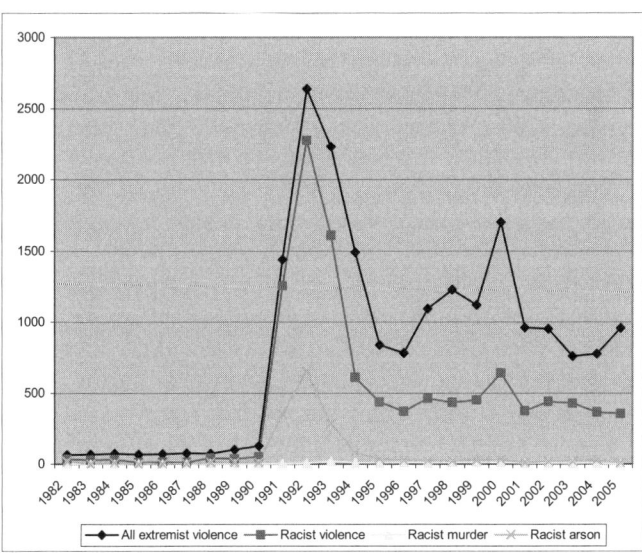

Graph 5.1 Extremist and xenophobic violence, 1982–2005
Source: Bundesminesterium des Innern: Verfassungsschutzberichte 1982–2005. Bonn, Berlin 1983–2006

The trends in Graph 5.1 demonstrate also that the eruption of hate violence at the beginning of the 1990s was almost exclusively affecting foreign nationals, but that from the mid-1990s on right wing extremist violence diversified. However, while violence against foreign nationals still accounts for the bulk of right wing violence in Germany, diversification of right wing violence; including murder, include some 70 incidents between 1991–1999. Almost half of the murder victims are foreign nationals, most of them belonging to visible minority, another 20 per cent of the victims are homeless people, a group which is particularly targeted by extremist skinhead groups (Emundts, 2000).

The outbreak of violence at the beginning of the 1990s not only coincided with substantial changes in immigration patterns during the 1980s but also parralled the substantial number of conflicts within the political system as to which approach was best suited to address immigration policies and in particular asylum policies. The so called "Asyldebatte" (debate on Asylum) then resulted in significant changes of those statutes regulating political asylum. These changes were by no means introduced in a consensual process. Opponents of the new Art 16a GG brought a case to the German constitutional court claiming that Art. 16 a GG was violating the basic principles of the constitution itself. This appeal however was turned down (Hailbronner, 1996). Thus, Germany has seen a shift from very liberal to much stricter asylum laws. The main aim was to reduce the number of asylum seekers significantly. What can be seen from Graph 5.2 is that the trend in xenophobic arson follows the number of asylum seekers and the debates on political asylum and thus underlines the assumption that supremacist groups and individuals may construct systems of justification based on the basis of views that depict asylum seekers and the other as bringing with them dangers and risks.

No type of official statistics be it crime or judicial statistics, can for the racial or ethnic composition of a population. What is available is the variable "nationality" or "citizenship" which may be used as a proxy in analyzing racial or ethnic segments in German society. Post-war Germany has experienced a rather short history of with immigration starting around 1960 and some significant changes in immigration patterns occurring especially since the end of the seventies. Another characteristic of ethnic and foreign minorities in Germany may be found in the structure of historical relationships between countries of origin of immigrant minorities and Germany. Unlike other European countries, there is no serious history of colonialism which may represent an important pull-factor for migration and shape the relationship between immigrant minorities and the society at large. The ethnic composition of immigrants and motivations for migration changed significantly over the last 20 years. First, countries from which the migrant work force originated have changed with South-Eastern European countries replacing South-West European countries. At the beginning of the 1960s approximately 60 per cent of the foreign population came from countries of the European Community. In the 1990s their share has dropped to some 27 per cent. Turkish immigrants and immigrants from former Yugoslavia now account for almost half of the resident foreign population in Germany. Furthermore, immigrants from Third World countries make-up substantial proportions of the immigrant population. Migration then at the end of the eighties has spread to Eastern European countries, thus adding to ethnic and cultural diversity of immigrant populations. With the change in the ethnic composition of immigrants a shift in the motives for migration and legal aspects of immigration has been associated.

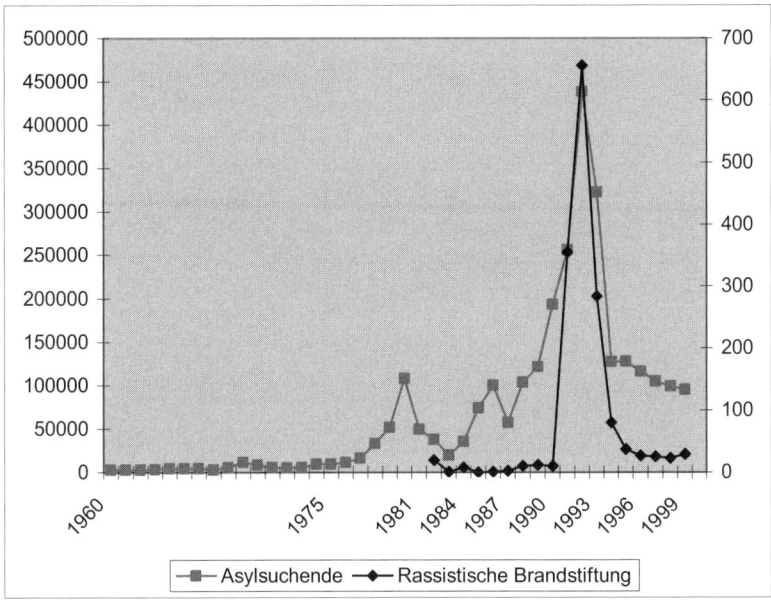

Graph 5.2 Trends in the number of asylum-seekers and xenophobic arson
Source: Bundesminesterium des Innern: Verfassungsschutzberichte 1982–2001

Finally, regional differences in the density of foreigners have to be addressed as metropolitan areas and the western part of Germany are the favorite places to which immigrants are attracted. In the 1990s just approximately 2 per cent of the foreign population lives in the "new Bundesländer", that is, in the eastern part of Germany (the former German Democratic Republic with a share of approximately 20 per cent of the population). However, Germany at large belongs to those European countries with the highest proportion of visible minorities. The occurrence of crimes against foreign nationals displays significant regional disparities.

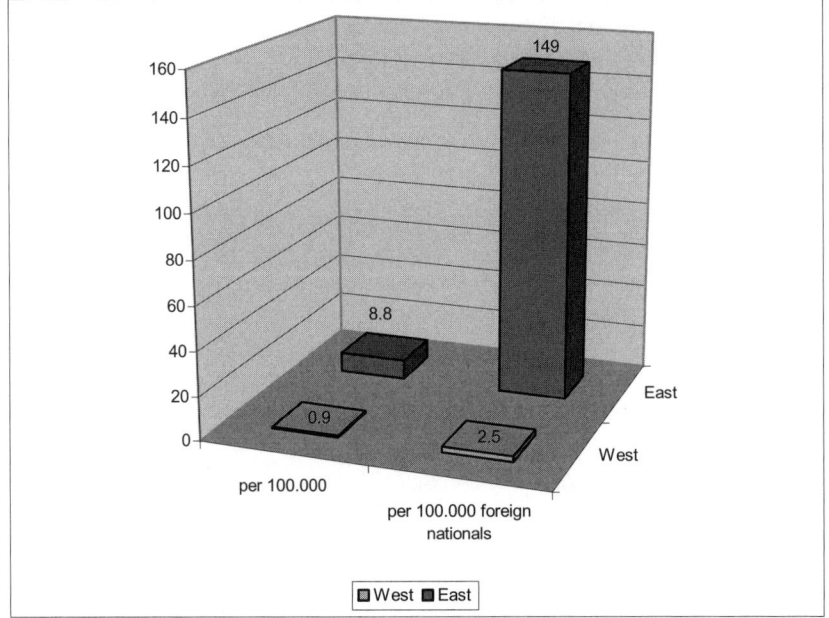

Graph 5.3 Xenophobic crime in East and West Germany (2005)
Source: Bundesminesterium des Innern: Verfassungsschutzbericht 2005. Berlin: BMI, 2006, p. 31; Statistisches Bundesamt: Bevölkerung und Erwerbstätigkeit. Ausländische Bevölkerung, 2005. Weisbaden: Statistisches Bundesamt, 2006

Although, in terms of absolute numbers most crimes committed against foreign nationals with an extremist or political motivation are counted in the west of Germany, in relative figures a completely different picture emerges. As can be seen from Graph 5.3, the risk for foreign nationals to be victimized by violent extremist crime in the east of Germany is by far exceeding risks encountered in the west.

According to official sources in 2005, an examination of the distribution of types of right wing extremist crime along various criminal offence statutes shows that incidents of racial hatred (i.e., extremist propaganda) was the most common type of offences (N= 10,881) followed by racially motivated propaganda such as the display and distribution of Nazi swastikas and other fascist propaganda (N= 2,957). Moreover, besides distribution of such propaganda material it is essentially the criminal offence of provocation of racial hatred which contributes to the overall number of hate crimes as defined by police and intelligence services (see Berline BMI, 2006: 24; Bundesministerium des Innern: Verfassungsschutzbericht, 2005).

In terms of the type of victims of right wing extremist violent crime, based on data from the same sources, foreign nationals (or immigrants stand out as victims, followed by political opponents (mostly individuals from leftist groups or members of mainstream political parties) were most likely to be victims of right wing violence.

Information on perpetrators of racist violence demonstrates that it is in particular:

a. young men.
   b. coming from disadvantaged environments.
   c. not affiliated to organized right wing organizations, and
   d. involved also in other type of crimes (and violence) who become known as suspects of racist crime and racist violence.

It does not come as a surprise that racist propaganda crimes can often be traced back to individuals affiliated with extremist organizations. While there is a dearth of victimization surveys and/or general surveys on racial victimization, especially in Germany; survey research has tended to demonstrates notable differences in the extent of racial violence and harassment suffered by various ethnic minorities.

Surveys show also that the proportion of immigrants who perceive German society as discriminating and hostile increased during the peak in racist violence experienced in 1993 and decreased afterwards. The rate of immigrants perceiving hostility towards them is particularly marked in the group of Turkish origin (Anhut/ Heitmeyer 2000, p. 21).

Explaining Racist Violence

A review of the other countries represented in this collection will reveal that different explanations of racist violence exist. They exist because given that racial victimization is a social construct it must be examined and understood within the social, organizational, economic and political environment. It is also plausible to link explanations of racial violence to the explanation of violence at large.

In Germany, disadvantagous social conditions such as unemployment, poor housing and poor school achievements have been assumed to play a role in explaining racist violence. In particular it has been hypothesized that individuals living in such conditions are easily affected by political campaigns suggesting that they are competing with immigrants about jobs and other resources. With that scapegoating is highlighted as a major source of racist violence and discrimination at large (Albrecht, 1997). More recently it was also argued that experienced disadvantages may result in shame and that shame then is transformed into rage which again is directed against minorities that are perceived to be more successful.

Furthermore, structural assumptions refer to a social and political process, which sets up immigrants and minorities as scapegoats and convenient enemies. The possible sources of such hostilities and ultimately violence certainly are located somewhere in the process of developing into modern and then into late modern societies (Young, 1999). Crime and crime control related accounts of late modernity (or of the last three decades of the 20th century) sometimes give an (unfounded) impression as if it was actually late modernity or the last three decades of the 20th century (that is socio-economic and cultural changes characterizing late modernity) when waves of violence have been launched, new paths to violence have been opened (Young, 1999) and instability and crisis have been produced by a hitherto unknown extent (Hobsbawm, 1994). European history from the Middle Ages through Enlightenment and beyond demonstrates the successful search for folk devils, scapegoats, and the demonization of the other and permanent exclusion of the stranger.

There exists a considerable body of research on the emergence and the consequences of cognitive biases and attitudes/perceptions displaying prejudice, labeling and discrimination in Germany (Boehnke, Fuß and Hagan, 2002). But, there is until now no conclusive research that could demonstrate how cognition, attitudes and perception are related to racist and violent behaviour. This may be explained by a bias in social science research which puts the focus on the emergence of extremist, racist or xenophobic attitudes and perceptions (see the summaries in Melzer/Rostampour, 2002) while the behavioural dimension has been neglected (Ohlemacher, 2001). This again is certainly explained by the fact that severe racist violence is rare, even when resorting to self-report studies on racist violence. A second problem, in Germany, is linked to establishing causal relationships which would require longitudinal (prospective) studies on how sequences of acquiring attitudes, building up affiliation to various groups and organizations as well as violent behaviour are developing over time (Boehnke, Fuß and Hagan, 2002). The explanatory power of theoretical approaches to attitudes and perceptions (e.g., the authoritarian personality approach, Adorno, 1950; Bromba and Edelstein, 2001), moreover, is rather poor (Melzer and Rostampour, 2002).

As regards the prevalent approach in explaining youth violence towards minorities in Germany, that is the hypothesis of frustration-aggression as well as learning theories, these are not specific, but general and up to now did not do too well in accounting for violence and in particular in predicting violence. However, as obviously racist violence overlaps with violence at large it seems worthwhile to study racist violence also from the perspective of general theories of violence.

For Germany it has been argued that re-unification and related and rapid socio-economic and cultural changes could have exerted a particular impact on a cohort of young people particularly exposed to such influences because of finding themselves in a period of search for identity (Bromba and Edelstein, 2001). Such assumptions on particular impacts of rapid social and cultural change may tentatively explain high rates of incidence of xenophobic violence in the east of Germany.

There is then a trail of explanation provided by the concept of culture conflict which can be followed in order to understand the nature and the extent of risks and dangers for social stability and integration at large. These dangers and risks are the product of collective reactions in terms of violent behaviour justified with defending cultural or national identities. It may be argued that in modern industrialized countries such as Germany, the locus of stability and integration is not anymore a culture based on shared values and collective morals (Brock, 1993). This type of culture has been replaced by a material culture (Heitmeyer, 2001) which is not dependent on shared values or cultural consensus but allows for individual choices in life-styles and orientations (Heitmeyer, 1995; Moeller, 1993). Under the conditions of stable economies which provide for the material basis of this mechanism of integration, the potential of cultural conflicts should be deemed to be rather low. Violence against minorities may therefore be conceived as a consequence of rapid socio-political transition and its effects in terms of social disintegration. Elevated levels of violence are to be interpreted also as indicators of cultural disintegration or cultural segregation. Moreover, these signs could be understood also as indicating basic discrimination in the general population. We may notice recently new sociological concern for these phenomena which were thought to belong to the past (Friedrich-Naumann Stiftung, 1993). Obviously, these outbursts of violence affecting foreign and ethnic minorities refer partially to a "conscience collective" emerging around the issues of the nation, the nation state as well as cultural and racial differences (Moeller, 1993, p. 43). It has been deplored that modern sociological theory cannot account for such developments because of the emphasis which is laid by sociology on describing and explaining post-industrial societies (Hondrich, 1992). Nationalist ideologies which seemed to have been overcome by structural changes in modern societies and their concern for rationality are on the rise again in virtually all major European countries and these changes are obviously beyond the reach of sociological explanations (Brock, 1993).

Summarizing the state of theorizing in the field of racist crime as it relates to Germany, it may be concluded that theories of racist violence and racist behaviour at large as well as tests of such theories are poorly developed – and not just for Germany. This holds in particular true for approaches to explain the increase of racist violence in the last few decades (Heitmeyer, 1994). The state of theories corresponds to the state of theoretical thinking observable in areas that are close to the phenomenon of racist violence, that is modern terrorism (Albrecht, 2002).

Social, Cultural and Political Reaction to Racial Victimization

A multitude of organisations and initiatives have developed since the first massive signs of racist crime after the 1990 German re-unification became visible (Rieker, 2002). These include the Alliance for Democracy and Tolerance; Young People for Tolerance and Democracy – against Right-wing Extremism; Xenophobia and Anti-Semitism; XENOS – Plural Living and Working; CIVITAS – Initiative against Right-wing Extremism in the New Federal States; ENTIMON – Together against Violence and Right-wing Extremism; Federal Programmes to Encourage Right-wing Extremists to Leave the movement, such as the EXIT program.

In addition to the grass root initiatives, victims of racist crime have received special attention. In the Federal Budget 2001, 10 million DM were provided for the establishment of a hardship fund for victims of right-wing violence, 5 million DM were provided for measures of assistance for the victims. Until the end of 2001 about 2.64 million DM have been claimed.

For the year 2002 the federal government has provided an additional 2.5 million Euro for this purpose. In 2001, 210 applications for compensation have been submitted: 121 applications (in favour of 151 persons) were acceded, 52 applications were rejected, 31 of the latter because no extreme right-wing background was obvious and 7 because the crime happened before 1 January 1999 (32 applications are still being processed). The compensations amounted to 500 to 500, 000 DM (Printed matter of the German parliament 14/8537 and 14/7058). In the meantime there are – especially in the Eastern federal states – various advice centers for victims of extreme right-wing violence. These centers offer various types of assistance either by an outward approach of potential victims or by being consulted by advice-seeking victims: legal advice, assistance in the search of witnesses, accompanying to authorities or court proceedings, finding appropriate medical or psychotherapeutic help, assistance in the application for compensation as well as for the coverage of legal expenses, providing contacts with initiatives that assist victims locally.

It is the objective to shift the emphasis from concentrating on the perpetrator to promoting processes of increasing solidarity in the social environment of the victims, to extend alliances against exclusion, to strengthen democratic structures and to weaken the right-wing power ("Focussing on the victims" (Die Opfer in den Blickpunkt rücken; www.kamalatta.de/opferperspektive/Opferperspektive.html); for details on the protection of victims see Printed matter of the German parliament 14/7058, Right-wing extremism in North Rhine Westphalia, Printed matter 13/1146, chapter 9 "Protection of victims", pp. 138–142) (see Box 2).

Box 2: Public Backlash to Xenophobia

In autumn 2003 a small Asian fast food outlet and a Turkish Kebab takeaway in a small town in the state (Land) of Brandenburg were attacked with firebombs and burned down completely causing also the loss of livelihood of the victims. Police investigated the case and found out that three young men and a young woman (aged between 17 and 26) carried out the attacks. A xenophobic motive was established through confessions and additional evidence linking some of the suspects to right wing extremist groups. In the ensuing criminal trials the offenders have been convicted and sentenced to prison terms between 2 and 3 years. The city administration responded (also to broad media coverage) by arranging a local donation account and collecting within some two weeks 2700 € for assistance to the victims. The local crime prevention council provided for counseling of victims and channeled the cases to the National Victim Assistance Organization "Weisser Ring" which subsequently managed the financial arrangements necessary to rebuild the takeaways. The racist incidents gave also rise to the foundation of a local initiative still active today in local anti-racist policies.

Source: Bürk-Matsunami, T. and Selders, B.: Fremdenfeindliche und rechtsextreme Übergriffe auf Imbissbuden im Land Brandenburg. Ein Forschungsbericht) www.aktionsbuendnis.brandenburg.de/media/1235, 23 October 2006

With regard to political responses, since the early 1990s most German states have established police units specialized on the investigation, repression and prevention of racist crime.

Programmes and initiatives to reduce and to prevent racial violence can be roughly collapsed into the following categories:

a. Awareness programmes aiming at changing cognitions, attitudes and behaviour of groups at risk (in particular young men from deteriorated neighbourhoods)

and school children and students, the public at large and particular professions (police).
b. Proactive social street work aimed at difficult to reach violent youth (see Albrecht and Kilchling, 2004).
c. Proactive community work in order to strengthen high risk communities in coping with racial discrimination and racial violence.
d. Victims of racial violence support and compensation schemes.
e. Increasing political, professional and social participation of groups at risk (in particular integration of ethnic minorities in police and judicial professions) through promoting integration of groups at risk through nationalization and political participation.
f. Promoting integration of (immigrant) minorities in particular through reducing legal pressures on immigrants and asylum seekers.
g. Supporting hard-core right wing activists in exiting extremist organizations.
h. Discouraging violent offenders through anti-aggression training/therapy and through establishing specialized police forces concentrating investigative efforts on racist or extremist violence.

Although, a lot of resources have been vested in all types of programmes aimed at prevention and repression of racist violence it must be noted that there is no evaluation research available that could be used in assessing impacts, efficiency or cost effectiveness of programmes implemented (Roth, 2003). The lack of sound evaluation research has recently led to a debate on whether programmes against right wing extremism should be funded through the Federal Budget at all. However, a decision of the Federal Government has now underlined that there will be financial support during the next budgetary years in a size comparable to what has been invested over the last several years.

Insofar, we do not know much about the results of anti-racist policies and programmes except that services can be delivered to victims. Basically, anti-racism policies in Germany are not led by scientific information but are rather guided by normative theory and ideology. A research agenda insofar has still to be developed.

Summary: Conclusion and Future Directions

The phenomenon of racist violence compared to some other countries represented in this text, is under-researched in Germany. As a result, we do not know much about incidence or prevalence about the development and trends in racist violence. This is largely due to the fact that the conventional information systems entrusted documentation of crime and criminal offenders are not yet capable to produce information that could be used to produce informative accounts of the nature and extent of racial violence in Germany. In particular, it is the lack of differentiated population statistics that does not allow one to calculate group specific rates of racist violence.

Available knowledge nevertheless suggests that racist violence represents but a minor part (approx. 1 per cent) of all violence documented on the basis of police statistics and survey research in European societies and that minorities are not more at risk than are majority groups. Notwithstanding this fact, racist violence has a destructive impact in terms of elevated levels of fear and insecurity among minorities which is expressed in a variety of ways. Given the current state of affairs regarding racial victimization in Germany (see Henning, 2001), there is a need for further research on the relationship between violence, racism and the community. In particular, questions should be studied that are related to the plausible assumption that racist violence and the messages sent out by such violence have a potential of polarization and escalation. Furthermore, research efforts should deal with the question of how communities can respond efficiently to racial crime. Theoretical discourses and empirical research on racist violence are clearly biased towards violence exerted by majority groups against minorities.

It is suggested to introduce systematic data collection with interviews with a selection of key persons (e.g., police, social workers, NGOs and community organizations members) or panels of key persons in each country. The key person approach has been successfully used in various areas and could be also adopted in monitoring closely changes in racist crime. The response to racist violence in terms of investigation and prosecution of racist crimes and racial violence is up top now with a few exceptions not covered by research. Available research in Germany shows that rates of conviction are rather low although in general they do not seem to be under average. Data are also interpreted as indicating that for some racist crimes mediation and victim offender reconciliation seem to be appropriate responses (Albrecht and Kilchling, 2002).

In terms of consequences of enforcement of criminal law against racist crime and racist violence we may separate effects in terms of recidivism, (negative) general deterrence, (positive) general prevention in terms of norm building and norm validation. Currently, there is no available research in these areas making it difficult to identifty, let alone devise constructive intervention strategies to combat racial victimization. A study from Germany – based on a qualitative approach – concludes that research evidence speaks against both, individual and general deterrence related effects (Heitmeyer and Müller, 1995). The authors of the study conclude also that there exists no empirical basis justifying demands for increasing criminal penalties against racist violent offenders (Heitmeyer and Müller, 1995: p. 178).

Finally, it is difficult to assess the potential of German criminal law and German criminal law enforcement to effectively address policy aimed at positive norm building and norm validation. Although, sociological and legal theory plausibly state that criminal norms need being routinely confirmed through sanctioning infringements, there exists no conclusive evidence as to the type of sanctions nor the intensity of punishment needed to maintain a process of norm validation. To this end, the issue of racial victimization while evident in Germany, has no clear solution. Hopefully through collaborative and international efforts such as that represented in this text, we will begin to not only address some of the fundamental hurdles but also being to identify actions and policies that can transcend social, cultural and political boundaries and serve to confine racial hatred and its consequences effectively.

References

Adorno, T., et. al. (1950). *The Authoritarian Personality*. New York: Harper.
AI Report (2001). Germany (www.amnesty.org). Date retrieved 23 October 2006.
Aktion Courage – SOS Rassismus (1999). Polizeiübergriffe gegen Ausländerinnen und Ausländer. Dokumentation: Bonn.
Albrecht, H.-J. (1997). Ethnic Minorities, Crime and Criminal Justice in Germany. In: Tonry, M. (ed.): *Crime and Justice. A Review of Research*, 21, Chicago: University Press, pp. 31–99.
Albrecht, H.-J. (2002). Terrorismus und kriminologische Forschung – Eine Bestandsaufnahme. In: *Schweizerische Zeitschrift für Kriminologie*, 1, pp. 5–17.
Albrecht, H.-J. (2002). Polizei, Diskriminierung und Fremdenfeindlichkeit in multi-ethnischen Gesellschaften. In: Donatsch, A., Forster, M., Schwarzenegger, C. (eds.): *Strafrecht, Strafprozessrecht und Menschenrechte*. Zürich: Schulthess, pp. 355–372.
Albrecht, H.-J.(2004). Eine kritische Bilanz – Die Zentrale Stelle Ludwigsburg für NS-Verbrechen. Tribüne – Zeitschrift zum Verständnis des Judentums 43, pp. 188–194.
Albrecht, H.-J. (2006). Illegalität, Kriminalität und Sicherheit. In: Alt, J., Bommes, M. (eds.): *Illegalität. Grenzen und Möglichkeiten der Migrationspolitik*. Wiesbaden: VS Verlag für Sozialwissenschaften, pp. 60–80.
Albrecht, H.-J. and Kilchling, M. (2002). Rechtsextremistische Gewalt, strafrechtliche Sozialkontrolle, Täter-Opfer-Ausgleich und Wiedergutmachungsansätze. In: *Recht der Jugend und des Bildungswesens*, 50, pp. 82–93.
Aly, G. (ed.) (1988). *Feinderklärung und Prävention. Kriminalbiologie, Zigeunerforschung und Asozialenpolitik. Beiträge zur nationalsozialistischen Gesundheits- und Sozialpolitik*, Band 6, Berlin.
Anhut, R. and Heitmeyer, W. (2000). Desintegration, Konflikt und Ethnisierung. In: Heitmeyer, W. and Anhut, R. (eds.): *Bedrohte Stadtgesellschaft. Soziale Desintegrationsprozesse und ethnisch-kulturelle Konfliktkonstellationen*. Weinheim, München: Juventa, pp. 17–75.
Arad, Y. (ed.) (1987). *Documents of the Holocaust. Selected sources on the destruction of the Jews of Germany and Austria, Poland, and the Soviet Union*. Jerusalem: Yad Vashem.
Arnold, H. (1986). Kriminelle Viktimisierung und ihre Korrelate. In: *Zeitschrift für die gesamte Strafrechtswissenschaft*, 98, pp. 1014–1058.
Arquilla, J. and Ronfeldt, D. (eds.) (2001). *Networks and Netwars: The Future of Terror, Crime, and Militancy*. Washington: Rand.
Bauman, Z. (1992). *Dialektik der Ordnung. Die Moderne und der Holocaust*. Hamburg: Europäische Verlagsanstalt.
Bauman, Z. (2000). Social Uses of Law and Order. In: Garland, D., Sparks, R. (eds.): *Criminology and Social Theory*, Oxford: Oxford University Press, pp. 23–45.
BayObLG, Bayerisches Oberstes Landgericht (1994). *Neue Zeitschrift für Strafrecht* 14, pp. 286–287.
Beck, U. (2002). *Das Schweigen der Wörter. Über Terror und Krieg*, Frankfurt: Edition Suhrkamp.

Bergmann, W. (2004). Die Verbreitung antisemitischer Einstellungen in der Bundesrepublik Deutschland. In: *Bundesministerium des Inneren* (ed.): Texte zur Inneren Sicherheit. Extremismus in Deutschland. Erscheinungsformen und aktuelle Bestandsaufnahme. Berlin: GGP Media.

Bjorgo, T. (1997). *Racist and Right-Wing Violence in Scandinavia. Patterns, Perpetrators and Responses* Oslo: Tano Aschehoug.

Bliesener, Th. (1992). Psychologische Hintergründe der Gewalt gegen Ausländer. In: DVJJ-Regionalgruppe Nordbayern (ed.): *Ausländer im Jugendstrafrecht. Neue Dimensionen. Erlangen*: DVJJ, pp. 15–32.

Boehnke, K., Fuß, D. and Hagan, J. (2002). Jugendgewalt und Rechtsextremismus – Soziologische und psychologische Analysen in internationaler Perspektive. In: Boehnke, K., Fuß, D. and Hagan, J. (eds.): *Jugendgewalt und Rechtsextremismus*, Weinheim, München: Juventa, pp. 21–30.

Bowling, B. and Phillips, C. (2003). Racist Victimization in England and Wales, in: Hawkins, D.F. (ed.): *Violent Crime. Assessing Race & Ethnic Differences*, Cambridge: Cambridge University Press, pp. 154–170.

Brock, D. (1993). Wiederkehr der Klassen? Über Mechanismen der Integration und Ausgrenzung in entwickelten Industriegesellschaften. *Soziale Welt*, 44, pp. 177–198.

Bromba, M.and Edelstein, W. (2001). *Das Anti-demokratische und Rechtsextreme Potenzial unter Jugendlichen und Jungen Erwachsenen in Deutschland*. Bonn: BMI.

Brustein, W. and King, R. (2002). Antisemitismus in Europa vor dem Holocaust. In: Boehnke, K., Fuß, D., Hagan, J. (eds.) *Jugendgewalt und Rechtsextremismus*, Weinheim, München: Juventa, pp. 257–282.

Bundesgerichtshof (BGH) (1971). *Neue Juristische Wochenschrift*, 59, p. 571.

Bundeskriminalamt (2001). *Rechtsextremismus, Antisemitismus und Fremdenfeindlichkeit*. Neuwied, Kriftel: Luchterhand.

Bundesministerium des Innern. Verfassungsschutzbericht 2005. Berlin: BMI 2006.

Busch, H. (2000). Andere Länder – ähnliche Sitten. Polizeiübergriffe und Kontrolle in Großbritannien und Frankreich. CILIP, 67, pp. 49–53.

Cernyak-Spatz, S.E. (1985). *German Holocaust Literature*. New York: Lang.

Christie, N. and Bruun, K. (1991). Der Nützliche Feind. Die Drogenpolitik und ihre Nutznießer, Bielefeld: AJZ-Verlag.

Coenders, M., Lubbers, M. and Scheepers, P. (2004). Majorities' attitudes towards minorities in Western and Eastern European Societies: Results from the European Social Survey 2002–2003. Report 4 for the European Monitoring Centre on Racism and Xenophobia. University of Nijmegen: Nijmegen.

Comité de prevention de la torture. (1991). Rapport au gouvernement de la République française relatif a la visite effectuée par le C.P.T en France du 27 octobre au 8 novembre 1991. Strasbourg: Conseil de l'Europe.

Crawford, A. (1999). Questioning Appeals to Community Within Crime Prevention and Control. European Journal of Crime Policy and Research, 7, pp. 509–530.

Dünkel, F. (2005). Young migrants and members of ethnic minorities as victims and offenders of violent crimes: an international comparative survey in the region of the Baltic Sea. In: Queloz, N. (Hrsg.): *Délinquance des Jeunes et Justice des*

Mineurs. Les Défis des Migrations et de la Pluralité éthnique. Bern: Stämpfli, pp. 185–220.
Emundts, C. (2000). Blutspur rechter Gewalt. *Die Woche*, 33, 11 August, p. 3.
EUMC. (2005). Racist Violence in 15 EU Member States. A Comparative Overview of Findings from the RAXEN National Focal Points Reports 2001–2004. Summary Report. Vienna: EUMC.
Europäische Kommission gegen Rassismus und Intoleranz. (2004). *Dritter Bericht über Deutschland*. Strasbourg: Council of Europe.
European Monitoring Centre (2005). *Racist Violence in 15 EU Member States*. Vienna: European Monitoring Centre.
Findeisen, H.-V., Kersten, J. (1999). *Der Kick und die Ehre. Vom Sinn jugendlicher Gewalt*, München: Kunstmann.
Fletcher, I. (1994). Strafverschärfung bei aus Hass begangenen Verbrechen, zu einem problematischen Urteil des amerikanischen Supreme Court. *Strafverteidiger* 14, pp. 105–106.
Friedrich-Naumann-Stiftung (1993). Dokumentation. Rechtsextremismus und Gewalt. COMDOK.
Frommel, M. (1994). Alles nur ein Vollzugsdefizit? Warum die Strafjustiz nicht angemessen auf die Gewaltverbrechen gegen Auslaender reagiert. *DVJJ-Journal*, 1, pp. 67–68.
Frommel, M. (1994). Fremdenfeindliche Gewalt, Polizei und Strafjustiz. *Kritische Justiz*, p. 323.
Goldhagen, D.J. (1996). *Hitler's willing executioners*. Knopf: New York.
Graebsch, Christine (ed.). (2000). *Experimente im Strafrecht – Wie genau können Erfolgskontrollen von kriminalpräventiven Maßnahmen sein?* Bremen: Bremer Institut für Kriminalpolitik.
Hailbronner, K. (1996). Das Asylrecht nach den Entscheidungen des Bundesverfassungsgerichts. *Neue Zeitschrift für Verwaltungsrecht*, pp. 625–631.
Hawkins, D.F. et. al. (eds.). (1998). Race, Ethnicity, and Serious Juvenile Offending. In: Loeber, R., Farrington, D. (eds.) *Serious and Violent Juvenile Offenders. Risk Factors and Successful Interventions*. London, New Dehli: Thousand Oaks, pp. 30–46.
Heitmeyer, W. (ed.). (1994). Das Gewaltdilemma. *Gesellschaftliche Reaktionen auf fremdenfeindliche Gewalt und Rechtsextremismus*. Frankfurt: Suhrkamp.
Heitmeyer, W. (ed.). (1995). Schattenseiten der Globalisierung. *Rechtsradikalismus, Rechtspopulismus und separatistischer Regionalismus in westlichen Demokratien*. Frankfurt: Suhrkamp.
Heitmeyer, W. (2004). Gruppenbezogene Menschenfeindlichkeit. Die theoretische Konzeption und empirische Ergebnisse aus den Jahren 2002, 2003 und 2004. In: Heitmeyer, W. (ed.): *Deutsche Zustände*. Frankfurt: Suhrkamp, pp. 13–35.
Heitmeyer, W. and Müller, J. (1995). *Fremdenfeindliche Gewalt junger Menschen. Biographische Hintergründe, soziale Situationskontexte und die Bedeutung strafrechtlicher Sanktionen*. Godesberg: Forum Verlag.
Hobsbawm, E. (1994). *The Age of Extremes*. London: Michael Joseph.

Hondrich, K.O. (1992). Wovon wir nichts wissen wollten. *Die Zeit*, No. 40, 25. 9. 1992. im extremistischen Spektrum Berlins. Berlin: Senatsverwaltung für Inneres.

Jacobs, J.B. (1993). The Emergence and Implications of American Hate Crime Jurisprudence. *Israel Yearbook on Human Rights* 22, pp. 113–139.

Jobard, F. (2001). L' usage de la force par la police. Paris: Edition de la Découverte.

Kerner, S.R. (1994). Kriminologische Erklärungsansätze für Fremdenfeindlichkeit, Rechtsextremismus und Gewalt. der Kriminalist, 26, pp. 147–151.

Krone, G. (1980). Die Volksverhetzung als Verbrechen gegen die Menschlichkeit : unter Berücksichtigung der soziologischen, psychologischen und sozialpsychologischen Gesetzmäßigkeiten des zugrundeliegenden Aggressionsprozesses sowie des historischen und kriminologischen Hintergrundes von § 130 StGB. Mainz: Universität Mainz 1980.

Kubink, M. (1997). *Fremdenfeindliche Straftaten*. Berlin: Duncker und Humblot.

Lipsey, M.W. and Wilson, D.B. (1998). Effective Intervention for Serious Juvenile Offenders In: Loeber, R., Farrington, D. (eds.) Serious and Violent Juvenile Offenders. Risk Factors and Successful Interventions. London, New Dehli: Thousand Oaks, pp. 313–345.

Lüdemann, C. (1992). Zur „Ansteckungswirkung" von Gewalt gegenüber Ausländern – Anwendung eines Schwellenwertmodells kollektiven Verhaltens. *Soziale Probleme* 3, pp. 137–153.

Melzer, W. and Rostampour, P. (2002). Schulqualität und Rechtsextremismus. In: *Recht der Jugend und des Bildungswesens*, 50, pp. 41–58.

Moeller, K. (1993). Rechtsextremismus und Gewalt. Empirische Befunde und individualisierungstheoretische Erklaerungen. In: Breyvogel, W. (ed.) *Lust auf Randale. Jugendliche Gewalt gegen Fremde*, Bonn: Verlag Dietz, pp. 35–64.

Neubacher, F. (1998). *Fremdenfeindliche Brandanschläge*. Mönchengladbach.

Ohlemacher, T. (2001). Fremdenfeindliche Gewalt, Rechtsextremismus und neue Rechte immer mal wieder – mehr von demselben. *Soziologische Revue*, 24, pp. 48–57.

Rieker, P. (2002). Aktionsprogramme gegen Rechtsextremismus und Fremdenfeindlichkeit – Überblick und Einschätzungen. *Recht der Jugend und des Bildungswesens*, 50, pp. 30–40.

Rommelspacher, B. (1993). Männliche Jugendliche als Projektionsfiguren gesellschaftlicher Gewaltphantasien. Rassismus im Selbstverständnis der Mehrheitskultur. In: Breyvogel, W. (ed.): *Lust auf Randale. Jugendliche Gewalt gegen Fremde*. Bonn: Verlag Dietz, pp. 65–82.

Roth, R. (2003). *Bürgernetzwerke gegen Rechts. Evaluierung von Aktionsprogrammen und Maßnahmen gegen Rechtsextremismus und Ausländerfeindlichkeit*. Bonn: FES.

Seehafer, S. (2003). *Strafrechtliche Reaktionen auf rechtsextremistisch / fremdenfeindlich motivierte Gewalttaten – Das amerikanische „hate crime" Konzept und seine Übertragbarkeit auf das deutsche Rechtssystem*. Berlin: Humboldt Universität.

Senatsverwaltung für Inneres, Abteilung Verfassungsschutz. (2004). *Antisemitismus*. Berlin: Senatsverwaltung für Inneres.

V. Trotha, T. (2002). Über die Zukunft der Gewalt. *Monatsschrift für Kriminologie und Strafrechtsreform*, 85, pp. 349–368.
Van Donselaar, J. (2000). *Monitor Racisme en Extreem Rechts*, Leiden: Derde Rapportage.
Von Hirsch, A. et al. (1999). Criminal Deterrence and Sentence Severity, Oxford: Hart.
Weiss, J. (1997). *Der lange Weg zum Holocauste Geschichte der Judenfeindschaft in Deutschland und Österreich*. Hamburg: Hoffmann und Campe.
Young, J. (1999). *The Exclusive Society*. Thousand Oaks, Ca.: Sage.
Zick, A. and Küpper, B. (2005). Transformed Anti-Semitism – A Report on Anti-Semitism in Germany. Journal für Konflikt- und Gewaltforschung, 7, pp. 50–92.

Helpful Websites

www.amnesty.org – Amnesty International.
http://www.bmi.bund.de/ – Federal Ministry of the Interior.
http://eumc.eu.int/eumc/index.php – European Monitoring Centre on Racism and Xenophobia.
http://www.statewatch.org/ – Statewatch: Monitoring the State and Civil Liberties in the European Union.

Chapter 6

Greece

Vassiliki Petoussi-Douli

Introduction

On 1 January 2006, Rethymno, a small town in Greece woke up to the news of the murder of a young immigrant man. The night before and while new year's celebration was going on, a group of young Greek men and a group of young Albanian men engaged in a bar fight. People from both groups suffered rather minor injuries which were treated at the local hospital on an outpatient basis. After his release from the hospital, one of the Greeks – a young man serving his military service at the time – met with his father – an ex-*gastarbeite*r (foreign 'guest worker') – and a number of friends and acquaintances of various nationalities and decided to 'avenge' the 'insult they sustained.'

A few hours before sunrise six men and one woman, broke and entered into the home of an Albanian family of immigrants, yanked the sleeping father and son out of their beds, chased them to the roof, beat and injured the father and one of the perpetrators stubbed the son to his death. The coroner counted 17 stub-wounds caused by a knife-blade broken and stuck in the young man's body. The offender was 18 years old and the victim – whose participation in the fight that preceded the murder is uncertain – was a 17-year-old man supporting his family and paying the medical treatments of his ill father whose kidney problems necessitate regular blood transfusions (*Patris*, 2 January 2006).

This was a brutal and unusual crime compared to the typical murder case in Greece (see for example: Tsouramanis, 1998; Nova-Kaltsouni, 1998). It involved several people – two victims and seven offenders, among them a female immigrant – while victims and offenders were neither relatives nor long-time friends and/or acquaintances. The murder victim was repeatedly stabbed not shot to death. The offenders broke and entered into the home of the victims *in order* to commit the crime – their presence in the family's home was not coincidental. Differences in political, religious, cultural and ethnic backgrounds existed between victims and offenders as well as among offenders. Overall, this crime did not occur as 'an act of impulse due to loss of temper' – several hours had passed since the event that purportedly 'led' to the crime – but rather as an intentional act of revenge.

The news shocked the local community. Surprised and confused, people saw their town and their behavior attracting negative media attention and read flyers, signed by nationalists, 'demanding' that all "*these foreigners* who flock in the country to snatch the locals' jobs, disrespect the country and its people and cause trouble" be "sent back to where they came from." After the initial shock however, a large, peaceful, candlelight immigrant-led march was organized and large numbers of people attended public debates about racism, xenophobia, social exclusion, social inclusion, assimilation, human rights, and victimization of immigrants. On a different level, local State officials and politicians were eager to reassure the local community as well as the rest of the country that this was an 'isolated incident' in an otherwise 'harmonious' coexistence of ethnic Greeks and immigrants (*Kathimerini*, 3 January 2006; *Patris*, 10 January 2006).

As different as the many perspectives, attitudes and behaviors expressed, discussed and debated were, what is probably of relevant importance is that at the local, and later on at the national level, it became apparent – at least as a subject of matter and interest – that certain people, or rather certain groups of people, may and do become victims of crime and ill treatment *because of their social status and identity*. Much of the relevant discussions focused upon economic immigrants and their social status as potential source of victimization.

Aspects of immigrant victimization however, are not foreign to Greek society. Greece's long history of heavy emigration whose rate at times and especially between the 1950s and the 1960s, exceeded the country's population growth rate, lasted until the mid to late 70's (Filias, 1967; Merlopoulos, 1967; Fakiolas and King, 1996). Indispensable for the country's economy – emigrant remittances, for decades supported individuals and families left behind and helped improve the balance of payments of the Greek economy (Petropoulos, 1994: 14-15, Glytsos, 1994: 107-109, 126-127) – emigration had a lasting effect on Greece's national consciousness through the expansion of the notion of 'Hellenism' and 'Hellenic Diaspora' (Kasimis and Kassimi, 2004).

Members of the Greek Diaspora – similarly to emigrants of other nationalities – during the process towards social integration in the countries of destination, experienced exploitation, poor working conditions, adverse discrimination and prejudice (Gizelis, 1994: 34-35; Kousis, 1985: 109). Represented and reproduced in various forms of popular entertainment such as movies and songs, the 'sorrows' of *ksenitia* (foreign land and country), the life of the *gastarbeiter*, and the overall experience of *being an immigrant* became commonly shared knowledge (Laliotou, 2004; Kamboureli, 1991; Daniil, 1991; Eideneier, 1991). From this perspective, it can be argued that Greek society at large, was rather familiar with experiences of racism, prejudice, discrimination and immigrant victimization from the point of view of the victim.

Given the country's long tradition of emigration and the economic importance of tourism,[1] it can be argued that Greek society has for long been exposed to heterogeneity and multiculturalism. Since the 1990s, however, social expressions, realization and interpretation of heterogeneity and multiculturalism swiftly altered in Greece. Following the collapse of former Soviet Republics and the Albanian State in particular, Greek society was faced with large numbers of people who entered the country not as economically potent visitors returning to their home countries after

---

1 It is estimated that 15-20 per cent of the total economic activity in Greece is attributable to the tourist industry. In 2005, for example, proceeds from foreign tourists accounted for 6 per cent of the GNP of the country (Sabaniotis, 2006; WTTC, 2004).

a short period of time (*the tourists*), but rather as economically and/or politically and socially deprived people seeking refuge, residence, employment, education, health and social insurance for extended periods of time (*the immigrants*) increasing heterogeneity and necessitating cultural, economic, political and social adjustments. These rapidly increasing levels of heterogeneity, presented and continue to present significant challenges for Greek society at large and State administration in particular. Societal reactions to these challenges but most importantly, State administration responses, provided the general framework within which the phenomenon of racist victimization emerged in Greece and will be addressed in this chapter.

At the societal level, prejudice, discrimination, xenophobia and racism as well as fear of 'immigrant criminality' emerged as dominant among the public attitudes towards immigrants (Zarafonitou, 2006: 268). At times, such attitudes resulted in instances of immigrant victimization from individuals and/or small communities.

At the State level, State administration unprepared to deal with the influx of immigrants in the country and bound by the broader European legal and policy framework of intolerance towards illegal immigration, at best, followed suit and reacted, rather than anticipated and planned for emerging social changes and problems. As a result, State administration's actions, occasionally intensified immigration problems and contributed to instances of direct or indirect victimization of immigrants and other groups (asylum seekers for example) attempting to gain entrance and establish residence in the country (Gropas and Triandafyllidou, 2005, Papatheodorou, 2005a).

Along the same lines, application of enacted anti-discrimination, anti-racism legislation is limited. Additionally, scarcity and restrictions of appropriate official data, comparability (and reliability) problems of data collected from NGOs and international bodies and organizations combined with State, Police and State and police officials' reluctance to acknowledge the existence of the problem (Antonopoulos, 2006, 2005) limit the extent of accounts provided and hide aspects of racist victimization in Greece.

As noted in the Introduction to this volume, there are a host of different interpretations and definitions of the term racist victimization. Given the socio-economic, political, and cultural implications of immigration for contemporary Greece, as well as the focus of this volume, I concentrate on minority *ethnic* groups as victims of racist victimization. Thus, in this chapter, accounts of racist victimization in Greece will be limited to victimization of immigrants (and asylum seekers). Furthermore, although victimization of immigrants from individuals and/or communities will be mentioned, emphasis will be placed upon structural aspects of racist victimization as these relate to the existing legal framework and the implementation of relevant policies and procedures (i.e. regularization programs and granting of asylum) and State attempts to control illegal immigration in their interplay with media accounts of the phenomenon of immigration and the purported criminality of immigrants. In other words, in this chapter, I look into the ways the legal framework, media accounts as well as State and police officials' actions and abuses have contributed to, or present the potential of racist victimization as it relates to migrants to Greece.

Historical Overview of Racial Victimization

Given that Greece, until very recently, was characterized by high levels of religious, ethnic and linguistic homogeneity, studies of discrimination and inequalities tended to employ primarily socio-economic, political and gender perspectives (Moschonas, 1993; 2005; Samatas, 2003; 2004; Papageorgiou, 1992; 2006; Petmezidou-Tsoulouvi, 1992). Since the mid 1990s however, related largely but not exclusively to the social phenomenon of immigration, the focus of discrimination and inequality discourses incorporated issues of social inclusion and exclusion, racism, xenophobia and victimization (Hatziprokopiou, 2003: 1039; Triandafyllidou and Veikou, 2002; Tsoukalas, 1995; Triandafyllidou, 2000).

Despite the existence of a number of social groups subject to exclusion and victimization such as the Roma[2] for example, the largest social group (heterogeneous as it is) specifically linked to discrimination and racial victimization are economic immigrants. Based on the pertinent discourse as well as the manifestations of the phenomenon, the relevant victimization, tends to be primarily ethnic rather than racial in origin (see for example Iosifides and King, 1998; Lazaridis, 1999; Lazaridis and Psimmenos, 2000). Thus, the content, meaning and implications of racial victimization in Greece relate primarily to rapidly changing patterns of the social phenomenon of immigration in the country.

Immigration Patterns

The international oil crisis of 1973, the restoration of Democracy in 1974 and the adoption of restrictive migration policies by the European countries led to a reduction of Greek outflow migration. Greece's entry into the European Community in 1981 and its new economic prospects, further contributed to the reversal of migration patterns (Jordan et al. 2003; Fakiolas and King, 1996). Thus, between 1974 and 1985 approximately half of the Greek *gastarbeiters*, members of the Greek Diaspora and political exiles who emigrated during the post-War period returned to the country (Labrianidis et al., 2004: 1188; Kasimis and Kassimi, 2004). Moreover, around the beginning of the 1980s a small number of immigrants from Poland as well as Asian and African countries, holding legal work permits, entered Greece

---

2 The term Roma refers to diverse, complex and multidimensional communities differing in language, dialect, history, culture, religion, social class, educational and occupational status who identify themselves as Roma, Gypsies, Travelers, Manouches, Sinti and comprise a population of approximately 8-10 million people concentrated but not restricted in Central and Eastern European countries. The adverse living conditions of such communities – some are nomadic by culture and some sedentary – are addressed by European Union and Council of Europe initiatives and action plans. For additional information see for example Liegeois, 1994; Fraser, 1992; Acton and Mundy, 1997; Guy, 2001; Liegeois and Gheorghe, 1995. Official accounts of the number of Roma living in Greece range between 120,000-150,000 and 250,000-300,000 people. An NGO account (MRG, 1997: 155) brings the number of Roma in Greece to 500,000 while *the Greek Helsinki Monitor* estimates the Romani population to be around 300,000-350,000 representing approximately 3 per cent of the total population (European Roma Rights Center-Greek Helsinki Monitor, 2003).

and started working in construction, agriculture and domestic service (Kasimis and Papadopoulos, 2005, Jordan et al., 2003). Still, the numbers of 'foreigners' in the country remained low. According to the 1991 Census there were a total of 167,000 'foreigners' residing in the country representing approximately 1.75 per cent of the total population.

However, the decisive factor in the transformation of many Southern European countries, Greece among them, from emigration to immigration countries was the collapse of Central and Eastern European regimes in 1989. Subsequently to their European Union integration and the resulting transformations in their economy – e.g., expansion of the economy's tertiary sector and related demands for flexible labor – many Southern European countries comprised: "a 'special case of European capitalism' characterized by late industrialization, large agricultural and tourism sectors, speculative urban development and an extensive family-based informal economy" (Kasimis and Papadopoulos, 2005: 100). Equivalently, in these countries it emerged as a 'Southern European model of migration' (King, 2000) characterized by broad 'illegality' caused by state policies or lack thereof, multiplicity and heterogeneity of migrant population, gender asymmetry as the majority of migrants are male, differentiation of geographical, cultural and social origin of migrants and coexistence of migration and high unemployment rates (Kasimis and Papadopoulos, 2005; Iosifides and King, 1996).

In Greece, in particular, the establishment of the 'Southern European model of migration' was facilitated by several factors. The country's geographic location as the eastern 'gate' of the European Union, its extended coastline, its large number of small and dispersed little islands (many uninhabited), its easily crossed continental borders and a notable lack of patrolling and guarding mechanisms, made Greece an easily accessible country of intermediate or final destination of immigrants. Furthermore, the country's economic development since the 1990s, its large size of informal, family-based economy and the seasonal nature of tourism, agriculture and construction increased demands for a flexible, low-cost, even exploitable labor force, outside the influence of labor union organizations and protective legislation (Kasimis and Papadopoulos, 2005; Kasimis and Kassimi, 2004; Lambrianidis et al., 2004: 1188; Gropas and Triandafyllidou, 2005). Thus, Greece became a preferred intermediate or final destination for large numbers of immigrants.

In terms of their ethnic composition, economic immigrants who came to Greece during the 1990s originated mainly from neighboring Balkan countries, Albania in particular, as well as Eastern European and former USSR countries such as Russia, Ukraine and Georgia. Smaller numbers of immigrants came from Middle Eastern, Asian and African countries. The vast majority of economic immigrants who came to Greece during the 1990s had entered the country illegally – frequently crossing the northern mountainous borders on foot – and lived and worked in clandestine positions. Such were the numbers and the frequency of immigrant arrivals in the country that it is not an exaggeration to argue that during the 1990s, illegal migration became a massive, at times uncontrollable phenomenon (Kasimis and Kassimi, 2004).

Emergence of Racism and Xenophobia

The sudden, dramatic and massive influx of immigrants in the early 1990s caught the country's administration by surprise. The lack of a legislative framework coupled with lack of strategic planning and management resulted in frequent instances of administrative and political confusion (Gropas and Triandafyllidou, 2005). At the same time, and similarly to the situation in neighboring countries (e.g., Italy) negative stereotyping of immigrants proliferated in the media (Mai, 2002; Mai and Schwandner-Sievers, 2003). Media reports about a purported 'wave of immigrant criminality' in particular, had a catalytic effect in generating a form of 'moral panic' and reified negative stereotypes of immigrants – mainly those coming from Albania – who constituted and continue to constitute the majority of the immigrant population in the country. Overall, the dominant media representation of immigrants was that of 'deviant,' 'criminal,' 'armed and dangerous,' and/or 'mafiosi' (Konstandinidou, 2000). Toward the end of the 1990s, thus, immigration equated criminality in media representations and such representations functioned as the sub terrain of certain initial instances of immigrant victimization that attracted public attention.

One such incident occurred in March 1998 in the area of Kastoria in Northern Greece. On 20 March 1998, a police officer was killed during an armed encounter with drug traffickers, perceived to be illegal immigrants. Subsequently, a public protest against the 'wave of immigrant criminality' was held in Kastoria while several instances of beatings of immigrants occurred in various parts of the country (*Ta Nea* 21 March 1998: N17; *Ta Nea*, 26 March 1998: N17). Responding to these events the Ministry of Public Order while noting the potential that such exaggerating reactions may foster and generate racism and xenophobia, declared its commitment to 'combat criminality' related to illegal immigration (*Ta Nea*, 24 March 1998: N15).

Around the same time, on 22 March 1998, the Community Council of a small village in Northern Greece addressing what they called a 'wave of burglaries committed by illegal immigrants,' issued a decree *'restricting the assembly and the movement of Albanian immigrants after sunset in order to control criminality'* and unanimously decided to form a *'voluntary secret police to protect the community on a 24-hour basis'* (*Ta Nea*, 26 March 1998: N16). The Courts nullified the Community Decree and brought penal charges against the Chair and members of the Community Council. Contemporaneously, although not significantly digressing from an overall concern with crime and criminality, certain newspaper articles, contended with the link between criminality and immigration and warned about the glaring potential of institutionalization of racism (*Eleftherotypia*, 24 March 1998).

Almost a year and a half later, on October 1999, a series of explicitly racially motivated crimes occurred in the city of Athens. A 25-year-old man, who, according to his testimony, 'hated colored people,' in a period of three days killed two, a Kurd and an Iranian, and severely injured four immigrants who came from Nigeria, Pakistan, Georgia and Egypt (*Ta Nea*, 23 October, 1999: N22).

The above-mentioned incidents point to examples of how the purported link between criminality and immigration contributed to instances of immigrant victimization perpetuated by individuals or local communities. On a broader level, immigrant victimization, or the potential thereof, was linked to various legal and administrative measures aiming at 'combating immigrant criminality.' These measures were precipitated by reports on organized crime and corruption of State and police officials as well as a number of high-profile crime-events involving immigrants.

Annual Reports on Organized Crime – initially published towards the end of the 1990s – pointed to the existence of various, restricted in number ethnic groups, which specialized in organized crime activities such as illicit drugs and guns' trade and trafficking of human beings. Included in these reports were accounts of ethnic Greeks' extended involvement and leadership of such groups. Furthermore, *Annual Reports on Organized Crime* documented police and other State officials' membership in organized criminal groups or active support of relevant activities (mainly prostitution 'rings,' falsification of official documents such as passports, visas, etc., and facilitation of illegal entry). From this perspective, *Annual Reports on Organized Crime* expanded the link between immigration and criminality to organized crime and State and police corruption. Conversely, these reports provided a different perspective to this link; that of immigrant victimization primarily through trafficking and prostitution 'rings.'

In addition to reports on organized crime, certain high-profile crime events involving immigrants had direct and indirect adverse impact upon immigrant victimization. Failed police operations in a hostage situation[3] on 23 September 1998 and a public bus high-jacking incident[4] on 28 May 1999 contested police and State ability to establish a sense of public security (*Ta Nea*, 1 June 1999: N01; N16).

---

3 During this so-called "Niovis fiasco" a Romanian man with a history of armed robbery convictions, a series of escapes and the abduction of a police officer, in his attempt to escape police apprehension, armed with grenades held a family hostage in their home for several hours. Police operations which were broadcasted live ended with the deadly injury of one of the hostages, the severe injury of the abductor who died few days later in his prison cell under dubious circumstances and the injury of 10 police officers; among them the Chief of Police and the Deputy Chief of Police. As a result, several high-ranking police officers including the Chief of Police were immediately dismissed while during annual evaluations in March 1999 almost the majority of high-commanding police officers were replaced. To counteract 'immigrant criminality' and enhance police efficiency, additional State funds were allocated to police and cost-guard police training and modernization of equipment (*Eleftherotypia*, 24 September 1998a; *Eleftherotypia*, 24 September 1998b; *Eleftherotypia*, 25 September 1998).

4 In this incident a 24 year-old Albanian immigrant – Flamur Pilsi – who lived and worked in a small village in Northern Greece, hi-jacked a public bus and armed with grenades and guns held a total of nine people hostage as a restitution to fabricated, as he claimed, gun ownership charges brought against him by the police. Police operations and negotiations were again broadcasted, ransom was paid and free passage to Albania was granted. After crossing the borders, Albanian police officers killed Pilsi and one of the passengers. This incident caused much tension between Albania and Greece, it was exploited politically in view of the then upcoming European Parliament elections in which the then governing party was defeated and initiated a large 'sweep operation' (*Ta Nea*, 1 June 1999: N01; N16; *Eleftherotypia*, 30 May 1999). (For a discussion of this incident and its impact upon the perceptions of 'Us' vs. the "Other' for both Albanian and Greek public opinion and the State see Papailias, 2003.)

The outcome of a third high-profile crime incident[5] – the high-jacking of another public bus – heralded by the media as a 'big success' (*Ta Nea*, 16 July, 1999: N01), 'a message to all those who think that with a grenade and a Kalashnikov they can snatch millions and the lives of people' (*Ta Nea*, 16 July 1999: N19) was largely seen as an indication that police and State administration were making inroads in fighting immigrant criminality and guaranteeing public safety (*Ta Nea*, 16 July 1999: N20). Based on State officials accounts however, not only did illegal immigration, immigrant criminality and public safety maintained focal interest in the public and State agenda but even more so, the link between immigration and criminality was strengthened and purportedly compelled to immediate action. In the words of then Prime Minister Kostas Simitis, criminality is connected "with the wave of economic immigrants, is a source of insecurity and is viewed by the citizens as a threat for Greek society" (*Eleftherotypia*, 17 July 1999).

To deal with the phenomenon of illegal immigration as well as address public concerns over crime and criminality, administration responses focused upon intensification of border controls and implementation of strict enforcement measures (Gropas and Triandafyllidou, 2005). To strengthen border controls, *Border Guards*, a special police body – in which ex-military Special Forces personnel are recruited – was established in 1998 and staffed in 1999 with approximately 1,500 people (Rigakos and Papanicolaou, 2003; Petoussi, 2005).

Enforcement measures, on the other hand, materialized in large-scale police operations, the so-called 'sweep operations.' Based on data from the Ministry of Public Order it is estimated that between 1988 and 1997, approximately 95,000 people were deported through regular deportation processes, while approximately 1,500,000 immigrants (primarily Albanians) were *re-forwarded*[6] to the Greek-Albanian borders. Expensive – their estimated cost amounts to 1,594,685,004 drachmas or 4,679,927 euros – and socially harmful as they resulted in frequent and repetitive human and civil rights violations, 'sweep operations' failed nonetheless to produce the anticipated results since the majority of expelled immigrants usually re-entered the country at a later time (Bossis, 1999: 250-251).

Despite the heightened attention given to the phenomenon, research on immigrant criminality in Greece has shown that the overall arrest rate of immigrants is lower than their respective rate in the population. A relatively small number of illegal immigrants and other non-Greeks are arrested for organized crime violations

---

5 In this incident a 28 year-old Albanian man, Alexis, who had lived and worked in Greece for 12 years claimed that few days before the hi-jacking, he was arrested, had his work permit tore up by a police officer and was beaten and abused before being deported. He demanded money in order to replace his bank savings which he could no longer withdraw since he was deprived of his identification papers and free entrance into Albania where he claimed he was going to release the nine hostages. Assisted by one of the hostages, a young man serving his military service at the time, the police were able to neutralize the hi-jacker's grenades and release the hostages while a police sniper shot and killed the hi-jacker (*Eleftherotypia*, 16 July 1999).

6 This word represents literal translation of the Greek neologism *epanaproothisi* used to describe the speedy process through which people in *sweep operations* were found, arrested, loaded in buses and driven (*re-forwarded*) to the Greek – Albanian borders.

(Lambropoulou, 2003) while 'foreigners' in general tend to be arrested for property crimes and forgery (Balwin-Edwards, 2001). Estimates based on official police data show that apart from the crimes of murder and robbery for which immigrant arrest rates exceeds the relevant population rate (Karydis, 1998; Zarafonitou and Mantoglou, 2000) for the most part immigrants are arrested for violations of immigration law, a possible artefact of state policies on immigration (Karydis, 1996, 1998).

Despite their relatively low rates of criminal involvement, research shows that illegal immigrants are considered responsible for actual or perceived rises in criminality (unemployment as well). A victimization study conducted in Athens, during 1998, found that 20-26 per cent of respondents (depending on area of residence) considered the presence of 'large numbers of foreigners' in their area of residence as one of the major (if not the dominant) factors that contributed to the fear of criminal victimization (Zarafonitou, 2002: 127).

Overall, it can be argued that in Greece, the emergence of racial victimization in the form of immigrant victimization and/or the potential thereof, was framed by: State and administration inability to address evolving challenges related to immigration, the media generated 'moral panic' over the purported 'wave of immigrant criminality' and related public reactions to the influx of immigrants in the country.

Discussion of Racism and Racist Crime within the Legal Context

Within the context of a rather homogeneous society, in terms of ethnic origin, language and religion, rare were the instances that the Greek State had to explicitly recognize minority groups. Such is the case with the Muslims of Thrace the only religious group accorded the status of religious minority since ratification of the Lausanne Treaty in 1923. In contrast, groups such as Jews, Catholics and Protestants although acknowledged as religious communities they are not accorded similar status.

In the same venue, the Roma (or *tsigani* or *athigani* as they tend to identify themselves in Greece) are implicitly acknowledged as a racial minority group since *The Greek Ombudsman* in its *Annual Reports* characterizes instances of Roma discrimination as racist discrimination. In contrast, Greek legislation equates Roma to traveling nomads (Ministerial Decree A5/696/25.4 of 1983 on "*Health Protections of traveling nomads*"). Provisioned restrictions and discerning enforcement of the above mentioned Ministerial Decree have contributed to Roma concentration in secluded and isolated settlements of sub-standard infrastructure and in numerous instances of discrimination and victimization such as evictions and forced relocation (*The Greek Ombudsman*, 2001). Greece has been urged to abolish this Decree since it is considered as contributing to 'institutionalized apartheid' against Roma (ODIHR, 2001).

Although reluctant to officially recognize ethnic and racial minorities, Greece, in addition to the constitutional provision for "respect and protection of all persons within Greek territory irrespective of ethnicity, race or other differences," has explicitly criminalized racism in Law 927 of 1979. According to this law, intentional instigation of acts and behaviors that "…can cause discrimination, hatred or violence against individuals or groups on account of their racial or ethnic origin" is penalized as a felony. Prohibited and criminalized in the same law are also the constitution and/or participation in groups which "...pursuit organized propaganda or any other type of activities tending at racist discrimination."

Moreover, Law 927/1979 reproaches "the expression of ideas insulting individuals or groups because of their racial or ethnic origin while sanctioned are those who, in the course of their usual occupation or profession, deny goods and services or condition the provision thereof upon a person's racial or ethnic origin." However, the anti-discrimination law of 1979 has largely remained 'in the books.'[7]

Issues of racism are explicitly addressed in additional legislation recently enacted in Greece. After considerable delay and following legal action taken by the European Commission against Greece, Law 3304 transposed two EC anti-discrimination directives (2000/43/EC and 2000/78/EC) which promote the principle of equality of treatment without discrimination of ethnic or racial origin. Provisioned in the EC Directives and established by Law 3304 are two separate bodies responsible on the one hand for promoting the antidiscrimination principle and on the other for establishing relevant complaint procedures. Thus, within the Greek legal context there are two paths of redress to racist treatment and victimization available to persons residing in the country.

Specifically, *The Greek Ombudsman* handles discrimination complaints involving various administration branches and other public legal persons. Discrimination complaints involving natural and private legal persons are handled by the newly established Committee of Equal Treatment, under the Minister of Justice.

Directly addressing issues of particular relevance to immigrant victimization, anti-trafficking legislation was enacted in Greece in 2002. Greece is included among the 'preferred' transit or final destination countries of trafficking for economic and sexual exploitation (HRW, 2001; Ministry of Public Order, 2006). Given the magnitude of the problem – unofficial estimates bring the number of women victims of trafficking and sexual exploitation in Greece between 1993 and 1999 to over 35,000 – and further the fact that the vast majority of trafficked people are immigrants (Emke-Poulopoulos, 2001; Lazos, 2002a; 2002b; Lazaridis, 2001), it follows that legislation on trafficking has important implications for immigrant victimization.

Relevant Greek legislation, Law 3064 of 2002 defines trafficking of humans for the purpose of economic and/or sexual exploitation as a felony and gives special attention to minors. Of relevant importance is the legally accorded assistance to victims of trafficking aiming "...at the protection of their life, bodily integrity and personal and sexual freedom...." Additionally, the law entitles victims of trafficking to provision of food, shelter, health-care, psychological and legal support. Such assistance is of paramount importance for the safety and security of trial witnesses, victims of organized criminal activities. For the duration of the trial and until a court decision is finalized, deportation procedures of victims who are illegally in the country are halted while arrangements are made for safe return to their country of origin.

---

7 As of December 2006 a relevant search in a widely used Greek litigation database, did not retrieve any court decision applying this law.

Although not directly addressing issues of racial victimization, immigration legislation and policies are of vital importance to issues of immigrant victimization because their specifics have the potential either to circumscribe and prevent or tolerate and beget immigrant victimization (International Monetary Fund, 1999; Collinson, 1993; Fakiolas, 2003). Given the focus of this chapter on issues of immigrant victimization related to administration and State actions and policies, addressing aspects of Greek immigration legislation and policy contributes to an overall understanding of the general framework of the phenomenon in the country.

The massive, often uncontrollable influx of illegal immigrants during the late 1980s and throughout the 1990s that abruptly transformed Greece from a sender to a recipient country, necessitated the dual task of simultaneously meeting the emerging socio-political challenges and drafting an immigration agenda and policy. Lacking a strategic plan pertaining to reception of immigrants – previous pertinent planning aimed mainly at facilitation of emigration (Papatheodorou, 2005a) and later on, return migration (Tzortzopoulou, 2002) – and pressured by European Union's bipolar attitude towards migration – the principle of fair treatment of documented and intolerance of undocumented immigrants – initial Greek immigration legislation adopted a rather preventing, defensive and repressive approach towards immigrants (Koukiadis, 2005; Papatheodorou, 2005a).

This approach towards immigration is exemplified in the two initial regularization programs implemented during 1998 and 2001. The first such approach was based on laws enacted in 1991 and amended in 1996 and 1997. Although in principle the first regularization program was aimed at documenting and legalizing 'irregular' immigrants it lacked specific objectives. Nevertheless, it attempted to deal with the relevant issues in a sporadic and rather bureaucratically complex and lengthy manner. It is characteristic that work permits accorded from this first regularization program were issued two years later while in the meantime applicants, for all intense and purposes remained or regressed in a state of illegality (Papantoniou-Fragoudi and Leventi, 2000).

Simultaneously, implementation of the first regularization program largely materialized into 'massive legality controls,' which for the most part were executed as 'sweep operations' resulting in massive deportation of undocumented immigrants or immigrants who failed to produce legal papers upon demand, the majority of which returned shortly after expulsion (Gropas and Triantafyllidou, 2005; Bossis, 1999). Thus, within the context of 'moral panic' generated by the purported link between illegal immigration and criminality, discussed in the previous section, initial immigration policies were largely confused with crime prevention policies and transformed into suppressing mechanisms of zero-tolerance attitudes towards immigration (Papatheodorou, 2005a; 2005b).

Legislation of the second regularization program was enacted in 2001 and underwent five consecutive amendments between 2002 and 2004. Bureaucratically complex, perplexing and reiterating the rather preferential treatment of immigrants considered to be of Greek ethnic origin, the second regularization program was costly and marginally effective (*The Greek Ombudsman*, 2001). Positive legal provisions such as family reunification notwithstanding, the 2001 regularization program continued to move along the lines of curbing and reducing immigration. To that effect, the principle that public legal entities should refrain from providing services to irregular immigrants was reaffirmed and extended to hospitals, clinics and other health care facilities with the exception of emergencies and medical care of children (Fakiolas, 2003; Scordas, 2002).[8]

Overall, it can be argued that despite the existence of anti-discrimination and anti-racism laws and constitutional closures, existing Greek legislation does not fully safeguard against potential abuses of power with respect to policy implementation and application. Exemplified in the case of immigration, relevant legislation and overall policy have initiated, maintained and tolerated socio-political and economic conditions which create unfair competition between legal and illegal immigrants, fosters employers' reliance on cheap, flexible and exploitable labor (International Monetary Fund, 1999; Collinson, 1993) and generates patterns of demand which stimulate further (legal and illegal) immigration (Fakiolas, 2003). More importantly however, inadequate administrative treatment of illegal immigration and a deficient system of social protection hinders or imposes undue burden in the process of social inclusion of immigrants. Simultaneously, it produces rights' uncertainty for immigrants and leaves this group vulnerable to potential victimization (Papatheodorou, 2005a; Karydis, 2005).

Extent and Nature of Racial Victimization in Greece

Despite the importance of recent immigration and the application of two regularization programs, the extent and the characteristics of the phenomenon are not well documented in Greece. Multiple data sources and related comparability and reliability problems impede comprehensive accounts of the number and the characteristics of immigrants in the country. Nevertheless, a formal structure exists which attempts to formally document the parameters of the social phenomenon of immigration.

Data on immigration are collected from various Ministries (i.e., Ministry of the Interior, Ministry of Labor, Ministry of Education, Ministry of Public Order and Ministry Foreign Affairs, as well as other state agencies such as the National Statistical Service of Greece, the IKA Foundation (the primary Social Security Agency in the country), and the Hellenic Migration Policy Institute. Collectively, however, these data sources are neither comparable nor always publicly available. As a result, the numbers and social characteristics of immigrants in Greece are based on 'best estimates' rather than accurate measures (MMO, 2004: 1-3).

According to the 2001 Census the total number of foreigners – including immigrants – residing in the country are approximately 800,000 and represent 7.3 per cent of the total population. Other estimates, however, bring the total number of non-Greek nationals residing in the country – economic immigrants in their majority – to approximately 1.15 million representing approximately 10.3 per cent of the total population (MMO, 2004: 5). Agreement however exists as to the nationality distribution of the foreign

---

8 A third regularization program is under way at the time this chapter is written. Although pertinent legislation appears to generate from a specific immigration strategy, contested is its efficacy towards social inclusion of immigrants (Papatheodorou, 2005a: 1191).

population in Greece. Thus, Albanians constitute some 56 per cent of all immigrants, followed by Bulgarians (5 per cent), Georgians (3 per cent), Romanians (3 per cent) while Americans, Cypriots, British and Germans account for approximately 2 per cent of the total foreign population (MMO, 2004: 5).

Data availability, validity and reliability problems, complicate accurate descriptions of the extent and nature of racist victimization in the country. Consequently, in Greece, similarly to Italy, Spain and Portugal official data on racist victimization are not available (EUMC, 2005a). To that extent, international bodies and organizations compiling comparative descriptions of racist victimization, largely depend upon media reports of such instances (EUMC, 2005b). Additional sources of information include unofficial data collected from various NGOs, as well as "…the Greek Office of the UNHCR [which] retains records of human rights violations concerning asylum seekers and refugees, including incidents of acts of racist violence committed by public agents/authorities" (EUMC, 2005b: 86).

Partial, albeit official data upon which inferences can be made as to the extent and nature of racist victimization in Greece, are collected by *The Greek Ombudsman* and the Ministry of Public Order.

The *Greek Ombudsman,* founded in October 1998 as a constitutionally sanctioned independent authority, "investigates individual administrative actions or omissions, or material actions taken by government departments or public services that infringe upon the personal rights or violate the legal interests of individuals or legal entities" (http://www.synigoros.gr/en_what_is.htm). Investigations are initiated by citizen-submitted complaints and conducted by the pertinent Department of the institution (e.g., Department of: Human Rights, Health and Social Welfare, Quality of Life, State-Citizens Relations and Children's Rights).

Thus, data collected by the Ombudsman refer to administration activities and are restricted to cases reported by the citizens. Constructive mediation towards restitution in cases of civic and human rights violations for example, has augmented the Ombudsman's positive reputation among the general public and among socially vulnerable groups. The steady increase in the number of complaints submitted to the Ombudsman from economic immigrants in particular (*The Greek Ombudsman*, 2005) on the one hand testifies to its acceptance as a source of mediation and on the other, enhances relevant data reliability.

According to the Greek Ombudsman's (2005) summary statistics report, between the years 1998 and 2004, approximately 4.6 per cent of all complaints received, were filed by non-Greek citizens (see Table 6.1). Notable should be that reports filed by third-country citizens (that is, non-Greek, non-EU member states citizens) are increasing in absolute numbers and proportionally to the overall number of reports filed by non-Greek citizens. For example, while in 1998 only two third-country citizens had filed a report to the Office of the Ombudsman, in 2004 the relevant number increased to 818 representing 7.7 per cent of all reports filed (see Table 6.1).

Table 6.1 Number of reports per year and nationality of reporting persons, 1998–2004

Year	Number of reports	Number of reporting foreign nationals	EU citizens -15	Third country citizens	% reporting foreigners/ number of reports	% third country nationals/ number of reporting foreigners
1998	1,430	2	0	2	0.1	100
1999	7,284	79	10	69	1.1	87.3
2000	10,107	390	37	353	3.9	90.5
2001	11,282	499	29	470	4.4	94.2
2002	11,762	558	30	528	4.7	94.6
2003	10,850	552	28	524	5.1	94.9
2004	10,571	818	36	782	7.7	95.6
Total	63,286	2,898	170	2,728	5	94

Source: *The Greek Ombudsman* (2005)

Among the non-Greek citizens who submit complaints to the Ombudsman, approximately 29 per cent are Albanians, 6.5 per cent Bulgarians, 5 per cent Ukrainians, 4.2 per cent Romanians and 3.9 per cent Russians (see Table 6.2). According to the Ombudsman, complaints submitted by non-EU citizens such as Egyptians, Nigerians and Philippinos are increasing in numbers. Conversely, complaints submitted to the Ombudsman from citizens of countries that recently joined the EU (for example Poland and Cyprus) exhibit a sharp decrease.

As to the subject matter of complaints filed to the Ombudsman, they are distributed in the various thematic Divisions as follows: 4.3 per cent of reports relate to Social Security issues, 2.6 per cent concern citizen-State relations 0.8 per cent Children's Rights and 0.5 per cent Quality of Life matters. The Division of Human Rights receives the majority of reports filed by foreigners. For the years 1998 to 2004 the overall rate of such reports was 91.9 per cent while in year 2004 the proportion of reports relating to matters of human rights violations was 94.1 per cent. Furthermore, non-Greek nationals' reports over human rights violations, exhibit an increasing trend. In 2004 in particular, foreigners filed almost half of the complaints submitted to the Division of Human Rights.

Reports related to *entry and residence of third-country citizens* constitute approximately 3.87 per cent of all complaints submitted to the Ombudsman for the years 1998-2004 and 7.6 per cent of all reports for the year 2004. The same type of reports constitutes 23.7 per cent of all reports submitted to the Division of Human Rights (DHR) for the years 1998-2004. For the year 2004 reports on *entry and residence of third-country citizens* constituted 39.2 per cent of all reports to the Division of Human Rights. Other thematic categories within the Division of Human Rights which are of particular importance for foreign citizens and immigrants relate

Table 6.2 Distribution of reporting foreigners per citizenship 1998–2004

	Number of reporting foreigners		Distribution of citizenship	
Citizenship	1998-2004	2004	1998-2004	2004
Albanian	835	239	28.8	29.2
Bulgarian	187	81	6.5	9.9
Ukrainian	144	49	5	6
Romanian	123	31	4.2	3.8
Russian	113	38	3.9	4.6
Egyptian	94	51	3.2	6.2
Turkish	79	15	2.7	1.8
Polish	75	4	2.6	0.5
Pakistani	65	16	2.2	2
Georgian	56	12	1.9	1.5
USA	54	8	1.9	1
British	51	7	1.8	0.9
Syrian	49	12	1.7	1.5
Nigerian	49	19	1.7	2.3
Moldavian	49	22	1.7	2.7
Iraqi	48	10	1.7	1.2
Armenian	45	8	1.6	1
German	44	10	1.5	1.2
Cypriot	41	6	1.4	0.7
Philippino	33	14	1.1	1.7
Other	664	166	22.9	20.3
Total	2,898	818	100	100

Source: *The Greek Ombudsman* (2005)

to the *acquisition of Greek nationality,* various *administration measures against foreigners* such as deportation and *matters of asylum seekers and refugees* (see Table 6.3).

The 2005 *Annual Report of the Greek Ombudsman*, suggests that the majority (47.3 per cent) of cases handled by the Division of Human Rights, related to *entry and residence in the country*. The same report notes significant levels of state inefficiency in the implementation of 'normalization' procedures. According to the *Annual Report*, such procedures impose undue economic burdens upon economic immigrants while work and residence permits are short-term. Moreover, the Ombudsman's report tackles issues pertaining to adverse conditions of imprisonment – overcrowding for example – as these relate to violations of prisoner's rights. Conditions of imprisonment are particularly relevant to economic and illegal immigrants since they constitute the majority of prison population (*The Greek Ombudsman*, 2005).

Table 6.3 Thematic categories related to matters of foreign citizens, 1998–2004

Thematic Categories	% of reports to Omb.		% of reports to DHR	
	1998-2004	2004	1998-2004	2004
Reports to the Office of the Ombudsman	100	100		
Reports to Division of Human Rights (DHR)	16.29	19.41	100	100
Acquisition of Greek nationality	1.44	1.04	8.83	5.34
Issues of civil status of foreigners	0.09	0.08	0.52	0.42
Entry and stay of third country nationals	3.87	7.61	23.73	39.19
entry and stay of omogeneis foreigners	0.32	0.35	1.94	1.83
Issues of asylum seekers and refugees	0.33	0.41	2	2.11
Administrative measures against foreigners	0.74	0.49	4.55	2.53
Discrimination against foreigners	0.14	0.12	0.85	0.63
matters of stay and special rights of EU citizens	0.14	0.20	0.85	1.05
Total matters of foreigners of Human Rights Division	7.05	10.31	43.27	63.08
Children's rights	0.68	2.58	100	100.00
Receipt of undcragc foreigners and refugees	0.06	0.27	8.89	10.58

Source: The Greek Ombudsman (2005)

Another source of information related to instances of racist violence in Greece are data collected from the Ministry of Public Order's *Directorate of Internal Affairs* which was established in 1999 with the authority to investigate instances of corruption among the police. Since 2003, corruption by State employees came under the Directorate's authority as well. Corruption represents a significant social problem in Greece. It affects all levels of state administration, particularly the local level, while it borders 'normalized,' socially accepted behavior for at least some proportion of the population (see *The Greek Ombudsman*, 2005; Directorate of Internal Affairs, 2005).

However, corruption among the police, which differs from corruption among State employees, is of particular interest to the subject matter of this chapter since it exhibits increased potential for vulnerable social groups' victimization; illegal immigrants being one such group. Research has shown that police is considered as adopting differential behavior towards various social groups depending on the group's social status. Specifically, police behavior towards economic and illegal immigrants (particularly Albanians) as well as Roma is perceived as negative, discriminatory and potentially abusive (Petoussi, 2006: 624-625).

Based on available data, Internal Affairs (*The Incorruptibles* as the media and the public frequently refer to them) between 15 October 1999 and 31 December 2004, handled 2,922 cases, the majority of which (n=2,819) related to police matters.

Penal charges were filed in 962 of these cases, the majority (n=907) of which were brought against police officers and police civil personnel. Of these 962 cases, 773 were brought to court; 730 of the cases brought to court concerned police matters. Additionally, 309 arrests were made through *first instance process* (Directorate of Internal Affairs, 2005: 27).

Of particular relevance to the focus of this chapter is the distribution of the subject matter of reports to the Division of Internal Affairs. Thus, 7.24 per cent of cases investigated in 2003 and 9.6 per cent of cases investigated in 2004 pertained to police misconduct against immigrants (and foreigners in general), while, 3.6 per cent and 2.2 per cent of cases investigated during the respective years, involved exploitation of women (most likely immigrant women and victims of trafficking). Moreover, offenses such as forgery and subtraction of official documents, extortion, abuse of power, bridge of duty as well as a proportion of narcotics violations, which led to arrests of police officers and civic police personnel, for the most part, related to aspects of the phenomenon of illegal immigration (Directorate of Internal Affairs, 2005).

One of the issues related to the extent and nature of immigrant victimization in the country pertains to the treatment of asylum seekers and refugees. This issue has placed Greece under observation from various NGOs and international organizations. Based on data provided by the Ministry of Public Order and reported by the UNHCR, Amnesty International notes:

> ... documented [is] a sharp decrease in the rate of recognition of refugees in the last two years. According to the UNHCR, by the end of 2004, 5,328 asylum applications were pending at first instance and around 2.500 at the review stage, while another 100 applications were pending before the Council of State for administrative review. Of those applications, 4,469 had been lodged during 2004. Another 50,000 people had expressed their wish to file an application but had not been able to lodge their applications yet. During that year, 11 people were recognized as refugees under the Refugee Convention and 22 were granted protection under humanitarian status, while two were naturalized. Another 3,731 applications were rejected and in 623 cases the examination was stopped before a decision was reached ... (Amnesty International, 2005: 2).

Furthermore, in comparison to other European countries, relatively few claimants are granted asylum in Greece. For example, in 2004, the average recognition rate (including humanitarian status) for all 25 EU member States was 26.4 per cent (UNHCR, 2005: 4) while in Greece the equivalent rate was 0.88 per cent (see Table 6.2). Furthermore, in 2005 the average recognition rate was 1.9 per cent and until June of 2006, it was 1.5 per cent. Additionally, as reported by Amnesty International (2005: 2) Greece's recognition rate in 2004 is among the lowest of 148 countries reviewed by UNHCR.

Explanations for this comparatively low recognition rate can be found in the relevant legal provisions and the application thereof. In relation to legal provisions, Greece, overall, follows international legal standards. However:

> ...a weak point of Greek asylum legislation is that the Ministry of Public Order decides both at first and second instance on asylum applications [while] there is no independent

appeals body, as is best practice in other EU countries.... Currently, the composition of the Greek Appeals Board comprises two officials who are closely associated with the Ministry of Public Order, two officials from the Ministry of Foreign Affairs and two non-government members, representing UNHCR and the Athens Bar Association (UNHCR, 2005: 4).

An additional legislative problem is related to the 'interruption' of asylum claims. Again, the United Nations notes:

> as of early 2004 persons returned to Greece under the "Dublin II" Regulation are usually informed upon arrival at the airport that their asylum procedure has been 'interrupted' because they left their declared residence address without informing the police. Consequently, they are detained and frequently deported, without having their asylum application examined in substance either by Greece or by they sending country. This often amounts to a breach of the 1951 Refugee Convention (UNHCR, 2005: 5).

Concerns have been raised over the extent to which legally provisioned procedures are indeed followed in each and every case of asylum seekers. As Amnesty International reports, frequently, legal procedures in Greece are not clearly explained to asylum seekers. Interpreters are rarely present during the required interview while lawyers are also infrequently present for consultation. Although definite numbers are not provided, Amnesty International notes that at times, people wanting to file asylum applications are discouraged or even misguided as to what is required and/or how to proceed (Amnesty International, 2005).

Finally, related to the extent and nature of racist victimization in the country, are the conditions of detention for people who enter and/or remain illegally in Greece. Persons who enter or remain illegally in Greece after their arrest are held in detention centers usually under substandard conditions. Overcrowding, insufficient medical treatment and lack of facilities which would allow the separation of men, women and unaccompanied minors are few of the commonly identifiable problems. At the other end of the continuum however, it should be noted that, in view of State structural support it is not uncommon for local communities (which often are small, rural, isolated island communities with limited resources) and detaining police officers alike to provide food, shelter and clothing to refugees, asylum seekers and trafficked persons illegally entering the country (UNHCR, 2005; Amnesty International, 2005).

Social, Cultural, and Political Reaction to Racially Motivated Victimization

As mentioned earlier in this chapter, the sudden influx of immigrants that occurred in Greece during the 1990s was met with overtly negative media coverage and ambivalent State responses. Despite the continuing administrative vacillation towards asylum seekers and refugees, compounded with lack of official data and limited focused research, civil society, media and the political class have started to openly react against racism, xenophobia and incidents of racist and immigrant victimization. One such example can be found in the reactions following an incident that occurred in September 2004.

On 5 September 2004, a football match between the national teams of Albania and Greece took place in Tirana, Albania. During the match's opening ceremony the Albanian fans disrupted the playing of Greece's national anthem generating thus, much tension between Greek and Albanian spectators. The Albanian national team won the game and Albanians living in Greece celebrated their team's victory in large open-street gatherings. Mutual provocations between groups of Albanians and Greeks and extremist right-wing Greek groups' aggravation instigated multiple violent incidents in various parts of the country (*Eleftherotypia*, 6 September 2004). Largely tolerated by the police, these incidents resulted in the death of one Albanian man, the hospitalization of 70 people and the arrest of 8 immigrants (RAXEN, 2005: 40).

The government and the country's political parties immediately, openly and explicitly condemned the eruption of racist violence and the related supportive ideology and practices – police tolerance of September 2004 violent clashes, in particular. To this approach, only few isolated exceptions were found in the positions of G. Karatzaferis, leader of the political party LAOS. (People's Orthodox Alarm)[9] and N. Psomiadis, the Prefect of Thessaloniki, who equated immigrants in the country to 'an open wound' (RAXEN, 2005). Citizens of Thessaloniki in Northern Greece contested Psomiadis' anti-immigrant, racist remarks and disrupted a Prefectural Council meeting in protest. Few days later, some 3,000 people in Athens, marched to protest against racist violence and discrimination. Simultaneously, the *Albanian Migrants Forum*, a NGO in Greece, issued a press release opposing fanaticism and nationalism expressed from both sides in the aftermath of the September 2004 incidents (RAXEN, 2005). Concurrently, in public debates and media accounts that followed the soccer-game related violent incidents, concerns were raised over what appeared to be a tendency towards 'mainstreaming' of racism and xenophobia (RAXEN, 2005).

In spite of the isolated incidents of racist violence and generally noted administration inefficiencies of the Greek State to comprehensively deal with immigration and immigrant victimization, there have been a number of positive developments addressing racial discrimination (EUMC, 2005a). For example, the *Action Plan for the Social Integration of Immigrants*, which was adopted in 2002 although not fully implemented, provides for measures to facilitate and safeguard documented immigrants' inclusion to labor market, access to health and social services, promotion of social dialogue and combating of racism and xenophobia (Gropas and Triandafyllidou, 2005). The third legalization program which is currently under way, although not without problems, appears to have the potential to instate a national immigration strategy which at a minimum will set specific standards and procedures for acquisition of work and resident permits reducing thus, the potential of exploitation and discrimination (Gropas and Triandafyllidou, 2005; Papatheodorou, 2005a).

---

9   LAOS (the party's acronym, is pronounced the same as the greek word *laos* meaning people) is a right-wing, extremist political party which during the Greek national elections in 2004 received 2.2 per cent of the popular vote – although not enough to gain a seat in the National Parliament. However, in the European Parliament elections, achieved 4.15 per cent of the electorate vote, enough to gain one seat in the European Parliament

Furthermore, Law 3304 of 2005, which ratified EC anti-discrimination directives, (2000/43/EC and 2000/78/EC), promotes the principle of equal treatment irrespectively of racial or ethic origin, religious or other beliefs, disability, age and sexual orientation. In the same law, special attention is given to protection against racism and discrimination in the fields of employment, social insurance, professional training, education, health and access to good and services (ENAR, 2005).

Given that a number of incidents of racist victimization are associated with police attitudes and behavior, special attention has been paid to legislation concerning use and discharge of firearms by the police as well as efforts to enhance police training and professionalism. Towards this end, the Chief of Police issued an official dictum on the treatment and respect of immigrants and other foreigners. Moreover, the Ministry of Public Order in cooperation with various NGOs, has organized training sessions on matters of human and civil rights as well as treatment of immigrants and foreigners in general (EUMC, 2005b).

Many of these efforts were initiated in response to international sanctions and criticism against police practices in Greece and several are funded through various EU funding programs. Furthermore, legislation and training on issues of human trafficking has been of primary importance and significance to the State, the police, political parties and civil society as well (EUMC, 2005b).

EU funding and cooperation between NGOs, public bodies and private organizations has had a significant impact in including matters of racism, xenophobia, discrimination, human and civil rights into the public agenda. Several such opportunities were presented in 2004 since upon completion of various EU funded projects, numerous conferences were organized, press releases were issued and best practice guides related to immigration and victimization were published. More importantly, the above-mentioned cooperation resulted in the establishment of structures and/or services providing specialized assistance to victims of trafficking, racial violence and discrimination (RAXEN, 2005).

Attempts are also being made by the various political parties for increased participation of foreigners residing in the country to actively engage in party[10] and government representation while a significant number of social, cultural and political groups of immigrants and foreigners formed various associations in the country. For example, there is a number of associations of Albanian, Russian, Georgian, Pakistani and other immigrants. There is at least one Albanian daily newspaper and two Russian weekly newspapers published in their respective language while at least one publisher (www.picturebooks.gr) has issued a series of bilingual childrens' books featuring Aesop's myths in Greek and Albanian. Further, through cultural, social and political events, festivals, and other initiatives (for example the Anti-Racist Festival held in Rethymno, Crete yearly) various ethnic or other groups are now engaging in dialogue with one another and with the Greek community at large while at the same

---

10 Within the same context, the Roma of Greece, on 15 January 2006 founded a political party with the intend to participate in the next national elections and hopes to gain a parliamentary seat "... since by shear numbers [they] can collect the necessary votes" (*Ta Nea*, 16 January 2006: N16).

time increase their potential for social activism and social integration (RAXEN, 2005).

Towards the goal of elimination of discrimination, prejudices and fear of the 'other' all these constitute positive steps with the potential to affect broader social and political attitudes towards ethnic minorities in Greece.

Conclusion

Greece's abrupt transformation from a sender to a recipient country of migration marked the decade of the 1990s and posed significant challenges for State administration and society at large. An essentially homogeneous society, within a period of 5 to 10 years, Greece rapidly increased in diversity and heterogeneity as the proportion of foreign population in the country augmented to almost 10 per cent of the total population. Fleeing oppressing regimes and/or adverse economic conditions in pursuit of a better life, the vast majority of 'aliens,' facilitated by the country's location and geographical characteristics – easily crossed mountainous borders and numerous islands many of which are uninhabited – entered and remained in the country illegally. Structured and organized around safeguarding political regimes against 'internal political enemies' (see, for example, Samatas, 2004) and preventing and controlling small scale conventional crime such as street crime, property crime, smuggling of goods, etc. Greek policing bodies – the police and coast guard police in particular – lacked necessary resources and experience in dealing with illegal entries of large numbers of people and even more so with related forms of organized criminal activities such as trafficking.

More importantly the existing legal, administration and policy framework on migration although aptly facilitated emigration, it was inadequate to regulate immigration. Additionally, State and administrative attempts to generate the appropriate legal framework and devise a competent migration strategy were required to comply with EU mandates for 'zero-tolerance' of illegal immigration (Papatheodorou, 2005a). To that extent, attempted legalization programs did not produce the expected results while on the other hand, administration attempts to control and regulate illegal immigration materialized into rather suppressive measures of large-scale deportation operations.

In analogy to neighboring countries with comparable models of immigration, negative stereotyping of immigrants emerged within Greek society. Amplified by media accounts of a purported – rather imaginary – 'wave of immigrant criminality' and reproduced in public discourse, the negative stereotyping of immigrants appeared to be gaining an obstructive momentum towards a reproached 'mainstreaming' of immigrant discrimination tolerance.

Within this context, Greece, not unlike other countries exhibiting similar patterns of immigration, experienced instances of racial victimization primarily in the form of immigrant victimization. The emergence of racial and immigrant victimization however, did not remain without resistance and opposition. Civil society, researchers, political parties and immigrant associations in synergy with local communities and policy makers, openly and explicitly discuss issues of immigration and racial victimization and undertake actions against social exclusion and discrimination, towards social inclusion and integration.

To that extent, it can be argued that Greek society holds an ambivalent, albeit dynamic, position towards the 'others.' For example, various opinion polls and studies find that negative stereotypes against immigrants persist among the general population (RAXEN, 2005) and research shows that one's fear of victimization relates to the presence of immigrants in his or her area of residence (Zarafonitou, 2002). On the other hand, based on opinion polls, the majority of Greeks, tend to view the social integration of immigrants positively while a significant proportion of the population would welcome the election of immigrants in local government bodies as well as the National Parliament (RAXEN, 2005). This ambivalent attitude towards immigrants is further reflected in research which shows that although a proportion of people who employ immigrants hold negative attitudes towards them, in their majority, employers of immigrants tend to perceive immigrants' contribution in a rather positive manner (Kasimis and Papadopoulos, 2005: 120).

Despite the noted ambivalence and even prejudice and discrimination towards immigrants, clear signs of successful integration of immigrants into Greek society are not lacking. For example, research on social integration of Albanian immigrants in Thessaloniki, Greece shows that they gradually become accustomed to the host country's culture and way of living. However, what appears to be of particular significance for the successful integration of Albanian immigrants (and immigrants of other ethnic origins as well) is the securing of legitimate employment and residence and proper education for their children (Hatziprokopiou, 2004; Labrianidis and Lyberaki, 2001).

The importance of legitimacy of residence and employment is further verified from research on legal immigrants' sense of security and conversely, fear and experience of victimization. The sample included in this study – immigrants holding legal work and residence permits – tended to exhibit patterns of sense of security and insecurity, similar to respective patterns of samples of national Greeks. However, this research shows that the single most important factor related to immigrant's sense of security relates to their legal status pertaining to residence and employment (Zarafonitou, 2006: 284).

The findings of these studies point to a central characteristic of racial/immigrant victimization in Greece. That is, although instances of racial/immigrant victimization perpetrated by individuals or small groups and local communities have been documented, arguably, the primary source or potential of immigrant victimization relates to State administration and State officials' implementation of relevant policies and procedures exemplified in the ineffectiveness of the two regularization programs, the punitive approach to controlling immigration, the lack of official documentation of racial victimization, instances of police and state officials' corruption and the inadequate procedures of granting asylum and refugee status as described in previous sections of this chapter.

As noted previously in this chapter, however, even though there is much room in Greece for improving the legal framework pertaining to entry, stay, legalization and social integration of immigrants and other foreigners in the country, legal safeguards against institutionalization of racism and discrimination have been implemented at the level of constitutional, civil and penal law. Although not sufficient to safeguard against racism and discrimination, Greece's legal provisions nonetheless, may, at a minimum, impart the message of intolerance to discrimination and prejudice, grant victims avenues of restitution and largely delineate policy making and implementation.

Recently undertaken efforts aiming at the establishment of a strategic plan towards immigration, and civic society's active engagement towards social integration of foreigners, have placed issues of prejudice, discrimination, xenophobia and racial victimization on the public agenda. Greek State and society, although still perplexed in the face of increasing diversity, appears to be engaging in dialogue with the 'others.' Hopefully, the outcome of this dialogue will result in successful social integration of the 'others' and minimization if not elimination of racial victimization.

References

Acton, T. and Mundy, G. (eds) (1997) *Romani Culture and Gypsy Identity*. Hatfield: University of Hartfordshire Press.

Amnesty International. (2005) *Greece: Out of the Spotlight: The Rights of Foreigners and Minorities are Still a Grey Area*. Available on the internet at: http://web.amnesty.org/library/index/engeur250162005. Retrieved on 12 July 2006.

Antonopoulos, G.A. (2005) "The Limitations of Official Statistics in Relation to the Criminality of Migrants in Greece." *Police Practice and Research* 6(3): 251-260.

Antonopoulos, G.A. (2006) "Greece: Policing Racist Violence in the 'Fenceless Vineyard'", *Race & Class,* 48(2), 92-100.

Baldwin-Edwards, M. (2001) "Crime and Migrants: Some myths and realities" Presentation to the International Police Association, 17th Greek Section Conference, Samos, Greece, 4 May.

Bossis, M. (1999) *Security Issues in the New World Order.* Athens: Ekdoseis Papazisi [in Greek].

Collinson, S. (1993) *Europe and International Migration*. London and New York: Pinter.

Daniil, G. (1991) "The Greek Poets of Canada (selection)." In Fossey J. M.(ed.) and Morin, J. (ass. ed) *Proceeding of the First International Congress on The Hellenic Diaspora: From Antiquity to Modern Times* Montreal, 17-22.iv.1988; Athens 26-30.iv.1988. Volume II: *From 1453 to Modern Times*. 445-482. Amsterdam: J.C.Gieben [in Greek].

Directorate of Internal Affairs (2005) *Annual Report 2004*. Available on the internet at: http://www.ydt.gr/main/Attachments/Attachment12367_ekthesi2004.pdf. Retrieved on 11 July 2006

Eideneier, N. (1991) "The Poetic Language of Immigration – Greek Literature on the Subject of *Gastarbeiters* in Germany and Greece." In Fossey J. M. (ed) and Morin, J. (ass. ed) *Proceeding of the First International Congress on The Hellenic Diaspora: From Antiquity to Modern Times* Montreal, 17-22.iv.1988; Athens

26-30.iv.1988. Volume II: *From 1453 to Modern Times*. 483-492. Amsterdam: J.C.Gieben [in Greek].

Eleftherotypia 25 September 1998. Marnellos, G. "Only the leadership of ELAS paid for the fiasco"; Roubanis, Gr. "Tough critique from the opposition parties" http://archive.enet.gr/1998/09/25/on-line/keimena/fpage/fpage.htm Retrieved on 19 December 2006.

Eleftherotypia 24 September 1998a. Kyriakopoulos, K., Morou, A, Marnellos, G, Tsatsis, Th., Vagena, D, Zarakovitou, A "The Deadly Fiasco" http://archive.enet.gr/1998/09/24/0n-line/keimena/fpage/fpage/htm. Retrieved on 19 December 2006.

Eleftherotypia 24 September 1998b. Roubanis, Gr. "On national network" http://archive.enet.gr/1998/09/24/on-line/stiles/sfigmos.htm. Retrieved on 19 December 2006.

Eleftherotypia 16 July 1999. Kyriakopoulos, K. "Operation lightning in 60 seconds" http://archive.enet.gr/1999/07/16/on-line/keimena/greece/greece1.htm. Retrieved on 19 December 2006.

Eleftherotypia 30 May 1999: front page. Marnelos, G., Kyriakopoulos, K. "Sweep operation after the blood" Kasdaglis, Chr. "Albanian front" http://archive.enet.gr/1999/05/30/on-line/keimena/fpage/fpage.htm Retrieved on 19 December 2006.

Eleftherotypia 17 July 1999. Sokos, P. "Speeds up tougher" http://archive.enet.gr/1999/07/17/on-linc/kcimcna/fpage/fpage.htm. Retrieved on 19 December 2006.

Eleftherotypia 6 September 2004. "National Doping." Available at the internet http://www.enet.gr/online/online-print?id=25595660 Retrieved on 23 December 2006.

Eleftherotypia 23 March 2006. Polymilis S. "Crime and Punshment" http://archive.enet.gr/1998/03/24/on-line/stiles/kafenio.htm Retrieved on 21 June 2006.

Emke-Poulopoulos, I. (2001) *Trafficking in Women and Children: Greece a Country of Destination and Transit.* Athens: Institute for the Study of the Greek Economy (IMEO)-Greek Society of Demographic Studies.

ENAR. (2006) *Responding to Racism in Greece.* Athens: European Network Against Racism. Available on the internet at: http://www.enar-eu.org/en/publication/national_leaflets. Retrieved on 29 June 2006.

EUMC. (2005a). *Racism and Xenophobia in the EU Member States: Trends, Developments and Good Practice. Annual Report 2005-Part 2.* European Monitoring Centre on Racism and Xenophobia. Available on the internet at: http://eumc.eu.int. Retrieved on: 6 December 2006.

EUMC. (2005b). *Racist violence in 15 EU Member States: A Comparative Overview of Findings from the RAXEN National Focal Points Reports 2001-2004.* European Monitoring Centre on Racism and Xenophobia. Available on the internet at: http://eumc.eu.int. Retrieved on: 6 December 2006.

European Commission (2004) *The Situation of Roma in an Enlarged European Union.* Luxembourg: Office for Official Publications of the European Communities. Available on the internet at http://www.errc.org/cikk.php?cikk=2119 Retrieved on 20 December 2006.

European Roma Rights Center-Greek Helsinki Monitor (2003) *Cleaning Operations: Excluding Roma in Greece*. Country Reports Series No 12. Budapest: ERRC. Available on the internet at: http://www.errc.org/cikk.php?cikk=115. Retrieved on 20 December 2006.

Fakiolas, R. and King, R. (1996) "Emigration, Return, Immigration: A Review and Evaluation of Greece's Postwar Experience on International Migration." *International Journal of Population Geography* 2(2): 171-190.

Fakiolas, R. (2003). "Regularising Undocumented Immigrants in Greece: Procedures and Effects." *Journal of Ethnic and Migration Studies* 29(3): 535-561.

Filias, V. (1967) "Emigration – Its Causes and Effects." *Essays on Greek Migration Series No1* pp.11-38. Athens: Social Sciences Centre.

Fraser, S.A. (1992) *The Gypsies*. Oxford, UK: Blackwell Publishing.

Gizelis. G. (1994) "Changes in Greek Cultural Identity and their Consequences upon Return Migrants." *The Greek Review of Social Research* 84-85: 34-42 [in Greek].

Glytsos, N.P. (1994) "Income and Remittances of Greek Immigrants of Australia and their Impact on Greece's Paying Balance." *The Greek Review of Social Research* 84-85, 106-131 [in Greek].

Gropas, R. and Triandafyllidou, A. (2005) "Migration in Greece at a Glance." *ELIAMEP Hellenic Foundation for European & Foreign Policy*. Available on the internet at: http://www.eliamep.gr/eliamep/files/Migration%20in%20Greece_Oct%202005%20(2).pdf. Retrieved on 22 March 2006.

Guy, W. (ed) (2001) *Between Past and Future: The Roma of Central and Eastern Europe*. Hatfield: University of Hartfordshire Press.

Hatziprokopiou, P. (2004) "Albanian Immigrants in Thessaloniki Greece: Processes of Economic and Social Incorporation." *Journal of Ethnic and Migration Studies* 29(6): 1033-1057.

HRW (2001) "Memorandum of Concern: Trafficking of Migrant Women for Forced Prostitution in Greece." Human Rights Watch. Available on the internet at: http://hrw.org/backgrounder/eca/greece/greece_memo_all.pdf. Retrieved on 11 January 2007.

International Monetary Fund (1999) *Shadow Economies around the World*. Washington DC: IMF.

Iosifides, T. and King, R. (1996) "Recent Immigration to Southern Europe: The Socio-economic and Labour Market Contexts." *Journal of Area Studies Southern Europe in Transition* 9: 70-94.

Iosifides, T. and King, R. (1998) "Socio-spatial Dynamics and Exclusion of three Immigrant Groups in the Athens Conurbation." *South European Society and Politics* 3(3): 205-29.

Jordan, B., Stra°th, B and Triandafyllidou, A. (2003) "Contextualising Immigration Policy Implementation in Europe." *Journal of Ethnic and Migration Studies* 29(2): 195-224.

Kamboureli, S. (1991) "A Palindromic Journey: Eyeing the Greek Immigrant Writer." In Fossey J. M. (ed) and Morin, J. (ass. ed) *Proceeding of the First International Congress on The Hellenic Diaspora: From Antiquity to Modern Times* Montreal,

17-22.iv.1988; Athens 26-30.iv.1988. Volume II: *From 1453 to Modern Times*. 433-444. Amsterdam: J.C.Gieben.

Karydis, V. (1996) *The Criminality of Immigrants in Greece: Problems of Theory and Anti-crime Policy.* Athens: Papazisi [in Greek].

Karydis, V. (1998) "Criminality or Criminalization of Migrants in Greece?" In Ruggiero, V. and South, N. (eds) *The New European Criminology* London and New York: Routledge.

Karydis, V. (2005) "The Issue of Second Generation: Crime and Immigration." In Pavlou, M. and Christopoulos, D. (eds) *Greece of Immigration.* Athens: Kritiki-KEMO [in Greek].

Kasimis, Ch. and Kassimi, Ch. (2004) "Greece: A History of Migration." *Migration Information Source* Washington, D.C.: Migration Policy Institute. Available on the internet at: http://www.migrationinformation.org/feature/print.chm?ID=228. Retrieved on 10 April 2006.

Kasimis, Ch. and Papadopoulos, A.G. (2005) "The Multifunctional Role of Migrants in the Greek Countryside: Implications for the Rural Economy and Society." *Journal of Ethnic and Migration Studies* 31(1): 99-127.

Kathimerini 3 January 2006 Souliotis, G. "Fear of Vendeta between Greeks and Albanians in Rethymno." http://www.kathimerini.gr/4dgi/_w_articles_ell_1_ 03/01/2006_168744. Retrieved on 19 December 2006.

King, R. (2000) "Southern Europe in the Changing Global Map of Migration." In King, R., Lazaridis, G. and Tsardanidis, C. (eds) *Eldorado or Fortress? Migration in Southern Europe* Basingstoke: Macmillan.

Konstandinidou, Ch. (2000) *Social Representations of Crime: Images of Albanian Immigrants in the Athenian Press* Athens: Sakkoula [in Greek].

Koukiadis, I. (2005) "EU Directions in Relation to Immigration Policy: Meteor Step between Xenophobia and Multiculturalist society." In Kapsalis, A. and Linardos-Rylmon, P. (eds) *Immigration Policy and Immigrants' Rights* Athens:INE/GSEE-ADEDY [in Greek].

Kousis, M. (1985) "Greek Immigrant Women in Philadelphia during the 1970s." *The Greek Review of Social Research* 59: 105-115 [in Greek].

Labrianidis, L., Lyberaki, A. (2001) *Albanian Immigrants in Thessaloniki.* Thessaloniki: Paratiritis [in Greek].

Labrianidis, L., Lyberaki, A., Tinios, P. and Hatziprokopiou, P. (2004) "Inflow of Migrants and Outflow of Investments: Aspects of Interdependence between Greece and the Balkans." *Journal of Ethnic and Migration Studies*, 30(6): 1183-1208.

Laliotou, I. (2004) *Transatlantic Subjects: Acts of Migration and Cultures of Transnationalism between Greece and America.* Chicago: University of Chicago Press.

Lambropoulou, E. (2003) "Criminal 'Organizations' in Greece and Public Policy: from Non-real to Hyper-real?" *International Journal of the Sociology of Law* 331: 69-87.

Lazaridis, G. (1999) "The Helots of the New Millennium: Ethnic-Greek Albanians and 'Other' Albanians in Greece." In Anthias, F. and Lazaridis, G. (eds) *Into*

the Margins: Migration and Exclusion in Southern Europe 105-121. Aldershot: Ashgate.
Lazaridis, G. (2001) "Trafficking and Prostitution: The Growing Exploitation of Migrant Women in Greece." *The European Journal of Women's Studies* 8(1): 67-102.
Lazaridis, G. and Psimmenos, I. (2000) "Migrant Flows from Albania to Greece: Economic, Social and Spatial Exclusion." In King, R., Lazaridis, G. and Tsardanidis, C. (eds) *Eldorado or Fortress? Migration in Southern Europe.* 170-185. London: Macmillan.
Lazos, G. (2002a) *Prostitution and Trafficking in Modern Greece-The Prostitute.* Athens: Kastaniotis [in Greek].
Lazos, G. (2002b) *Trafficking in Greece in 2002.* Athens: STOPNOW-KEDE. Available on the internet http://www.stop-trafficking.org/database/STOPNOW_REPORT_en_2002.pdf. Retrieved on 20 December 2006.
Liegeois, J-P. (1994) *Roma, Gypsies, Travelers, Socio-Cultural Data, Socio-Political Data.* Brussels: Council of Europe.
Liegeois, J-P. and Gheorghe, N. (1995) *Roma/Gypsies: A European Minority.* London: Minority Rights Group.
Mai, N. (2002) "Myths and Moral Panics: Italian Identity and the Media Representation of Albanian Immigration." In Grillo, R.D. and Pratt J. (eds) *The Politics of Recognizing Difference: Multiculturalism Italian Style.* 77-94. Aldershot: Ashgate.
Mai, N. and Schwandner-Sievers, S. (2003) "Albanian Migration and New Transnationalisms." *Journal of Ethnic and Migration Studies* 29(6): 939-948.
Merlopoulos, P. (1967) "Emigration in Greece During the Post-War Years." *Essays on Greek Migration Series No1* 39-54. Athens: Social Sciences Centre.
Ministry of Public Order (2006) *Annual Report on Organized Crime in Greece for the year 2005. Open edition.* Available on the internet at: http://www.ydt.gr/main/Section.jsp?SectionID=14636. Retrieved on 17 October 2006.
MMO (2004) *Statistical Data on Immigrants in Greece: An Analytic Study of Available Data and Recommendations for Conformity with European Union Standards.* Final Report. Athens: Hellenic Migration Policy Institute and Mediterranean Migration Observatory. Available on the internet at: http://www.mmo.gr/pdf/general/IMEPO_Exec_Summary_English.pdf. Retrieved on 22 March 2006.
Moschonas, A. (2005) *Social Classes and Strata in Contemporary Societies* Athens: Odysseas [in Greek].
Moschonas, A. (1993) "Social Complexity and Contemporary Greek Society: Interpretive Approaches." In Sakellaropoulos, Th. (ed) *Contemporary Greek Society: Historical and Critical Approaches.* Athens: Kritiki pp. 247-295 [in Greek].
MRG. (1997) *World Directory of Minorities.* Minority Rights Group International London: MRG.
Nova-Kaltsouni, X. (1989) "The Criminal Engagement of Women." *Greek Review of Criminology* 3-4: 177-181 [in Greek].
ODIHR (2001) *Human Dimension Implementation Meeting Consolidated Summary.* Office for Democratic Institutions and Human Rights. Warsaw 17-21 September.

Available on the internet http://www.osce/org/documents/odihr/2001/09/1805_en.pdf. Retrieved on 20 December 2006.
Papageorgiou, Y. (1992) "The Women's Movement and Greek Politics." In Bystydzienski, J (ed) *Women Transforming Politics: Worldwide Strategies for Empowerment* Bloomighton: Indiana University Press.
Papageorgiou, Y. (2006) *Hegemony and Feminism* Athens: Gutenberg [in Greek]
Papailias, P. (2003) "'Money of *Kurbet* is Money of Blood': The Making of a 'Hero' of Migration at the Greek-Albanian Border." *Journal of Ethnic and Migration Studies* 29(6): 1059-1078.
Papantoniou-Fragoudi, M. and Leventi, K.M. (2000) "The Reguralisation of Aliens in Greece." *International Migration Review*, 34(3): 950-955.
Papatheodorou, Th. (2005a) "The New Institutional Framework for Immigrants: between Legality, Strictness and Control." *Poiniki Dikaiosyni*, 10: 1185-1192 [in Greek].
Papatheodorou, Th. (2005b) *Public Safety and Crime Prevention Policies*. Athens: Nomiki Vivliothiki [in Greek].
Patris, 2 January 2006. Pervolarakis, Th. "Racist Crime with a 17 year-old Albanian Victim." http://www.patris.gr/articles /76600/33495 Retrieved on 19 December 2006.
Patris, 10 January 2006. Sarhianakis, M. "Some Thoughts on the Occasion of a Murder." http://www.patris.gr/print/77068/0. Retrieved on 19 December 2006.
Pctmezidou-Tsoulouvi, M. (1992) *Social Inequalities and Social Policy* Athens: Exantas [in Greek].
Petoussi, V. (2005) "Greece. Hellenic Republic." In Das, D. and Palmiotto, M.J. (eds) *The World Police Encyclopedia* New York, NY: Routledge Taylor and Francis Group.
Petoussi, V. (2006) "Aspects of the Relationship between Youth and the Police." In Koniordos, S., Maratou-Alipranti, L., Panagiotopoulou, R. (eds) *Social Developments in Contemporary Greece*. 603-639. Athens: Ant. N. Sakkoulas Publishers [in Greek].
Petropoulos, N.P. (1994) "Social Mobility of Greek Immigrants in the Host Countries: A First Comparative Analysis." *The Greek Review of Social Research* 84-85: 13-27 [in Greek].
RAXEN. (2005) *National Focal Point for Greece*. European Racism and Xenophobia Information Network. Report prepared by Pavlou, M, Mavromamati, D., Theodoridis, N. Antigone Information & Documentation Centre. Available on the internet at: http://www.antigone.gr/RAXEN_Publications.html Retrieved on 19 December 2006.
Rigakos, G.S. and Papanicolaou, G. (2003) "The Political Economy of Greek Policing: Between Neo-Liberalism and the Sovereign State." *Policing and Society* 13(3): 271-304.
Sabaniotis, Th. (2006) "Greek Tourism in the Context of International Competition" *Eurobank Research Economy & Markets* 8 (25 October): 1-17 [in Greek].
Samatas, M. (2003) "Greece in 'Schengenland': Blessing or Anathema for Citizens and Foreigners' Rights?" *Journal of Ethnic and Migration Studies* 29(1): 141-156.

Samatas, M. (2004) *Surveillance in Greece: From Anticommunist to Consumer Surveillance*. Athens: Pella.

Scordas, A. (2002) "The New Immigration Law in Greece: 'Modernization on the Wrong Rrack.'" *European Journal of Migration and Law* 4(1): 23-48.

Ta Nea 21 March 1998: N17 "They arrested the murderers." http://www.tanea.gr/print.php?3=A&f=16094&m=N17&aa=1.

Ta Nea 24 March 1998: N15. "Albanians were saved from lynching." http://www.tanea.gr/print_article.php?e=A&f=16096&m=N15&aa=1. Retrieved on 21 June 2006.

Ta Nea 26 March 1998: N16. Glentzakis, P. "Community on patrol against Albanians." http://www.tanea.gr/print.php?e=A&f=16097&m=N16&aa=1. Retrieved on 21 June 2006.

Ta Nea 26 March 1998: N17. "Protest in Kastoria." http://www.tanea.gr/print_article.php?e=A&f=16097&m=N17&aa=2. Retrieved on 19 December 2006.

Ta Nea 1 June 1999: N01 "Albanian Fever hits the government." http://www.tanea.gr/print_article.php?e=A&f=16451&m=N01&aa=1. Retrieved on 19 December 2006.

Ta Nea 1 June 1999: N16. Papachristos, G. "Mutual accusations two weeks before elections" http://www.tanea.gr/print_article.php?e=A&f=16451&m=N16&aa=1 Retrieved on 19 December 2006.

Ta Nea 16 July 1999: N01 "Finally a big success." http://www.tanea.gr/print_article.php?e=A&f=16490&m=N01&aa=1.

Ta Nea 16 July 1999: N19. Nesfyge, L, Hatzidis, K, Kantouris, K, Kehagia, V. "Finally they have sent a message." http://www.tanea.gr/print_article.php?e=A&f=16490&m=N19&aa=1 Retrieved on 26 June 2006.

Ta Nea 16 July 1999: N20. Nesfyge, L. Hatzidis, K., Kantouris, K., Kehagia, V. "Dead the Albanian abductor-Safe the hostages who heroically helped the police." http://www.tanea.gr/print_article.php?e=A&f=16490&m=N20&aa=1 Retrieved on 26 June 2006.

Ta Nea 23 October 1999: N22. "A 7-hour itinerary of a racist amok." http://www.tanea.gr/print.php?e=A&f=16574&m=N22&aa=1. Retrieved on 19 December 2006.

Ta Nea 16 January 2006 "The Roma founded a political party." Available at the internet at http://www.tanea.gr/print.php?e=A&f=18439&m=N16&aa=3 Retrieved on 22 December 2006.

The Greek Ombudsman. (2001) *Annual Report. Abridged English Language Version*. Available on the internet at: http://www.synigoros.gr/annual01_en/en_2001.pdf. Retrieved on 20 December 2006.

The Greek Ombudsman. (2005) *Annual Summary Report*. Available on the internet at: http://www.synigoros.gr/annual_05/perilipsh_2005.pdf . Retrieved on 11 July 2006.

Triandafyllidou, A. (2000) "Racists? Us? Are you joking? The Discourse of Social Exclusion of Immigrants in Greece and Italy." In King, R., Lazaridis, G. and Tsardanidis, C. (eds) *Eldorado or Fortress? Migration in Southern Europe*. 186-205. London: Macmillan.

Triandafyllidou, A. and Veikou, M. (2002) "The Hierarchy of Greekness: Ethnic and National Identity Considerations in Greek Immigration Policy." *Ethnicities*, 2(2): 189-208.

Tsoukalas, C. (1995) "Free Riders in Wonderland; Or of Greeks in Greece." In Constas, D. and Stavrou, T. (eds) *Greece Prepares for the Twenty-First Century*. 191-222. Washington DC: The Woodrow Wilson Centre Press.

Tsouramanis, X. (1998) *Murder in Greece: A Criminological Approach*. Athens-Komotini: Ant. N Sakkoula Publishers [in Greek].

Tzortzopoulou, M. (2002) "The Position of Immigrants in Greece." In Mouriki, A. Naoumi, M., Papapetrou, G. (eds) *The Social Portrait of Greece. 2001*. 205-210. Athens: EKKE [in Greek].

UNHCR (2005) "*2004 Global Refugee Trends: Over view of Refugee Populations, New Arrivals, Durable Solutions, Asylum-Seekers, Stateless and other persons of concern to UNHCR*" Population and Geographical Section Division on Operational Support. Geneva: UNHCR.

WTTC (2004) "Competitiveness Monitor 2004." *World Trade and Tourist Council*. Available on the internet at: http://www.wttc.org. Retrieved on 17 December 2006.

Zarafoniou, Ch. (2002) *Fear of Crime: A Criminological Approach and Inquiry based on an Empirical Study of the Phenomenon within the City of Athens*. Athens-Komotini: Ant. N Sakkoulas Publishers [in Greek and English].

Zarafonitou, Ch. (2006) "The (in)security of Immigrants: A Criminological approach." *Poinikos Logos* 1: 267-286 [in Greek].

Zarafonitou, Ch. and Mantoglou, A. (2000). "The Social Representation of Crime and the Criminal." In Kourakis, N. (ed) *Criminal Policy II*. Athens: A. Sakkoulas [in Greek].

Helpful Websites

www.greekhelsinki.gr – Greek Helsinki Monitor.

http://www.antigone.gr/ – Antigone: Information and Documentation Centre on Racism.

http://www.synigoros.gr – The Greek Ombudsman.

http://www.gcr.gr/ – Greek Council for Refugees.

http://www.eliamep.gr – Hellenic Foundation for European & Foreign Policy.

http://www.mmo.gr – Mediterranean Migration Observatory.

http://eumc.eu.int/eumc/index.php European Monitoring Centre on Racism and Xenophobia.

http://www.statewatch.org/ – Statewatch: Monitoring the State and Civil Liberties in the European Union.

Chapter 7

Japan

Mark Fenwick

Introduction

Any consideration of racial victimization in Japan is rendered difficult by government policies that for much of the period since 1868 (i.e., the Meiji Restoration and the "opening" up of Japan after nearly two centuries of isolation), and particularly since 1945, have promoted a myth of homogeneity that has denied diversity and obscured the existence of minority groups. Although, there has been some progress in recent years in state recognition of such groups, an ideology of mono-ethnicity remains a central aspect of modern Japanese notions of self-identity. This conception of the nation as a single people has a number of implications for any discussion of racial victimization. In particular, the emphasis on homogeneity means that reliable official information on racially motivated crime is extremely difficult to come by and consequently any meaningful analysis of the extent of such crimes is difficult to determine. Although crime statistics on foreign offenders are widely disseminated and have become a central element in the current law and order debate (see http://www.debito.org/TheCommunity/crimestats.html for an annotated translation of the 2003 figures), reliable information on crimes committed against members of different ethnic groups is not readily available. Moreover, in spite of constitutional guarantees, Japan has no specific criminal laws focusing on racially motivated crimes, nor, unlike other OECD (Organization for Economic Co-operation and Development) members, does it have any legislation dealing with racial discrimination.

This chapter will suggest that the myth of homogeneity has served to conceal a social reality that is somewhat more complicated. Although Japan may not have the ethnic diversity of modern Europe or North America, it does have a degree of diversity that is not normally recognized or acknowledged either domestically or internationally. On the specific question of racially motivated crimes it will be suggested that although there is not a widespread problem of violent crimes in Japanese society, anecdotal evidence derived from both the mass media, academic commentators, NGOs, and, in particular a recent UN report (see Diene, 2006), suggests that minor forms of racial discrimination and victimization are a routine feature of everyday life in a Japanese context. The fact that there are not crimes of a more serious nature may simply be a function of the fact that serious violent crimes of any kind remain relatively rare in Japan (for a recent and systematic review of post-war Japanese crime rates, see Park, 2006).

Examples of victimization of minority groups will be taken from: (i) minority groups who possess Japanese nationality (i.e., the Buraku people, the Ainu and the Okinawans); (ii) descendants of people from former Japanese colonies, most obviously the Korean minority (*zainichi*), who although born and raised in Japan do not possess Japanese nationality but have special permanent resident status; and (iii) foreigners and migrants from other countries. In particular, the final part of the chapter will seek to demonstrate how the current law and order debate has focused on criminal acts committed by foreigners, and that this perception of the foreigner-as-criminal has resulted in criminal justice policies and rhetoric that are in some cases quite clearly discriminatory against foreign residents. In that sense, the central contention of this chapter will be that the most pernicious examples of racial victimization in a Japanese context have been perpetrated by state agencies and that, by and large, civil society remains relatively free of violent racially motivated crime. The question posed by this discussion is whether this situation will continue given the climate of fear generated by political elites that now surrounds foreigners.

Traditional forms of Racial Victimization in Japan

The myth of homogeneity is one of the key features of post-war Japanese national identity (see Weiner, 1997 for an overview of this issue). Moreover, it is a view that for a long time was embraced by western commentators on Japan, most obviously the tradition of social anthropology initiated by Ruth Benedict (1946) in her classic study of Japan, *The Chrysanthemum and the Sword*. To illustrate the central tenets of this view of Japan, it is worth focusing on the writings of former Japanese Prime Minister, Nakasone Yasuhiro (see Hood, 1998). Not only is Nakasone one of the leading figures in post-war Japanese politics but his views on race and Japan are representative of a powerful current of thinking in modern Japanese society (see Box 3).

Box 3: Yasuhiro Nakasone: 27 May 1918

> The former Prime Minister of Japan from 1982 to 1987 is perhaps best known for pushing through the privatization of state owned companies, and for helping to revitalize Japanese nationalism during and after his term as prime minister. One of his first political forays, and sign of things to come, occurred in 1952 when he accused Emperor Hirohito for Japan's defeat in World War II. He went on to hold several prominent Ministerial positions before becoming prime minister. While prime minister he established a close relationship with US President Ronald Reagan as well as with China and he made significant inroads with his various privatization initiatives throughout the country. However in 1987 he along with other LDP lawmakers was implicated in the Recruit (a real estate and telecommunication company) scandal; an insider trading and corruption scandal that led to the Nakasone and other prominent politicians to resign. Nakasone went on to serve in the Diet until 2003 when he officially retired from politics.

Nakasone was prime minister from December 1982 to November 1987, one of the longest terms of the post-war period. Usually, an LDP (Liberal Democratic Party, *Jimintô*) President (which for most of the post-war period meant also being Prime Minister due to the LDP's control over Japanese politics) has been limited to a maximum of four years in office. However, due to high levels of popularity, Nakasone was given the honor of a one-year extension. After stepping down as Prime Minister, Nakasone has continued to exert great influence over Japanese politics both through his public pronouncements, but, perhaps more importantly in a Japanese context, private maneuverings. Now one of grandees of the LDP, he is a regular and influential media commentator on politics and society.

A key tenet of Nakasone's political ideology has been the concept of "healthy" (*kenzen*) nationalism, which Nakazone has defined as follows: "It is when a race of people who share a common destiny are aware that they share a common destiny and make every effort to enable the country to grow and prosper politically, economically, and culturally". (Nakasone, 1987: 10). The mantra of Nakasone is that Japan is a mono-ethnic society. "Japan has one state, one ethnicity, one language ... it is very good that we are a mono-ethnic country, and it's something that we should be proud of" (quoted in Yoshimura, 1988: 36).

In developing this political philosophy, Nakasone has often contrasted Japan with other countries (most frequently, the United States) that do not consist of a single race that "share a common destiny". Infamously, in September 1986, for example, Nakasone told an LDP research meeting that, 'it is only Japan that has become a highly educated society. Because of the considerable presence of blacks, Puerto Ricans and Mexicans in the United States, the average intelligence level is extremely low" (quoted in Yoshimura, 1988: 38). Nakasone went on to suggest that high crime rates and other social problems in the US were also connected to the presence of these different racial groups. These comments soon appeared in the US media, and Nakasone was eventually forced into retracting them and issuing an apology. Although as Hood (1999: 12) correctly points out, "a large number of Japanese actually agreed with the comments, but were merely angered by the embarrassment that it has caused Japan by him making them". In giving expression to the belief that Japanese people belong to one race, Nakasone was, and remains, a powerful spokesman for the influential notion that Japan is a mono-ethnic society.

And yet, over the last decade both within Japan and abroad, this kind of view has been subject to extensive criticism in the contemporary academic literature on the politics of race and nationalism in Japan (see, for example, the essays collected in Weiner, 1997, for a sample of this literature). One of the most penetrating of these critiques is John Lie's (2004) *Multiethnic Japan.*

The starting point of Lie's analysis is the observation that there is something curious about the fact that a nation comprising of Ainu, Okinawans, Koreans, Chinese, children of mixed ancestry and foreigners, "around 5 per cent of the total population" (Lie, 2004: 3) behaves as though mono-ethnicity were an undisputable fact. Although one can question Lie's figure of 5 per cent as being at the top-end of the range, his basic point – namely, that the notion of homogeneity is deeply flawed as an empirical description of social reality – is well made.

Lie (2004) goes on to suggest that this type of "discourse of Japaneseness" emerged as the dominant response to the question of Japanese identity in the post-war period and that it has served to replace pre-war Japan's nationalism, Emperor worship and militarism with a post-war ideology centred around economic growth, uniqueness and racial purity.

Lie (2004) seeks to undermine the myth of homogeneity through a series of specific examples of heterogeneity that, in many cases, would come as a surprise to Japanese readers. Few would have suspected, for example, that Seibu department store was founded by a Japanese of Korean descent; or that Kitano "Beat" Takeshi, arguably the leading entertainer and film director in Japan since the 1980s, is part Korean. The actress Matsuzaka Keiko, the singer Misora Hibari and the wrestler Rikidozan are all of Korean ancestry; Sumo superstar Taiho's father was Russian; and the baseball star and coach, Oh Sadaharu, is of Taiwanese origin. All of these figures (and others) widely regarded as symbols of the Japanese 'race' are, in fact, the opposite, namely symbols of its multi-ethnicity.

Historian Sakai Naoki (2006) also suggests that the notion that Japan is a uniquely homogeneous nation-state is a post-war invention. Japan's loss of a multiethnic empire in 1945 overturned a sense of national identity that posited Japan as a great melting pot of peoples along the lines of the United States. After 1945, the myth of homogeneity replaced what could be termed the multiculturalism of imperial Japan. The myth of homogeneous Japan gained such popularity that claims it is a recent construct surprises Japanese and foreign observers alike, but an increasing body of scholarship supports Sakai's and Lie's claims.

Sakai suggests that the Empire left many legacies that undermine the myth of homogeneity. Post-war writer, Kazue Morisaki, for example, born in colonial Korea to a Japanese father and a Korean mother, struggled to reconcile her own background with the post-war sense of nation that denied ethnic diversity and propagated notions of homogeneity (Sakai, 2006: 135). The fact that Morisaki was a baby of the empire who felt as much if not more of an affinity for the land where she was raised than for Japan made it impossible for this reflective writer to accept the standard post-war definition of what it meant to be Japanese. As a pre-war imperial power, the post-war idea of "one nation, one people" was not only incompatible with the Japanese Empire's, albeit hypocritical, concept of a "Greater East Asian Co-Prosperity Sphere", it conflicted with the reality of post-war society. Much of the culture was a byproduct of the Asian mainland. Whether examining writing (Chinese characters, *kanji*), dishes (*ramen*), games (*pachinko*), or genres (*enka*), one constantly encounters clear examples of ethnic heterogeneity and cultural hybridity in post-war Japanese society.

Ethnic Diversity and Racial Victimization: A Rich History

Giichi Nomura, leader of the Ainu Association of Hokkaido was one of those who criticized Nakasone at the time of his comments on Japan and the United States:

> Does [he] really think that Japan is a mono-ethnic state? In Hokkaido there are the Ainu people, and in Okinawa there are residents who have their own history and culture.

[There are also] the peoples of North Korea, South Korea, China, and Taiwan who, while maintaining their own life customs, have naturalized in Japan or are engaged in making a living as permanent residents; is he [Nakasone] saying that these peoples are the same people as the so-called Yamato people? (Nomura, 1986: 7).

Nomura implored Nakasone "to recognize the existence of ethnic minorities in Japan, and to sweep away the heretofore concept of mono-ethnic state that is used toward these ethnic minorities". "Japan is definitely not mono-ethnic", we need "a society in which the multiple peoples (*fukusu minzoku*) residing in this country are able to speak their respective mother tongues, while living together using Japanese as a common language" (Nomura, 1986: 7).

According to figures from the 2003 census, Japan has a population of 127.7 million, out of which 98.45 per cent are Japanese nationals. The Japanese population includes one indigenous population, the Ainu, estimated at between 30,000 and 50,000 people: they live predominantly in the island of Hokkaido and represent the second largest minority group among Japanese citizens. Also there are also the indigenous peoples of Okinawa, the Ryukyu. There is also the Buraku population, which although not a distinct ethnic group as such, is certainly a minority group that has been subject to discrimination both historically and recently. Amongst the foreigners, who do not represent more than 1.55 per cent of the population, Koreans are the largest foreign community (607,419 in 2004), followed by the Chinese, Brazilians and Filipinos. In this section, each of these groups will be introduced in order to substantiate the diversity of contemporary Japan, and examples of on-going victimization presented. The key point is that although this victimization very rarely, if ever, takes the form of serious or violent crime, it nevertheless is a persistent problem that has been obscured by the state's emphasis on mono-ethnicity.

Much of the evidence of such victimization will be taken from the 2006 report of the UN Special Rapporteur on Discrimination and Racism, Doudou Diene (2006). This report proved to be particularly controversial as it was extremely critical of the Japanese government's record in tackling discrimination. Although the report was welcomed by most minority groups and political progressives, it was the subject of vitriolic criticism by nationalist commentators. And yet, as David MacNeill (2006) in his commentary on the reaction to the report within Japan points out, much of this right-wing criticism was less concerned with disputing the substantive findings of Diene but to point to the racism of US and European societies, "suggesting they fix their own back yards before trampling into Japan's". Although Diene's report is not without difficulties, it is wrong to dismiss it as some have as the work of a politically naïve visitor being unduly influenced by politically biased representatives of Japanese minorities.

i. The Ainu

In the fifteenth century, the Yamato people of Honshu (the largest of the four main islands that comprises modern Japan) started to occupy the southernmost part of the island of Hokkaido, ancestral land of the Ainu people. Between the seventeenth and the nineteenth centuries, the Ainu in Hokkaido were put into forced labor, deprived of their resources, prevented from practicing their traditional activities (Siddle, 1996: chapters 1–2). After 1868, the Japanese occupied the whole of Hokkaido and it was fully assimilated. The motive for the occupation was largely economical, since Hokkaido was rich in the kind of natural resources necessary for the rapid industrialization that the Meiji oligarchs recognized as being essential for Japan to avoid being colonized by western powers. The Meiji state adopted an official policy of forced assimilation with regard to the indigenous peoples of Hokkaido. This culminated in an 1899 law that forcibly relocated Ainu and expropriated swathes of their land, much of which was of religious significance to the Ainu (Howell, 2004). The inevitable consequence of these policies was the almost complete destruction of traditional Ainu society, culture and language. For much of the twentieth century, the existence of the Ainu was not acknowledged by the Japanese state (Cheung, 2005). It was only in 1997 that a law for the promotion of the Ainu culture was enacted, but even this law failed to recognize the Ainu as an indigenous people (for a commentary and critique, see Siddle, 2002, 2003). The government established a Foundation for Research and Promotion of Ainu culture, the promotion of the Ainu language and culture, research on the Ainu and the dissemination of knowledge about Ainu traditions.

According to a 1999 survey conducted by the Hokkaido prefectural government, 28.1 per cent of the Ainu people interviewed indicated that they had experienced discrimination or known someone who had experienced discrimination (Diene, 2006: para. 43). The situations in which discrimination was experienced were, in order, at school, regarding marriage and at the workplace. The survey indicates that 95.2 per cent of Ainu children go to high school, compared to the local average of 97 per cent. The difference becomes very significant in access to university level education: 16.1 per cent of them go to university, as opposed to the local average of 34.5 per cent (Diene, 2006, para. 43). In his commentary on the evidence, the Special UN Rapporteur continues:

> The discrimination faced by Ainu children at school is a serious concern. Ainu children are despised in such a strong way that some of them leave school because such persecutory treatments become unbearable. This affects the life of the entire family, which is sometimes forced to move to another region. Another consequence is that children tend to be ashamed of their identity: therefore, they tend to assimilate into the mainstream culture, and lose their culture and their pride in it. Many Ainu adults also hide their identity for fear of discrimination in finding employment or accommodation ... On the identity side, the Japanese have built a number of prejudices to justify the historical oppression of the Ainu, spreading the idea that they were not intelligent, had a barbaric culture, and had a different appearance. These prejudices continue to be used to denigrate them and make them ashamed of their origins (Diene, 2006: para. 44–46).

Moreover, land expropriations have continued until relatively recently. Most controversially, the Nibutani dam project involved the expropriation of land that included several important sacred sites, for the construction of a dam. Although the expropriation was subsequently declared illegal on the grounds that the Hokkaido development agency had failed to consider the cultural significance of the land in performing the balancing of interests required by the Land Expropriation Law, the dam construction proceeded and has never been reversed (on this case, see Levin, 2001). Today their distinctive culture has all but been wiped out yet some of their songs, stories, distinctive dances, and some Ainu festivals and crafts have been preserved primarily to capitalize on tourism.

ii. Okinawans

The "Ryukyu Kingdoms", home of the Okinawan peoples and an independent nation from the fourteenth century was conquered by the government of Japan and annexed in 1879. The collection of islands to the southwest of Japan main island were formally known as the Ryukyu Islands and more recently as the Nansei Islands. As in the case of the Ainu various assimilative policies were adopted that sought to prohibit Ryukyu dialects, traditional customs, and lifestyles. During the final months of the war, the battle for Okinawa proved to be one of bloodiest battles of the Pacific campaign. The civilian population of Okinawa were caught in the crossfire. During the fighting, over a quarter of a million Okinawans were forced into US detention camps in order to get them out of the way of the fighting, yet an estimated 150,000 died from artillery attacks or because locals were often indistinguishable from Japanese soldiers (Feiffer, 2001). Unlike the Japanese mainland which was handed over to Japanese control in 1952, Okinawa remained under US occupation until 1972. And yet, in one sense, the occupation continues for Okinawans since one-fifth of the best land on their island is still occupied by the US military as well as Japanese forces. Since 1972, the majority of the United States military bases in Japan have been concentrated in Okinawa, which covers only 0.6 per cent of Japanese territory. These bases affect the environment, indigenous culture and custom of the Okinawa people, and are a source of lingering resentment. Tensions between Okinawan prefectural government and central government in Tokyo continue run high on occasion (Hein, 2003). The fact that the central government of Japan has tended to concentrate many of the American based forces in Okinawa with a minimal presence on the mainland is considered by some natives of the Ryukyus as discriminatory against the islanders. In additional, among some political circles, people from the Ryukyus are not considered to be "real" Japanese.

iii. Koreans

Of the approximately, two million documented foreigners in Japan, 607,419 are Koreans, or *zainichi*. The Japanese word *zainichi* itself means "staying in Japan". For example, *zainichi-gaikokujin* refers to "foreign nationals living in Japan". However, "zainichi" on its own usually refers to *zainichi* Koreans because of their significant presence. Strictly speaking, the term *zainichi* refers only to long term, permanent residents of Japan who have retained either their North or South Korean nationalities, not ethnic Koreans who have acquired Japanese nationality through naturalization. Most *zainichi* families can be traced back to wartime labor. Between 1939 and 1945, labor shortages caused by war led to a series of official policies that recruited Koreans often forcibly to work in Japan. Those who were brought to Japan were forced to work in factories, in mines and as laborers, often under appalling conditions. Most of the wartime laborers went home after the war, but, for various complex reasons, some remained in Japan and chose to retain their Korean names and nationality.

Discrimination against *zainichi* has been well-documented (see Ryang, 2004 for an overview). Most notoriously, was the requirement that, along with other foreign residents, all *zainichi* had to be fingerprinted by the local government. This practice, which was only abolished in 1999, came to symbolize the systematic discrimination against *zainichi*. Of course, this was only one aspect of a much more wide-ranging problem. More recently, in his assessment of the current situation with regard to *zainichi*, UN Special Rapporteur Diene, points to a number of problems ranging from relatively poor living conditions (para. 54), lack of access to pension rights and other social benefits (para. 56), lack of recognition of and financial support for *zainichi* schools (para. 57), and a failure to acknowledge wartime atrocities committed against Korean people (para. 59). On the specific issue of violent crime, he mentions attacks, although – perhaps unfortunately – he fails to provide any concrete examples:

> While some situations of discrimination against Korean children have recently been solved, for example concerning their right to participate in school sports federations, violence against Korean schoolchildren continues to increase. Some children suffer insults or are physically abused simply because they are Koreans. But the most serious expression concerns girls wearing national Korean dresses, who have had their clothes ripped or cut in public places during daytime. Children are now scared of showing their identity or of wearing their traditional dress (Diene, 2006: para. 58).

iv. Burakumin.

A final example of minority groups within Japan is that of the Buraku people (see De Vos, 1971; Upham, 1987; McLauchlan, 2003; and Neary 2004, for general accounts of the Buraku issue). Although Burakumin are ethnically and linguistically indistinguishable from other Japanese, they have been regarded as a distinct group or caste and have undoubtedly been discriminated against. Historically, Buraku are descendants of the outcastes from the Tokugawa period (1603–1867) who were regarded as unclean due to Shinto concepts of filth and the stigma attached to the killing of animals. Burkau (then known as *dowa*) engaged in professions that involved slaughtering animals. Due to this perceived pollution many Burakumin were excluded from religious ceremonies and subject to discriminatory laws that limited areas in which they could live. The precise origins and status of Buraku are contested, but the salient points on are, to quote Reber (1999) that:

> (1) the status of outcast existed over the course of several centuries in Japan, (2) the vestiges of discrimination against these outcasts remain, and (3) none of the historical explanation of why the status of outcast existed in the past justify the continuance of this status today (Reber, 1999: 304).

Discrimination against Buraku people continued well into the twentieth century. Following a scandal in 1975 revealing that private detectives were selling to companies and potential marriage partners directories known as "Buraku lists", which included information on Buraku community locations, names of households, etc., the Osaka prefectural government adopted a municipal ordinance, which prohibited such lists. This, however, did not mark the end of the problem. In 2000, the Osaka prefectural government conducted a study on the situation of the Buraku people. It revealed that, while there had been improvements in relation to housing and infrastructure, the progress had not been sufficient in the field of education and employment, or concerning changes in the mentalities of non-Buraku people. It revealed that 20 per cent of them were still reluctant to accepting a marriage with a Buraku person and that 40 per cent did not want to live in a Buraku area. Consequently, the prefecture is now working on promoting the integration of the different communities as a means to eliminate prejudice, and on human rights education (Diene, 2006: paras. 35–37). Again to quote the UN Special Raporteur:

> The daily manifestations [of discrimination] include graffiti, posters and Internet messages insulting Buraku people, treating them as dirty and requesting them to leave, and discriminatory practices, mainly in the field of employment and marriage. Employers continue to enquire on the origins of the job applicants, but there is no local or national legislation that prohibits this practice, except for the prefectures of Osaka, Fukuoka, Kumamoto, Tokushima, Kagawa and Tottori. Regrettably, the "Buraku lists" are also used by marriage partners, who inquire as to the origins of their future spouse. According to a recent survey, 78 per cent of the population of Osaka indicated that they would see a marriage with Buraku people as problematic: this shows how profound the discriminatory mentality against Buraku people is. Discouragement of marriages is a major obstacle to the integration of Buraku people into the rest of the Japanese society (Diene, 2006: para. 36).

In each of the above cases, therefore, we see the continued persistence of discrimination against minority groups whose existence has been obscured by the myth of homogeneity.

Racial Victimization in Japan within a Criminal Justice Context

In this final section, the focus will be on criminal justice issues. In particular, it will be suggested that a recent yet persistent trend in the contemporary law and order debate has been to consistently portray foreign residents in Japan as a criminogenic population, and that this has resulted in a number of new policies, many of which, although popular, are clearly discriminatory and victimize foreign residents. The background to the emergence of this new discourse on the foreigner as criminal has been declining public confidence in the performance of crime control policies. Rising crime rates combined with a clearance rate that has fallen dramatically to a little over 20 per cent in the past decade appear to have damaged public confidence in the Japanese criminal justice system and social control mechanisms more generally (Park, 2006). This confidence has been further damaged by a string of scandals among the political elite as well as involving the police (Sugita, 1999) that have severely damaged their legitimacy. A survey conducted by the *Yomiuri* newspaper and reported on 14 March 2001 reported that 60 per cent of those surveyed said their trust in the police had "declined in recent years" and that 40 per cent of those surveyed said they "did not trust the police at all" (*Yomiuri Newspaper*, 14 March, 2001: 1). Other developments have compounded concerns about criminal justice more generally and prompted reforms that have resulted in a more punitive, expressive system of criminal justice. For example, the lack of disclosure of information to victims in criminal proceedings, as well as public perceptions of inadequate sentencing by the judiciary have led to the emergence of a vocal victim's rights movement that elicits extensive public support and has prompted the government to consider enacting a new victims rights law. A series of high profile murders by juvenile offenders and mentally-ill offenders have led to reforms in how the criminal justice system deals with these two classes of defendant that shift the balance away from the "psy"-professions towards a more punitive approach.

Of course, the economic and social background to these crime control developments is a decade long recession and a process of "de-subordination" that has increasingly undermined the respect for authority and hierarchy that has been a legacy of Japan's Confucian history. Urbanization and, in particular, the rapid expansion of the Tokyo metropolitan area has meant that community based crime prevention measures have lost their effectiveness as a result of more anonymous and individualistic patterns of social life. A detailed analysis of this crisis in crime control and its social causes is beyond the scope of this chapter. However, what is relevant is how this crisis seems to have resulted in the emergence of a new and emotionally charged political discourse on crime that focuses attention on foreign criminals as being behind the recent crime wave. In this sense, the kind of politicization of crime that has occurred in the US, the UK and other countries has also occurred in albeit in a nascent way in Japan.

The Situation of 'Foreign' Residents

One key element of this new populist, political discourse on crime is the emphasis it places on crimes committed by foreign residents. This section will consider the statements of one of the most popular and high profile politicians in Japan, the Governor of Tokyo, Shintaro Ishihara in order to illustrate this new discourse. First elected Governor in 1999 and re-elected by a landslide in April 2003, Ishihara became famous as a university student when his book, *Taiyo no Kisetsu* ("Seasons of the Sun"), won the prestigious Akutagawa Award in 1955. Shintaro and his younger brother Yujiro became national celebrities when they stared in a film based on the book. While Yujiro concentrated on his career as an entertainer (he went on to become one of the most popular actors in post-war Japan before his death in 1987), Shintaro focused on writing novels and a burgeoning political career, becoming a government minister in the 1980s before quitting national politics in 1995 in protest at the "lack of vision" of his fellow legislators.

Ishihara is well known for being out-spoken. With Sony's Akio Morita he co-wrote in 1989 *The Japan That Can Say No*, a book widely interpreted as anti-American. He has also claimed that the "Rape" of Nanking was a "fabrication" and suggested that Japan's occupation of Korea was a "merger" initiated at the request of the Korean authorities. Less controversially, he has called on the US to give up its air base at Yokota, believes that poor people "should eat barley instead of rice", and has spoken openly about the ineptitude and corruption of the national government.

In spite of these opinions, – perhaps even because of them – Ishihara has proved to be extremely popular with a wide cross section of the electorate. Most political analysts agree that his electoral success is partly a vote against the traditional style of Japanese politicians in favor of blunt talking and clear expression. In a culture that places an overwhelming emphasis on indirectness and subtly of expression, Ishihara's personal style may appeal simply because it marks a refreshing break from the norm. It may also be that he has been very successful in articulating popular discontent during a period of economic contraction and social uncertainty. Many of his more xenophobic statements may resonate with ideas that many individuals have some sympathy for but are unwilling to articulate in public. Ishihara's style has been adopted by a number of other "celebrity" politicians who have managed to succeed in gubernatorial elections across the country.

In this context, however, what is important is the centrality of crime to Ishihara's political rhetoric, and, in particular, the theme of crime committed by foreigners. To illustrate the kind of position he takes, I will consider one representative example, an article, *Nihon yo: Uchinaru Bouei wo* ("Japan: Defend the Home Front") published in *Sankei Shimbun* on 8 May 2001. Ishihara begins the article with a nostalgic longing for a lost past:

> When I look at the country that Japan has become, it seems obvious to me that the forces binding us together as a nation have become weakened. As a result, we have lost many of our irreplaceable virtues and beautiful traditions. Some of the factors causing this loss come from within, while others come from without. One of our vanishing virtues is the blessing of public safety that has been admired by people of other lands, but today seems well on its way to becoming a rapidly-disappearing legend. Factors leading to the breakdown of public safety also come from both within and without, but in this modern era of internationalization, the nature of crime in this country is undergoing major changes (Ishihara, 2001: 6).

This theme of the decay of traditional virtues is a familiar one in nationalist discourse, and it provides the basis for the identification of the cause of this decline as something external and alien. Ishihara develops his argument by describing how on a visit to the National Police Agency Headquarters in Tokyo, officers described a case in which a murder victim had the skin stripped from his face so as to conceal his identity. According to Ishihara, the police were convinced that the killer was Chinese:

> This conjecture was based on the fact that this type of modus operandi is simply not used by Japanese people. In due course, the perpetrators were captured, and, just as had been suspected, the crime was one of revenge among Chinese criminals. There is fear – and not without cause – that it will not be long before the entire nature of Japanese society itself will be altered by the spread of this type of crime that is indicative of the ethnic DNA of the Chinese (Ishihara, 2001: 7).

The jump from what may well have been a reasonable conjecture on the part of the police based on the circumstances of the particular case to the assertion that this type of crime will soon become commonplace as a result of the "ethnic DNA" of Chinese, is striking. It brings us to Ishihara's main claim, namely that as a result of increased internationalization Japanese cities are likely to be overrun by illegal Chinese migrants who are genetically predisposed to criminal activity.

> Let me also note that in the Tokyo areas of Shinjuku, Ikebukuro, and Roppongi you wouldn't even think you were in Japan during the hours from after midnight until early dawn. It may seem ironic or even comical, but the truth is that even the Japanese gangsters hesitate to enter these outrageous areas. Probably most of the foreigners gathering there have illegally entered the country or are illegally overstaying their visas (Ishihara, 2001: 7).

To be sure, Ishihara is not alone in adopting this kind rhetoric about foreign crime. In fact, it has become almost routine to find articles or speeches by politicians that are either explicitly or implicitly predicated on the assumption that crime rates amongst the foreign population are disproportionately high. In another high profile incident, Kanagawa Governor Matsuzawa Shigefumi was recently forced to apologize after he described foreigners as "a bunch of sneaky thieves", when discussing the growing Chinese population in his prefecture.

Whether these claims about foreign crime rates have any statistical basis is unclear, as the official crime statistics make meaningful comparisons extremely difficult. To give just one example, the crime statistics have included visa violations in the category of "heinous crimes", meaning that over-staying one's visa (a crime that can only be committed by a foreigner) will be classified along with much more serious To take one final example, offences. And even if there was some basis for the suggestion that foreigners commit a disproportionate amount of crime then one would have to Many problems with the site, not least the lack of any formal criteria for determining who may be illegally overstaying and the fact that such note that the majority of foreigners in Japan are young people brought by the government to work in so-called "3k" jobs (i.e., *kitanai, kiken, kitsui* (dirty, dangerous and difficult)). That is to say, foreigners in Japan are disproportionately likely to be young, as well as economically and socially marginalized, so any comparison with rates of crime amongst the Japanese population *in general* is likely to be an unfavourable one.

Of course the question of whether Ishihara's fears have any basis in reality is perhaps of less significance than the social and political effects of this kind of rhetoric. It is certainly the case that this populist crime talk has changed the political context within which crime as well as immigration policy is being formulated in Japan. Undoubtedly, this has implications for the kind of criminal justice policies that are being implemented.

It seems clear that the police seem to be stressing the threat posed by foreign crime in crime prevention materials. The *Mainichi* newspaper reported on February 22, 2001 that Nagano banks and government offices displayed prefectural police notices about foreign money-snatchers. The article also mentioned December 2000 Tokyo Metropolitan Police flyers that suggested citizens call the police "if you hear someone speaking Chinese". In February 2000, the Shizuoka Police Department distributed to shopkeepers a handbook entitled "Characteristic Crimes by Foreigners Coming to Japan". It offers hints on dealing with local Brazilian and Peruvian customers: if a "group" of "two to four" foreigners park outside your store, "write down their license plate and report it to the police". More far-fetched was the recent revelation that the Police Research Agency had received a 175 million yen ($1.6 million) research grant to establish an index of "foreignness". Police would test minute samples of blood or other evidence from crime scenes to determine whether the suspect is foreign or not. Predicated on the spurious notion that Japanese DNA is somehow biologically different than that of foreigners, this kind of policy resonates with the kind of thinking associated with Ishihara.

On 16 February 2004, the Ministry of Justice's Department of Immigration unveiled a website (http://www.immi-moj.go.jp/zyouhou/index.html) for the public to notify authorities of suspected illegal migrants. "tip-offs" were anonymous. A number of human rights groups, including Amnesty International, criticised the site as being racist and discriminatory. After over a thousand complaints, the site was changed at the end of March to tone down the language.

The inevitable result of these kinds of policies has been a dramatic shift in Japanese attitudes towards foreigners in general. On 12 April 2003, a Japanese government survey was published that found that only 54 per cent of the public believed that foreigners should have the same right as Japanese (*Asahi Shimbun*, 13 April, 2003). This was down from past results of 65.5 per cent (1998) and 68.3 per cent (1993). A justice ministry official was quoted as citing "foreign crime" as the principle reason for these rapidly declining numbers. An alternative explanation would be that the stereotyping of foreigners by influential figures in Japanese politics and mass media has unnecessarily created this kind of moral panic. Keen to distract public attention from their own failings, most notably in the management of the economy, public officials have resorted to stereotyping of foreign residents. For the moment, it is unclear what effects this labelling will have, either in terms of the behaviour of foreign residents or Japanese population. Given the current climate of fear surrounding crime, however, it is not inconceivable that an unfortunate effect of this kind of rhetoric may be the emergence of something that for most of Japan's post-war history has not been a problem, namely racially motivated violent crime.

Conclusion

This chapter has suggested that although serious racially discriminated crime is not a serious issue in Japan, minor forms of racial discrimination are a routine part of everyday life for minority groups and foreign residents. Moreover, the chapter has argued that the Japanese state has compounded these problems, firstly, by systematically denying the existence of minority groups and, secondly, by blaming foreigners for the recent increase in crime. The chapter concluded with the suggestion that by labelling foreigners in this way, there is a danger that foreigners in Japan may become targets of more serious forms of victimization. Of course, it is always possible the Japanese government both at a national and local level may adopt more progressive policies. Certainly, in order for this to occur there would need to be internal pressure from the Japanese population, but international pressure may well also have an important role to play in this regard. It is worth noting, for instance, that

Japan's ratification of the International Convention on the Elimination of All Forms of Racial Discrimination in 1995 – 30 years after the Convention was concluded – coincided with Japanese efforts to increase its role in international affairs, most obviously the attempt to secure a permanent seat on the UN Security Council. If greater international pressure were brought to bear – particularly through the UN – perhaps the Japanese government would be motivated to enact legislation that would give genuine legal effect to the ideals of the Convention. Perhaps then, there would be a basis for cautious optimism about future developments. For the moment, however, the populist appeal of more nationalistic rhetoric leaves less room for hope.

References

Benedict, R. (1946), *The Chrysanthemum and the Sword* (Tokyo: Tuttle).
Cheung, S. (2005), 'Rethinking Ainu heritage: A Case Study of Ainu Settlement in Hokkaido, Japan', 11, *International Journal of Heritage Studies*, 197.
De Vos, G. (1971), *Japan's Outcasts: The Problem of the Burakumin* (Minority Rights Group).
Diene, D. (2006), *Report of the Special Rapporteur on Contemporary Forms of Racism, Racial Discrimination, Xenophobia and Related Intolerance, Doudou Diene, on his Mission to Japan* (New York: United Nations).
Feiffer, G. (2001), *The Battle for Okinawa* (New York: Lyon Press).
Hein, L. (2003), *Islands of Discontent: Okinawan Responses to Japanese and American Power* (New York: Rowman & Littlefield).
Hood, C. P. (1998) *Nakasone Yasuhiro and Japanese Education Reform: A Revisionist View*, University of Sheffield, Unpublished PhD. thesis, April 1998.
Hood, C. P. (1999), *Nakasone: Nationalist or Internationalist?* Unpublished paper.
Howell, D. (2004), 'Making useful citizens of Ainu in early twentieth century Japan', 1, *Journal of Asian Studies*, 5.
Ishihara, S. (2001), *'Nihon yo: uchinaru bôei wo'*, 'Japan! Defend the home front', *Sankei Shimbun*, 8 May 2001.
Levin, M. A. (2001), 'Essential commodities and racial justice: constitutional protection of Japan's indigenous Ainu people', 8, *New York University Journal of International Law and Policy*, 419.
Lie, J. (2004), *Multiethnic Japan* (Cambridge, MA.: Harvard University Press).
MacNeill, D. (2006), *The Diene Report on Discrimination and Racism in Japan*, available on-line at http://www.zmag.org/content/showarticle.cfm?ItemID=10066 (retrieved Oct. 09/06).
McLauchlan, M. (2003), *Prejudice and Discrimination in Japan: The Buraku Issue* (Edwin Mellen Press).
Nakasone Y. (1987), *My Political Philosophy* (Tokyo: LDP).
Neary, I. (2004), *The Buraku Issue and Modern Japan: The Career of Matsumoto Jiichiro* (London: Routledge).
Nomura, G. (1986), 'Ainu', *Asahi Newspaper*, 13 April 2003.

Park, W. (2006), *Senko Nihon Ni Okeru Hanzairitsu no Suii (Trends in Japanese Crime Rates Post-War)* (Tokyo: Shinzansha).
Reber, S. (1999), 'The Buraku mondai in Japan: historical and modern perspectives and directions fort the future', 12, *Harvard Human Rights Journal*, 297.
Ryang, S. (editor) (2004), *Koreans in Japan* (London: Routledge).
Sakai, N. (2005), *Deconstructing Nationality*, Ithaca (NY.: Cornell University Press).
Siddle, R. (1996), *Race, Resistance and the Ainu of Japan* (London: Routledge).
Siddle, R. (2002), 'An epoch making event? The 1997 Ainu Cultural Promotion Act and its impact', *Japan Forum*, 405.
Siddle, R. (2003), 'The limits to citizenship in Japan', 7, *Citizenship Studies*, 447.
Stevens, G. (2001), 'The Ainu and human rights: domestic and international legal problems', 21, *Japanese Studies*, 181.
Sugita, K. (1999), Looking into Japanese Police Corruption. http://www.tokyoprogressive.org/~tpgn/japan/japanesepolice.html (retrieved Oct. 09/06).
Upham, F. (1987), *Law and Social Change in Post-war Japan* (Cambridge, MA.: Harvard University Press).
Weiner, M. (editor) (1997), *Japan's Minorities: The Illusion of Homogeneity* (London: Routledge).
Yaguchi, Y. (2000), 'Remembering a more layered past in Hokkaido: Americans, Japanese and the Ainu', 11, *Japanese Journal of American Studies*, 109.
Yoshimura, K. (1988), *Sengo Sôri no Hôgen, Shitsugen* (Tokyo: Bunshun Bunko).

Helpful Websites

http://www.npa.go.jp/english/index.htm – National Police Agency.
http://www.immi-moj.go.jp/english/index.html – Immigration Bureau of Japan.
http://www.kantei.go.jp/foreign/index-e.html – Prime Minister's Office.
http://www.moj.go.jp/ENGLISH/index.html – Ministry of Justice.
http://www.imadr.org/tokyo/ishikawareport.html – Burakumin Liberation League Report.
http://www.debito.org/ – website of Arudo Debito, controversial activist against racial discrimination. Nevertheless, the site contains a lot of interesting and important information and examples on a range of issues connected to this topic, particularly discrimination against long-term foreign residents.

Chapter 8

United States of America

Ineke Haen Marshall and Amy Farrell

Introduction

The United States now counts over 300 million inhabitants. A significant portion of the current population are descendants of early Western European settlers, the so-called WASPs (White Anglo-Saxon Protestants), who – by most measures – remain the dominant group in American society, both in terms of numbers and in terms of power and influence. However, American society also includes an extremely complex patchwork of minority groups based on race, ethnicity, national origin, citizenship or religion. Some 'minorities' came to the United States a long time ago, others are foreign-born, recent legal immigrants, or immigrants without the proper documents. Some are white, others are people of color. Some come from Europe, others from Asia, South America, or Africa; they are political refugees, migrant workers, members of international organized crime groups, or highly educated professionals.

The United States is generally known as a 'nation of immigrants', a country which historically has been very hospitable towards most new immigrants, a 'melting pot' of many different religions, races, and cultural backgrounds. At the same time, the history of the United States is replete with examples of racism and exclusionary treatment of newcomers and other minority groups who were often seen as a threat to the American way of life. Indeed, the measuring rod for 'normal' behavior and appearance ("us") is the "Americanized" white (Northern and Western) European, which reduces, by definition, all other ethnic, national and racial groups to minorities ("them"). Thus, an interesting paradox presents itself. On the one hand, the United States proudly proclaims itself as one of the most democratic societies on earth; on the other hand, the United States is far from being a color blind society (see, for example, Kennedy, 1997, Feagin, 2000).

Virtually all minority groups in the United States have experienced – or continue to experience – exclusionary and discriminatory treatment, in the areas of housing, education, employment, safety, political and civic representation. Even more disturbing is the fact that American history is testimony to harsh, violent, and dehumanizing treatment – both organized and individual – of Native Americans (or American Indians), African Americans, Asian Americans, and Hispanics.[1] There is a

---

1 These groups represent the main ethnic and racial minority groupings in the US. It should be noted that these are very broad racial/ethnic categories (following the US Census), which ignore the diversity which exist within each of these groups (see, for example, Wakeling

plethora of detailed and often bone-chilling analyses and accounts of the whole gamut of victimization of members of these minority groups, ranging from humiliation and harassment, exploitation and intimidation to rapes and beatings, lynching and murders (see Finkelman, 1992; Shapiro, 1988). Because of the significance of race and ethnicity in American history, there is a huge volume of journalistic, political, scholarly, philosophical as well as fictional writing on the topic of racist violence and victimization.[2] In the next paragraphs, we will briefly touch on some of the main points of this body of writings.

Any review of writings on racist victimization must start – historically – with the systematic exploitation and brutalization of the original inhabitants of North America, the American Indians, *originally* the largest population group. Native Americans are currently one of the smallest minority groups – only 1.5 per cent of the US population – as a result of "massacres by the whites, economic base destruction, disease, war, famine, and interracial mixing" (Flowers, 1990: 3). Native Americans remain among the most marginalized groups in American society today, in terms of income, education, housing, health and criminal victimization.

There is a growing scholarly interest in documenting the plight of the Native American (see Nielsen and Silverman 1996; Ross and Gould, 2006), but there is no question that the minority group of African Americans or Blacks has received by far the most scholarly and political attention. Blacks now constitute 12.9 per cent of the American population. Unlike other immigrants, Blacks came to the United States against their will, in chains as slaves, forced into involuntary servitude. Black history is a history of exploitation, violation, victimization and exclusion. The doctrine of 'Black inferiority' – the idea that Black people were different or beneath whites – became a prominent ideology in justifying slavery and racism (Flowers, 1990: 8). Black slaves were viewed as property, without rights, and subject to cruelty, beatings, rape and murder. Even after the end of slavery, Jim Crow laws (a system of legal segregation first instituted in 1876 and remained in force until 1965) continued to treat African Americans as second class citizens, without basic civil rights (see Barnes, 1983 for further details). Mob violence of whites against Blacks, lynchings,[3] harassment, and intimidation were the order of the day. The *1964 Civil Rights Act* was a significant step in the elimination of formal segregation, but the 'doctrine of racial inferiority' supported the continued violence and intimidation of Blacks. Although blatant white racism no longer is tolerated, American society continues to be: "Two nations: Black and white, separate, hostile, unequal" as the telling title of an insightful work on racism in the United States (Hacker, 1992) describes it. It is true that, compared to 100, or even 30 years ago, Black Americans have made considerable progress on their long voyage to economic, educational and political

---

et al., 2001). The categories used by the US Bureau of the Census are: (1) American Indian or Alaska Native, (2) Asian, (3) Black or African American, (4) Hispanic or Latino, (5) Native Hawaiian or Other Pacific Islander, and (6) White.

2 For example, K. R. Johnson (2004), *The 'Huddled Masses Myth': Immigration and Civil Rights*, Philadelphia, PA: Temple University Press.

3 The greatest number of Black lynchings – 1,111 – occurred during the 1890s (Flowers, 1996: 9).

equality with their white counterparts. However, Blacks in the United States continue to experience a much lower quality of life (measured in terms of income, education, health, housing, and personal safety) than white Americans.

There is no doubt that both Native Americans and African Americans have a long and painful history of victimization and exclusion – both institutionally and individually. They are not the only ethnic minority groups who have suffered discriminatory treatment in the United States, however. The United States Census recognizes a third racial category of 'Asian Americans', including people from the Far East, Southeast Asia, or the Indian Subcontinent. This category includes not only Japanese and Chinese and Koreans, but also Indonesians and Indians along with Burmese and Thais, Filipinos and Pakistanis – a strange mixture of racial, national and cultural identities that together constitute 4.21 per cent of the American population. Some Asian American groups are doing extremely well, both socially and economically (e.g., the Japanese and Koreans), whereas others (some Chinese and Filipinos) barely are able to survive economically. This reinforces the point that it is not very useful to think in very broad ethnic or racial categories, for some groups of Asian descent are much more successful than white Americans. In this case, it is only appearance or skin color which designates this group as a visible minority. This fact notwithstanding, Asians living in the United States have been subject to legal discrimination, police harassment and hate crimes (Flowers, 1996; Hacker, 1992; Mann 1993; Marshall 1997) – both in the past and present.

Latinos or Hispanics are the fastest growing ethnic minority group in the United States. The category of Hispanics (or Latinos) includes a wide variety of Spanish-speaking groups: people of Mexican heritage, Puerto Ricans, Cubans, people from Central or South America; a mixture of long-term inhabitants of the US and newcomers, Latino immigrants and refugees, and their descendants (Parrillo, 1996: 131). In 2000, about 35 million people in the United States were Hispanic that is 12.5 per cent of the United States population. Most of the research and political interest has focused on Mexican-Americans. According to the 2000 United States census, there are almost 21 million people from Mexican origin living in the United States. Mexican immigrants account for the largest proportion of both legal and undocumented inhabitants; the United States government has recently stepped up its efforts to curb the influx from eager workers from "South of the border". These people who are willing to work for substandard wages are viewed as taking away jobs from Americans and, in general, as a drain on social services (a claim that is not supported by available evidence). Most vulnerable are those immigrants who have come to this country without proper documentation, making them subject to exploitation, fearful of the police and unlikely to publicly challenge their substandard treatment. Some national media are focusing relentlessly on undocumented workers from Mexico (for example, CNN's Lou Dobbs) and citizens' vigilante groups have made it their mission to patrol the borders with Mexico.[4] Since the early beginning of Mexican immigration into the United States, this group has been the target of

---

4 "Citizen border patrols" have sprung up around the country, influenced by the Minuteman Project, a para-militairy effort to seal the Arizona border. The Minuteman Project is a citizens' "Vigilance Operation monitoring immigration, business and

over surveillance, prejudice and discrimination. Paralleling the experiences of black Americans, Hispanics as a group are relatively powerless, they have been (or are) seen as 'different' often threatening, problematic, or deviant; they have been subject to discriminatory laws and regulations, prejudice and negative stereotyping; the focus of public fear and violence, and targets of political campaigns. On average, Hispanics living in the US are less educated, more likely to be unemployed, poorer, and less healthy than the non-Hispanic population.[5] Blacks, Hispanics, Asians and American Indians all have a relatively long history in the United States. However, the terrorist acts in the United States on 11 September 2001 proved a watershed event in minority group relations in the United States: hostility towards Muslims and Arabs increased (Helly, 2004: 24). Not only did the plane hijackings shatter the confidence and sense of invulnerability of the American population, it also led to the discovery of a 'new' minority group: Arabs or people from Middle-eastern descent.[6] Census 2000 data showed that less than 0.5 per cent of the American population self-identified as having Arab Ancestry. The social significance of being from Arab or Middle-eastern descent or Muslim has changed drastically since 9/11, with significant consequences for racist victimization (see for example, Welch, 2006).

The premise of this chapter is that a racist society produces racist violence and victimization. The United States' very complex immigrant heritage, together with its long and checkered race relations history, "makes this society a uniquely valuable source of insight and experience with regard to the volatile mixture of race, ethnicity, nationality, and immigrant status" (Marshall, 1997: xi). The majority of the huge amount of writings and experience in this area seems to agree on one basic point: the United States remains – at heart – a biased and racist society. This is not to deny that great strides have been made since the early settlers systematically exploited and killed masses of the original inhabitants of this nation (see Nielsen and Silverman, 1996).

Racism in the United States has become much less overt and blatant, and racist practices often are now against the law. But a society cannot erase its history overnight. Once racism becomes embedded in society, it tends to infect all of its people and institutions; it shapes a particular worldview handed down from

---

government"; it started in Arizona but now has chapters all over the United States (see www.minutemanproject.com)

5 www.census.gov/prod/2003pubs.p70-91.pdf and www.access.gpo.gov/eop/ca/pdfs/ch1/pdf

6 The US Office of Management and Budget is involved in ongoing research on the proper definition of an Arab ethnic category. Currently, the term 'Arab' is used to refer to the Arab-ancestry population in the United States (e.g., Lebanese, Egyptian, Syrian, Palestinian, Jordanian, Moroccan, Iraque or 'other Arab'). Ancestry refers to ethnic origin, descent, roots, heritage, or place of birth of the person or the person's ancestors. Although religious affiliation can be a component of identity, neither the ancestry question nor any other question on the 2000 census was designed to collect information about religion (Census 2000 Special Reports, We the people of Arab ancestry in the United States, issued March 2005 by Angela Brittingham and G. Patricia de la Cruz, US Department of Commerce, Economics and Statistics Administration, US Census Bureau). It should be noted that often religion (i.e., Muslim) is used interchangeably with ancestry (i.e., Middle-eastern or Arab).

generation to generation A racist society does not only encourage victimization of racial and/or ethnic minorities by the majority groups, it also shapes prejudice, stereotyping and hatred of the dominant (white) group among the minority groups. This prejudice and bias also fuels hatred among minority groups against other minorities. In today's America, a culture of racism and prejudice – fueled by fierce competition for scarce resources – pits different racial and ethnic minority groups against each other: Black gangs against Hispanic gangs in Los Angeles (Archibold, 2007), White and Mexican-American parents against busing their kids to schools in poor Black neighborhoods in Chicago (Wilson and Taub, 2007), or Black rioters who target Korean shops during the 1992 Rodney King riots in LA, to mention but a few examples.

"Racist Victimization": Hate Crime or Broader Than That?

In the Introduction of this volume, the meaning of 'racist' victimization has already been discussed in depth. We want to reiterate a few points. As has been recognized by different authors, the particular label used to refer to 'racist victimization' is culture-specific: Sometimes the term of xenophobic violence or ethno-violence is used, others use right-wing extremism and – in the United States – the most common term is 'hate crime' or 'bias crime'.[7] Following the distinguished Norwegian researcher on racist violence Tore Bjorgo (2003: 785), the essence of the definition of 'racist victimization' is that "victims are selected because of their ethnic, racial, religious, cultural or national origin. These victims are attacked not in their capacities as individuals, but as representatives of such minority groups". Racist victimization – whether it is referred to as xenophobic violence, ethno-violence, right-wing extremism, hate crime or bias crime – may take many different forms. For example, it may be the action of one isolated individual (e.g., the yelling of a racial slur during a sexual assault by a white man on a Black female), of a group of individuals (i.e., a dozen Black youngsters who chase a white "trespasser" out of their neighborhood), or the activities of an organized collectivity (such as a cross-burning or lynching by the Ku Klux Klan, or a Latino gang that selects a Black – any Black – victim to shoot in revenge for an assault by a Black gang on one of their fellow gang members). Students of racist violence, xenophobic violence, hate crime or right-wing extremist violence are, by definition, interested in the *motives* of the *perpetrators* (after all, there is a need for identification of a racist motive in order for something to qualify as a 'hate crime'). Although the motives of the perpetrator(s) are important, current research and writings in this field tends to focus mainly on the effects of violence and harassment on *victims*; it is recognized that: "[v]ictimization may involve both physical injuries to the body and a mental violation of the person's integrity" (Bjorgo, 2003: 789). In his discussion of British research, Bjorgo (2003: 789) states that the victimological perspective on racist victimization is often linked with a critical analysis of government and police response to racist violence. There is no doubt

---

7 In the US, the label 'hate crime' or 'bias crime' is not restricted only to criminal acts against various ethnic minorities, but is also applied to violence against homosexuals, women and religious minorities.

that the same observation applies to the United States, where much research focuses on the relationship between the police and minority populations in general. As the remainder of this chapter will show, American studies (as well as British studies – also, see Chapter 3 in this volume) "have concluded that racism within the police is very much part of the problem of violent racism" (Bjorgo, 2003: 790).

Our interpretation is broader than the FBI's (1999) working definition which is limited to behavior that is *criminal*: "A hate crime, also known as a bias crime, is a criminal offense committed against a person, property, or society which is motivated, in whole or in part, by the offender's bias against a race, religion, disability, sexual orientation, or ethnicity/national origin" (McDevitt and Balboni, 2000: 2). Most commonly, there is a rather narrow interpretation of racist victimization, that is, there has to be an explicit and manifest racial motive, *and* there has to be physical injury done to the victim. Racist victimization often is the acting out of feelings of individual prejudice and hatred, but it may also be a reflection of larger institutionalized forms of discrimination where racial minorities are systematically singled out for differential treatment. A case in point is racial profiling (discussed below). Thus, a case may be made to view all actions that systematically disadvantage – intentional or not – minority groups as examples of racist victimization. Consistent with the broader interpretation of 'racist victimization', in this chapter we will include racially motivated misbehavior by law enforcement. This means not only violent episodes (police brutality and use of deadly force by police), but also the 'less dramatic forms of harassment experienced on a more frequent basis by many minority members" (Bjorgo, 2003: 790), such as racial profiling, and over-and under policing of minority neighborhoods.

US Legislation on Hate Crime

"What is relatively new about hate crime is not its occurrence, but its widespread recognition and codification into law" (Shively, 2005: 2), so states a comprehensive summary and analysis of literature and legislation addressing hate crime in the United States.[8] Legal responses to racially motivated violence are not new. In the early 20th century numerous states adopted statutes aimed at preventing specific activities of racist organizations such as the Ku Klux Klan such as vandalism and the wearing of masks or hoods (see Levin, 2001). The date of the passage of the first contemporary hate crime statute is debatable, since some of the state civil rights statutes passed in the 1960s and 1970s could be regarded as hate crime laws (Shively, 2005: i). There appears to be some agreement, however, that the first state hate crime statutes were passed in 1981 (Shively, 2005: i).

Bias-motivated crimes are not separate offenses, but they acknowledge a specific motive for a crime (e.g., race, religion, sexual orientation, ethnicity, national origin, disability, with race representing the largest number of single-based bias-motivated offences according to FBI statistics, see next section below); this motivation is

---

8 Michael Shively, Study of Literature and Legislation on Hate Crime in America, June 2005, National Institute of Justice and Abt. Associates. This section draws heavily from this review.

considered more disruptive and harmful to society (Levin and McDevitt, 1993). It is the increased awareness of and discussion about the impact of such crimes that has prompted American federal and state legislation that distinguishes bias crime from other crimes (McDevitt and Balboni, 2000: 2).

Since the Washington and Oregon legislatures first passed hate crime statutes in 1981, up to 47 states (including the District of Columbia) have passed at least one piece of legislation addressing hate or bias motivated crime in some way (Anti-Defamation League, 2005, cited in Shively, 2005: 2, footnote 1).[9] In the United States, 'bias' crime is not limited to race or ethnicity, but also includes religion, sexual orientation, or gender. Not surprisingly, then, current debates on hate crime law include the set of traits covered (Shively, 2005). The majority of states have specific statutory provisions based on race, religion, and ethnicity; 32 protect sexual orientation; 27 gender; and 32 disability. Additionally, some states have enacted legislation requiring data collection, mandating law enforcement training, prohibiting paramilitary training, and providing for compensation to victims (ADL, 2005).

Federal hate crime legislation was introduced and debated as early as 1985, and the first federal statute, the *Hate Crime Statistics Act*, was passed in 1990 (see also next section). This has been followed by several other pieces of federal legislation (e.g., *Hate Crime Sentencing Enhancement Act* of 1992, *Violence Against Women Act* of 1998, *Church Arson Prevention Act* of 1994 and the *Violent Crime Control and Law Enforcement Act* of 1994).

Legislative responses to hate crimes have generally taken one of two tracks. Some have established an additional category of offence specifying that an existing criminal act was committed out of hatred. Others permit a sentencing enhancement for existing criminal offenses that can be shown to have been committed based in part on hatred toward a particular group. In both cases, statutes do not criminalize thoughts, beliefs, or legal forms of expression. Also in play are the application of civil remedies for hate crimes, and whether "hate speech" should be considered a criminal offence or should be protected as political speech under the First Amendment (see section on legal, social and political reaction to racist victimization later in this chapter).

State and federal hate crime legislation was critical in transforming both legal and popular understanding of bias motivated crime from a vague and controversial concept to a focused legal practice (Phillips and Grattet, 2000). Subsequent court decisions affirming the constitutionality of hate crime legislation have served to further institutionalize the concept of enhanced punishment for acts motivated by bias. The collection of statistics on the prevalence of bias motivated crimes has

---

9 The exact number of states with such laws is subject to interpretation, depending on what one considers a hate crime law. For example, by the ADL's count, all but one state had some form of hate crime statute through 2003. Forty-seven states (including the District of Columbia in this count) have criminal penalties for bias or hate motivated violence. Of the remaining four states, three have some other statutory provisions (such as civil remedies for offenses, or criminalization of institutional vandalism) linked to hate or bias motivation. Only Wyoming is devoid of any identified hate or bias related statute. However, applying a more stringent definition of hate crime requiring three criteria to be met, Jenness and Grattet (2001) regard only 41 states as having a hate crime statute (Shively, 2005, footnote 1: 2).

proved critically important to increasing public awareness and acceptance of hate crime as an important social problem.

Hate Crime Reporting and Statistics

In addition to the rapid spread of federal and state hate crime legislation over the past 20 years, the government also has heavily invested in data collection programs. In 1992 the United States, coordinated through the Department of Justice, began to collect and report on an annual basis hate crime statistics. The data collection represents a joint effort between the FBI and law enforcement agencies throughout the United States. In fact, the number two priority in the FBI's Civil Rights Program is the investigation of hate crimes.

Information about the character and prevalence of hate crime victimization in the United States comes from two primary sources: law enforcement reports of bias motivated crime incidents and self-reported hate crime victimization – both approaches have been funded by the United States government. Though each of these sources has strengths and weaknesses that limit the type of information they provide, they have significantly increased our knowledge about hate crime in the United States over the past two decades.

Prior to 1991, there were no "official" national hate crime data from which to form a picture of the size and shape of the problem, nor to observe trends (Shively, 2005). The *Federal Hate Crime Statistics Act* (HCSA) passed in 1990 (and amended in 1994 and 1996) charged the Attorney General to acquire data about crimes that exhibit prejudice based on race, religion, sexual orientation or ethnicity. The *Violent Crime Control and Law Enforcement Act* of 1994 expanded coverage of the HCSA to include crimes based on disability. Utilizing the FBI's existing Uniform Crime Reporting (UCR) Program, local, county, and state law enforcement agencies began to submit annual information about hate crime incidents occurring in their jurisdictions to the FBI. Incorporating the new hate crime data collection effort into the UCR program helped streamline data collection as the UCR program has been an accepted method for collecting crime data collection for over 70 years.

Today more than 17,000 local, county, and state law enforcement agencies participate in the UCR program. In addition to the national hate crime data collection program by the FBI, 24 states have adopted some type of mandatory hate crime reporting programs (ADL, 2005).[10] Though national hate crime data utilizing official police records allow for the collection of standardized information on hate motivated incidents, these statistics are limited to only those incidents that are known to the police. Many victims may not report a hate motivated crime to the police, particularly members of groups who have experienced historically negative interactions with law enforcement (Balboni and McDevitt, 2001).

In addition to hate crime data gathered from law enforcement agencies, the federal government, through the Bureau of Justice Statistics (BJS) has begun

---

10 By the end of the 1990s, as many as half of local law enforcement jurisdictions were not complying with the Act (McDevitt et al., 2000).

to collect data on the number of individuals who believe they were victims of a crime which was motivated by bias, whether or not the hate crime is reported to the police. Questions about hate crime victimization were incorporated into the National Crime Victimization Survey (NCVS) in 2000. The NCVS is an annual survey of approximately 49,000 households compromising approximately 100,000 persons nationwide which asks a variety of questions about their experiences with crime. The integration of hate crime questions into the NCVS provides the first mechanism for nationwide estimation of hate crime victimization based on self-reporting, rather than police reports. Self-report surveys of hate crime victimization have the potential to tap into victimization that is not identified by the police, but since hate crime is a rare event surveys of the general population may not reach a representative number of hate crime victims. Additionally, victims may not be able to accurately identify whether or not the crime they experienced was motivated by bias.

In addition to the police and self-report data collected by federal government agencies, some data are also generated by national advocacy organizations, such as the Anti-Defamation League and Southern Poverty Law Center, and state human rights commissions. The statistics gathered from these sources are in many cases different than those reported in the national hate crime statistics due to inconsistencies in reporting practices and definitions of hate crime but provide alternative estimates of the prevalence and nature of hate crime victimization (Shively, 2005). There is, of course, a large volume of anecdotal evidence on hate crime in the United States, including incidents covered by local and national media.[11]

Academic researchers have also begun to focus on bias crimes – both in terms of estimating its prevalence as well as in terms of developing theoretical explanations (see, for example, Welch, 2006). [It should be noted that the United States has a long history of academic research and theorizing on racism, violence, discrimination and prejudice, but the term 'hate crime' has only fairly recently become part of the American scholarly discourse.] Individual study estimates have varied widely depending on sampling and how hate crime was operationally defined (for more details, see Shively, 2005).

Extent and Nature of Racial Criminal Victimization (Hate Crime) in the United States

Hate crime statistics from the FBI provide a critical measure of the prevalence and distribution of hate crimes throughout the county.[12] Between 1995 and 2005, the FBI

---

11 One of the most discussed and most publicized hate crime in recent US history was the death of Matthew Sheppard, the result of anti-gay violence. A more recent case in the *Los Angeles Times* focuses on a court case where three white women were beaten by a group of black youth in Long Beach during Halloween ("Victims speak out in Long Beach Hate-Crime case"). Allegedly, racial slurs ("I hate....white people") were heard during the attack (http://www/latimes/com/news/printedition/california/la-me-lbhate 1 February 2007).

12 Despite the growth in the total number of agencies participating in the national hate crime reporting program, many law enforcement agencies from major cities report no hate crimes or surprisingly low numbers of hate crimes. Nearly 85% of participating agencies

reports the total number of hate motivated crimes reported in the national statistics remained relatively constant ranging from a low of 7,160 incidents (2005) to highs of 9,792 incidents (1999) and 9,721 incidents (2001) (see Graph 8.1).

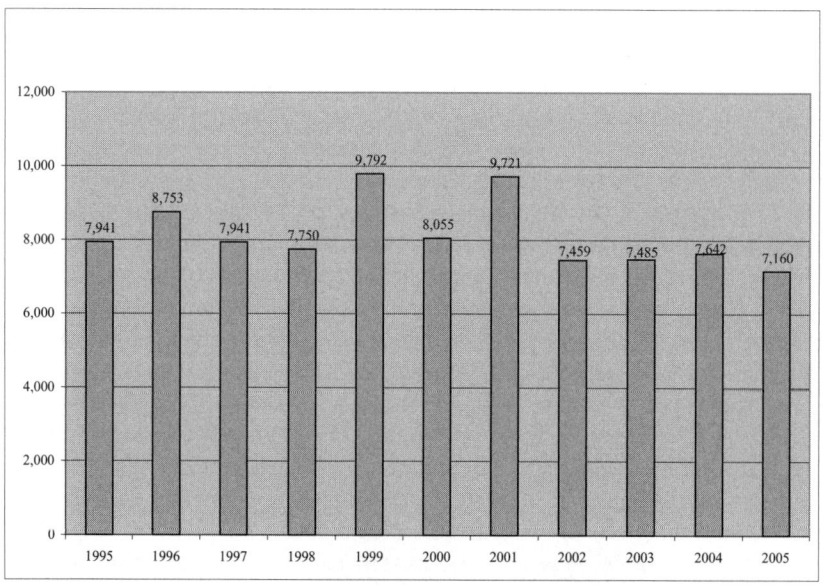

Graph 8.1 Total hate crime incidents by year, 1995–2005
Source: FBI (2006)

In addition to the prevalence of hate crime incidents, the national hate crime statistics provide useful information about the type of underlying crime that has been reported. In 2005, 30 per cent of all hate crime victimizations involved destruction of property or vandalism, 30 per cent involved actions intended to intimidate the victim, 18 per cent were simple assaults, and 13 per cent aggravated assaults (FBI, 2006).[13] These figures indicate that in 2005 almost one-half of all hate crimes reported nationally involved attempts to intimidate or physically harm the victim.

The Bureau of Justice Statistics estimates that between 2000 and 2003, 191,000 incidents of hate crime have occurred annually. They report that approximately 3 per cent of all violent crimes measured by the NCVS were motivated by bias

---

report no hate incidents in the most recent FBI report. While reporting no hate incidents may accurately reflect the number of hate crimes in many jurisdictions, scholars suggest that some agencies, particularly in larger, more diverse communities, are not fully and accurately collecting information on and reporting hate crime (McDevitt et al., 2003).

13 The remaining 7% of crimes were made up of 2% robbery, 2% burglary, 2% larceny-theft, 1% arson, and less than 1% homicide, rape and other crimes combined (percentages are rounded).

and 1 out of every 500 property crimes was a hate crime (BJS, 2005). The NCVS survey indicates that only 44 per cent of hate crime victims reported the crime to the police – suggesting the FBI statistics may greatly underestimate the total number of individuals victimized by hate crimes. Victims of hate crime report being threatened verbally or assaulted in over half of the hate motivated incidents.

According to 2005 hate crime statistics data as collected by the UCR Program of the FBI, over half (52 per cent) of all hate incidents are racially motivated (see Graph 8.2).

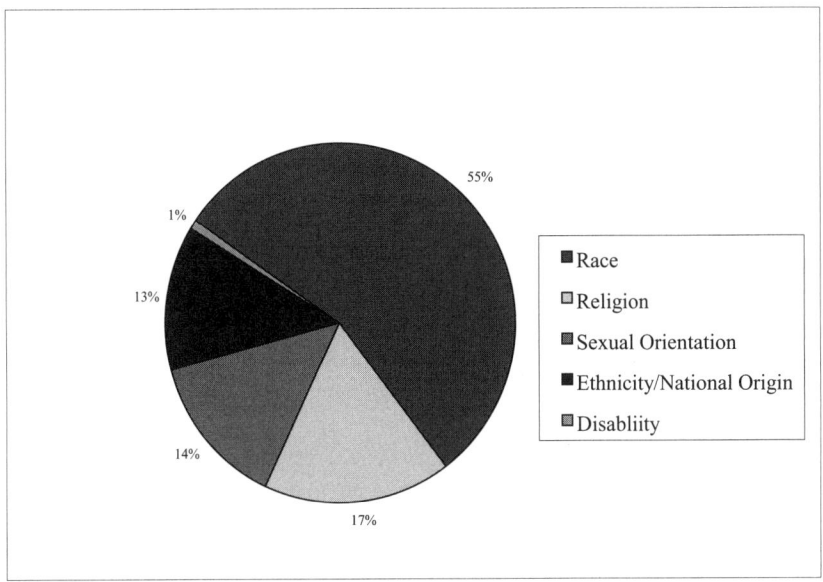

Graph 8.2 Reported hate incidents according to motivation 2005 UCR count and per cent of total incidents
Source: FBI (2006)

When incidents of ethnicity and nationality based hatred (13 per cent) are included, the figure rises to 65 per cent (FBI, 2006). Victims responding to the NCVS similarly reported that race was the primary perceived offender motivation. In addition to believing that a crime was motivated by bias against their own personal characteristics, nearly 33 per cent of hate crime victims perceived that their association with someone of a different race, for example a multiracial couple, was the motivation for their victimization. The FBI data from 2005 indicates that 68 per cent of racially motivated hate crimes were motivated by anti-Black bias, 20 per cent were motivated by anti-white bias, 5 per cent were motivated by anti-Asian bias, 2 per cent were motivated by anti-American Indian bias and 5 per cent were motivated by biases against multi-racial individuals (FBI, 2006).

Interestingly, the NCVS did not find significant differences in the vulnerability of victims by race or ethnic group. Whites reported being victimized at a rate of 0.9 per 1,000, Blacks at 0.7 per 1,000 and Hispanics at 0.9 per 1,000. Taken together the NCVS and FBI data suggest that though racial groups may not vary in their experiences of hate crime, white victims are less likely to report to the police or police are less likely to identify whites as victims of crime incidents motivated by bias.

State hate crime reports mirror the national findings, particularly the national police incident data. For example, in California between 1996 and 2005 hate crimes motivated by anti-Black and anti-Hispanic sentiment have consistently been the most common bias motivation categories across all hate crimes (California Department of Justice, 2006). Similarly, in Tennessee between 2000 and 2003 anti-Black motivated crime has steadily remained the most common form of hate crime representing over 23 per cent of all reported hate crime incidents (Tennessee Bureau of Investigation, 2003).

Racially motivated hate crimes have a number of serious consequences for victims. According to the NCVS survey, hate crime victims are more likely to experience violence than other crime victims not associated with bias motivation. In addition to experiencing more violence, limited research on hate crime indicates racially motivated hate crime appears to increase the potential vulnerability expressed by victims. A study of college students conducted by Craig (1999) examined Black and white student reactions to portrayals of hate motivated assault, general assault, and non-violent control scenes. Black students rated the likelihood that they would find themselves in a situation such as the hate motivated assault significantly higher than White students did. Additionally, Blacks students disproportionately suggested that the victim of the hate crime should seek revenge. Hate crime, and racialized violence in particular, targets core identity issues. The unique effects of these crimes on victims and the broader community, who share a racial identity with hate crime victims increase the urgency in which societies must act to prevent and respond to hate crime.

As noted before, there are many forms of racist violence that are not included in formal studies and statistics. A front-page article in the *New York Times* with the headline "A City's violence feeds on Black-Hispanic rivalry" (17 January 2007) documents the wave of bias-related attacks and incidents in Los Angeles, springing from rivalries between Black and Latino gangs, especially in neighborhoods where the black population has been declining and the Latino population surging. This is a significant development in view of the fact that – historically – most of the violent street crime in the United States has been intra-racial (i.e., Blacks victimizing Blacks, Latinos victimizing Latinos).

While race has been the overwhelming motivation for hate crime over the past 10 years, the proportion of reported hate crimes based on religion has increased throughout this 10 year period (from about 10 per cent in 1995 to about 17 per cent in 2005, see Graph 8.3). The proportion of reported hate crimes based on ethnicity/national origin has remained virtually the same between 1995 and 2005 (about 12–13 per cent), but there have been some marked fluctuations in that time period, most notably in 2001 (22 per cent).

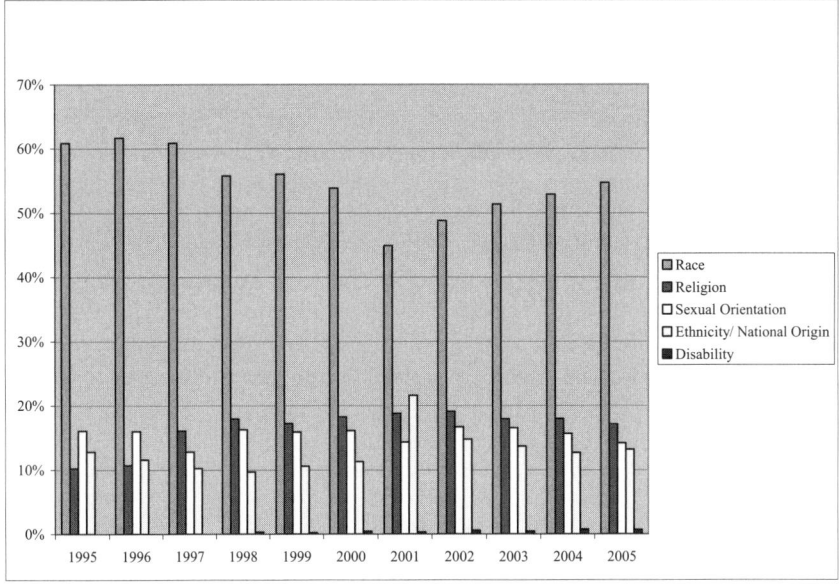

Graph 8.3 Hate crime by motivation
Source: FBI (2006)

Some suggest that this increase may be related to anti-Arab/Muslim sentiment following the events of 11 September 2001. The FBI hate crime data provide a breakdown of crimes motivated by religion as well as race. In 2001 there was a dramatic spike in the number of reported anti-Islamic hate crimes. Offences against this sector of the American society ranged from murder to assault, arson attacks, and attacks on places of worship. For example, in the first few weeks following 9/11, SAALT's (South Asian American Leaders of Tomorrow) surveys recorded over 100 attacks against Muslim places of worship and nearly 300 unprovoked assaults of Muslim. Furthermore, every city researched by the Human Rights Watch reported major increases in hate crimes directed towards people known or perceived to be of Arab/Muslim affiliation. Fortunately, since 2001, the incident rate of hate crimes against people of Islamic heritage has decreased but still remains significantly higher than pre-2001 levels. Similarly, California reported a surge of anti-Arab/Muslim or anti-Middle Eastern hate crimes against individuals and/or their property in 2001 which have decreased in each succeeding year (California Department of Justice, 2006).

Reports from advocacy groups such as the Arab American Anti-Discrimination Committee confirm with anecdotal information that reports of anti-Asian and anti-Arab harassment and intimidation have been on the rise since 2001. According to statistics gathered by the Council on American-Islamic Relations (CAIR), a national Muslim civil rights and advocacy group, as of February 2002 the number of hate crimes and 'anti-Muslim' incidents reported by American Muslims exceeded 1,700.

These ranged from public harassment and hate mail to bomb threats, death threats, physical assault, property damage and murder (Abdelkarim, 2003: 51).

In a recent publication, *Scapegoats of September 11th, Hate Crimes & State Crimes in the War on Terror*, Michael Welch (2006: 70) notes that reactions to the 9/11 attacks in the form of hate crimes and related hostilities have had an enduring impact on American society and its victims in particular through its accumulating negative effects on Muslims living in the United States. For example, the Council on American-Islamic Relations found that of the nearly 1,000 Muslim Americans surveyed 48 per cent felt that their lives had changed for the worse since 9/11, and 57 per cent reported experiencing "some acts of bias or discrimination, ranging from disparaging remarks for being Muslim to in some instances being victim of a hate crime" (Welch 2006: 70). Some scholars suggest that anti-immigration sentiment may exacerbate racially and ethnically motivated hate crime in the United States in the coming years, potentially broadening racial violence to include new immigrant groups (Perry, 2002).

Racial Profiling: Another Form of Racist Victimization?

The perceptions of individuals that they are stopped, searched and harassed by the police on the basis of their race is a complex problem facing police and communities they serve (Ramirez et al., 2000; Fridell et al., 2001). While the majority of police officers are hard-working public servants, who perform a dangerous job, the perception that some police officers are engaging in racial profiling threatens to create deep distrust between police and the public. In the late 1990s the American news media exploded with coverage of the problem of racial profiling. Allegations of bias became so common that the phenomenon was popularly described as "driving while Black" or "driving while brown" (Harris, 1999). Front-page news stories and editorials in both the national and local press illustrated that there were high social and individual costs associated with the perception that police profiled drivers based on their race. Racial profiling is generally understood as the practice of targeting or stopping a pedestrian or motor vehicle based primarily on the person's race, rather than any individualized suspicion. Although there have long been allegations of police targeting people of color, aggressive crime control strategies utilized by police in an effort to reduce crime rates heightened the perception that police may use traffic offenses as a pretext to conduct disproportionate numbers of roadside investigations of Black or Hispanic drivers and their vehicles. During the mid-1980's the Federal Drug Enforcement Agency developed a profile of drug couriers which included clues of drug trafficking such as signs of concealment in the vehicle, indications of fast, point-to-point driving, and certain behavioral cues. Named Operation Pipeline, DEA investigators trained local and state law enforcement to use the profile to determine whether or not drivers were suspicious. Information from investigators and participants in Operation Pipeline trainings suggest that the profile also included indications of race, age and gender characteristics of potential traffickers (Webb, 1999).

The perception that police engage in racial profiling when making decisions to stop individuals arises out of a long history of adversarial relationships between the police and disenfranchised communities. Conflicts between police and communities of color include police enforcement of Jim Crow segregation (see above); police participation in the suppression of the efforts to register black voters in the South; the Watts, Detroit, Newark, and other riots of the 1960s; the videotaped beating of Rodney King by officers of the Los Angles Police Department; and the shooting of an unarmed Black man, Amadou Diallo, by four New York City Police in 1999. Survey research on public attitudes towards the police has consistently shown that race is one of the strongest predictors of negative perceptions of police (Weitzer, 1999). For example, in a 1994 survey of police practices in Ohio, nearly half of all African American respondents indicated that they had been "hassled" by the police, compared to only 9 per cent of white respondents (Browning et al., 1994). National surveys indicate that a majority of Americans, regardless of race, believe that racial bias in police stops is a significant social problem. In US Gallup Polls from 1999, 2001 and 2003, almost 60 per cent of Americans surveyed believe that the practice of racial profiling is widespread. For African-American respondents, however, the perception that racial profiling is widespread actually increased from 77 per cent in 1999 to 85 per cent in 2003. Twenty-two per cent of Blacks reported that they had been unfairly treated by the police in the 30 days prior to the poll; the percentage reporting such unfair treatment increased from 15 per cent to 22 per cent between 1997 and 2003 (Ludwig, 2003).

Despite promises by federal officials to end the practice of racial profiling, including statement by President George W. Bush shortly after his taking office in 2000 decrying the use of profiles based on race, federal legislation such as the End *Racial Profiling Act* of 2004 which would allocate sufficient funds for its vigorous enforcement has yet to pass Congress. Even without federal legislation state and local law enforcement agencies have advanced a number of possible responses ranging from bans and policies to task forces and data collection. To date twenty-seven states have passed legislation banning the practice of racial profiling and in many cases creating systems of data collection and accountability to monitor biased policing.

In response to new data collection efforts by law enforcement, scholars have begun attempting to identify whether or not officers treat people differently in traffic stop contexts based on differences in immutable characteristics such as race. Recent studies of traffic policing in California (Cordner et al., 2000: Landsdowne, 2000), Ohio (Eck et al., 2004); Massachusetts (Farrell et al., 2004), and Missouri (Missouri Attorney General's Office, 2003) show that police stop African-Americans disproportionately, compared to whites according to the residential or driving population of a particular area. Other research examining the relationship between traffic stop demographics and roadway demographics based on observational methodologies has also found similar consistent disparities (Lamberth, 2003). While racial disparities in traffic stops can result from a number of factors that social scientists are just beginning to understand, bias on the part of an individual officer is one of several possible explanations for disparities in stops and searches. Continued vigilance to understand and address racially biased police practices is critical to law enforcement agencies committed to the principles of community policing. The growing concern about ethnic profiling (targeting Arabs and Middle Easterners) by law enforcement and government in the name of the war on terror is discussed in the next section.

Other Forms of Racist Victimization by Law Enforcement and the Government

The American system of criminal justice, including police, courts, and corrections, has historically showed extreme anti-Black bias. Although the most blatant forms of racial inequalities have been eliminated from the system, anti-Black (and anti-Hispanic) racism in the criminal justice system continues to exist in particular structural contexts. Institutional racism remains a reality in the American criminal justice system as our discussion of racial profiling has shown.[14] We already alluded to the tense relationship that exists between police and Blacks in the US. Many minority communities in America feel both over-policed and under-protected (Donziger, 1996: 160). Black Americans often feel verbally and physically harassed by the police; police protection in minority neighborhoods is viewed as worse than in white neighborhoods. Usually, the youngest and least experienced police officers are assigned to the most violent precincts – often with a primarily Black or Hispanic population. Police gang and drug sweeps in housing projects frequently involve blatant disregard for the residents' rights. Early studies have concluded that police officers were more likely to shoot and use excessive force when dealing with blacks; more recent research shows that the racial disparity in people shot and killed by police has declined (Walker, Spohn and Delone, 2000).

The problems related to policing racial minorities are likely to be exacerbated when communities contain large numbers of foreign-born minorities (Davis and Henderson, 2003: 565). Just as there are some well-known examples of police abuse of American-born Blacks (e.g., Rodney King), there also have been several well-publicized incidents of abuse by the police of immigrants. Two notorious allegations of police misconduct in New York City threw a national spotlight on police dealings with immigrants. In the 1997 Abner Louima case, New York police officers were accused (and convicted) of brutalizing a Haitian immigrant held at a Brooklyn precinct house. In the 1999 case of Amadou Diallo, four special unit New York police officers faced grand jury charges of second degree murder in the shooting of an unarmed West African immigrant. The two incidents tapped into deep-seated frustrations that immigrants and established minorities have harbored concerning their treatment at the hands of the police (Davis and Henderson, 2002: 565, cited in Marshall, 2007: 650).

Since 9/11, immigrant communities – particularly those with a large Arab-American population – have been particularly vulnerable to both legal and illegal discrimination and treatment by law enforcement. The events of 9/11 solidified the

---

14 In this chapter, we focus rather narrowly on ant-Black bias by police. We could expand this discussion to include the documented fact that offenders killing whites are more likely to receive the death penalty than those killing Blacks; that there is a proven anti-Black and anti-Hispanic bias in current drug legislation, and so on.

belief that recent immigrants and foreigners – particularly Muslims and Arabs – represent a major threat to US national security interests and to the democratic world order. After 9/11, law enforcement routinely has used ethnic profiling based on Muslim or Arabic background in several ethnic communities with a high population of Muslims Welch, 2006). The hostility towards Muslims in North America (and Europe) has increased tremendously since the terrorist acts on 9/11/2001 (Helly, 2004). In addition to claims of increased hate crimes and illegal discrimination, "Arab Americans have found themselves on the front lines of a host of derogations of civil liberties and new forms of discrimination in immigration policies and law enforcement" (Ibish, 2004: 26).

Welch (2006: 79) documents how: "acts of scapegoating and racial profiling" against Middle Easterners and South Asians in the wake of 9/11 have been committed by law enforcement officers, the National Guard, and transportation security personnel. He describes how the Department of Justice expanded its use of profiling in the war on terror by introducing a special registration program in December 2002. "The directive, intended to produce vital information about terrorist activity, was aimed at all non-immigrant male visitors who are over the age of 16 and entered the United States before 30 September 2002. Specifically, special registration applied to those males from countries that, according to the United States government, have links to terrorism, including 12 North African and Middle Eastern countries plus North Korea..." (Welch, 2006: 83). In additional to ethnic profiling targeting (perceived) Muslim groups, the United States government has been accused of other human rights violations because of arbitrary detention, abuse of detainees abusive interrogations and other procedural infractions involving Arabs and Middle Easterners (see also Ibish, 2004).

Legal, Social and Political Reaction to Racist Victimization in the United States

As we discussed in the introduction to this chapter, "racist victimization' (including hate crime) has existed in the United States virtually from its very birth as an independent nation. Still, its recognition as a genuine social problem is from a much more recent origin. The construction of 'racist victimization' as a recognized social problem in this country is the result of the complex – and by now intractable – interplay between scholars, human rights activists, civil rights groups, politicians, the media and other interest groups. It is, therefore, close to impossible to provide a clear and succinct, historically correct account of the legal, social and political reaction to racist victimization. At best, it is possible to make a few general observations.

First and foremost, in the United States, the primary response to racist victimization has been to criminalize it by enacting specific hate crime or bias crime statutes (see previous section). Rather than using the criminal law as the *ultimo remedium* (i.e., last resort), it is part of the American heritage to rely heavily on the criminal law to deal with social problems. As history has shown all too frequently, however, the criminal law is not a very effective, nor a very efficient tool to ensure conformity to unpopular rules. Not surprisingly, therefore, hate crime legislation – and its enforcement – has encountered many challenges and criticisms. An additional pitfall in the use of legal remedies in the fight against hate crime is that laws aiming to protect individuals from bias motivated crimes, and hate speech in particular, make visible a tension within American constitutional law between the State's interest in protecting an individuals right to free speech and expression (First Amendment) and equal protection of the law (Fourteenth Amendment). States have grappled with balancing the harms of speech or actions aimed at harming groups of people based on their personal characteristics such as race, ethnicity, national origin or religion with censorship of thought and expression. Since most hate crimes laws create sentence enhancements for bias motivation opponents claim the enhanced punishment targets the sentiment or expression rather than the act (e.g., assault, vandalism) which is already illegal. In Wisconsin v. Mitchell (1993) the US Supreme Court upheld the constitutionality of a state statue enhancing sentences for crimes motivated by racial bias, arguing that states have a compelling interest to protect individuals from attacks based on status characteristics such as race. The court's decision in Mitchell reaffirms the notion that racially motivated hate crimes at their core violate the principles of equality and equal protection of the law that are fundamental in American Constitutional law. Over the past decade courts have concluded that the majority of hate crime laws are in fact constitutional.

A second observation is that, more and more, American communities use a two-pronged approach, using both public education and enforcement. Supplementing criminal legislation, a considerable number of criminal justice initiatives are collaborative endeavors involving federal agencies (such as the ATF, FBI, or the Community Relations Service), large national non-governmental organizations (such as the Southern Poverty Law Center or the Anti-Defamation League), or state and community organizations (such as local advocacy groups). Most states and large cities have hate crime task forces involving coordination of effort across agencies and levels of government, and with independent community organizations (see Shively, 2005). A good example is California, a state with a very ethnically diverse population. The state of California uses a bottom-up as well as a top-down approach to combating hate crime. The governor established a bipartisan blue-ribbon commission to make recommendations, and established hate violence telephone hotlines to directly field public complaints. At the same time, there was very much a grass-root involvement in the anti-bias crime efforts of the state. The California Department of Fair Employment and Housing (DFEH), the state agency empowered to enforce civil hate crime violations and to provide remedies for victims of hate violence, has collaborated with the Fair Employment and Housing Commission and several Northern and Southern California bar associations to train attorneys to aid victims of hate violence.

Community-based organizations, religious groups, housing providers, and others who refer or assist hate violence victims attend training on the rights and remedies available under California and federal statutes. The Department distributes brochures that are written in several languages to help people understand their right to be free from hate violence and know what they can do if they are victimized [15] (see California Department of Fair Employment and Housing, 2003, for an example of a very thorough and informative public education pamphlet).

Thus, in the United States, the typical response to hate crime combines litigation, advocacy, education, and organizing. These comprehensive community strategies are supplemented, in some instances, by targeted efforts to teaching tolerance and appreciation for diversity and 'otherness' to groups considered to be especially high risk for getting involved in bias crime. The San Diego, California-based Pathways to Tolerance program is such an intensive intervention program for youth and young adults which uses a psycho-educational format to teach tolerance to youth and young adults who are referred by the probation department or Juvenile Court. The main goal of Pathways to Tolerance is to decrease participants' risk of committing a hate crime by increasing the participants' tolerance of those who are different. This change should be demonstrated through attitudes and behaviors (Misch et al., 2004). The success of this twelve-week group therapy program has not been clearly demonstrated, however. This leads to another point: there are very few well-designed evaluations of the various programs. Although there is a considerable body of work on "best practices" and many recommendations for how the criminal justice system can more effectively address, prevent, and respond to hate crime (see Shively, 2005 for a listing), dealing with racist violence remains more an art than a science at this point in time.

A comment needs to be made with regard to the role of the media. As we all know, the media play a crucial role in the 'claims-making' process involved in defining particular behaviors as 'problems' and worthy of further attention, be it political, public, or legal. Racism remains a somewhat taboo and certainly sensitive topic in the American mainstream media. Not all racist victimization incidents are made equal. The incident in LA involving the beating of three white girls by a group of Black youngsters on Halloween night (31 October 2006), for example, only received attention in the nation's leading newspaper, the New York Times, on December 3, 2006, several weeks after it happened One may only speculate about the reason for this delayed response; once possibility may be that 'reverse' racism was involved: 'liberal' media such as the New York Times would rather not report on anti-white violence (see http://www.laweekly.com/news/news/long-beach-hate-crime/15346/?page=2).

Although not flawless, the United States has a strong democratic tradition where human and civil rights activists, victim groups, religious leaders, social commentators, and local and national politicians are not afraid to voice their concerns about racialized violence and victimization. Were these voices rather timid and rare in the not too distant past, currently there is a very vocal and outspoken outcry against racist and ethnic violence. After 9/11, the national discourse has shifted to focus on the war on terror, anti-immigrant sentiments, prejudice and ethnic hatred. Political rhetoric is increasingly challenged by critical scholars who provide convincing arguments that

---

15 Informational materials, developed in collaboration with the State VictimCompensation and Government Claims Board (VCGCB), are available in English, Arabic, Bengali, Farsi, Gujarati, Hindi, Punjabi, Sinhalese, and Urdu. For more information, see www.dfha.ca.gov.

the "Bush administration's response to 9/11 was an extension of racialized patterns of fear mobilizing and scapegoating that have deformed American democracy long before that terrible day" (Simon, comment on cover of Welch, 2006).

Conclusion: Speculations about likely Future Developments

America is an immigration country, yet, at the same time, America is also a country with a strong nativist tradition.[16] The belief that 'original' Americans are superior and better than other 'newcomers' (no matter how long they have been in this country) has become very much engrained. This ideology has supported different forms of 'anti-immigration' policies throughout history (for example, restricting immigrants from China through the *Chinese Exclusion Act* of 1882). The anti-immigration attitude has tended to be directed to people of color, and from non-western cultures. Because of the events of 9/11, this latent anti-immigrant sentiment (against selected 'different' categories of newcomers) has been bolstered by a very strong new argument: the war on terror. The war on terror targets Arab and/or Muslim groups – the government – sanctioned differential treatment of these groups fortifies the prejudices extant in many Americans concerning outsiders. By making such practices routine and 'normal', demonization of Arab/Muslims in the United States becomes normal and acceptable; after all, these are dangerous people potentially out to destroy the US, or so it is said. Welch (2006) paints a convincing account of how the broader American culture enables the targeting of Middle Easterners and Muslims for individual and institutionalized victimization. Hate crime is a social practice "embedded in wider patterns of oppression and discrimination" (Welch, 2006: 63). Structural exclusion and cultural imaging characterize Arabs and Muslims in post 9/11 America, but the other minorities discussed in this chapter – Blacks, Hispanics, or American Indians – also continue to be systematically marginalized, making them vulnerable targets – and perpetrators – of racial violence.

American's distant and not-so-distant history of exclusion and differential treatment of ethnic and racial minority groups provides a very fertile soil for the continuing expression of hate crimes. Using people's race or ethnicity as a shorthand way of categorizing them as 'good' or 'bad' is as American as apple pie. Add to this mixture the reality of stark economic inequalities, the existence of many neighborhoods of concentrated disadvantage (often with sharp racial/ethnic divisions), the *de facto* racial and ethnic segregation in many cities, and the growing sense of feeling besieged by the outside world, this does not bode well for the future. That is the bad news. There is also some good news. That is, American society is also very resilient, open-minded, and humane at heart. As we have seen, there is a strong coalition of forces working to eliminate racist practices and violence; the chorus of voices critical of racism, scape-goating, and exclusion is becoming stronger (see, for

---

16 There is an extensive literature on the topic of 'nativism'. See, for example, Dale T. Knobel, America for the Americans: The Nativist Movement in the United States. New York, 1996; Juan F. Perea (ed.), Immigrants Out! The New Nativism and the Anti-immigrant Impulse in the United States. New York, 1997.

example, Lee, 2002). The pendulum is bound to swing back in the direction of more tolerance, rationality, compassion, and respect for equality and human rights.

Almost since its very foundation, it has been believed that the United States is a unique country, and that it in crucial ways is different and distinct from other Western countries (Shafter, 1991). Outsiders tend to view the United States as 'exceptional' – both positively (because of the availability of material wealth, opportunities for individual advancement, investments in science and technology) *and* negatively (because of its high crime rate, high proportion of teenage mothers, and stark economic inequality, to mention but a few examples). Indeed, for several decades, many (mostly Western European) observers used the United States as a deplorable example of a country divided by racism and exclusionary treatment of selected ethnic minority groups and newcomers. Unfortunately, the United States can no longer be used as an exceptional case when it comes to racism and bias crime: as the other chapters in this book show, racism and hate crime have become global phenomena. All we can hope for is that tolerance, rationality, compassion, and respect for equality and human rights similarly will soon be a global reality as well.

References

Abdelkarim, R. (2003). Surge in hate crimes followed by official U.S. targeting of Muslim, Arab men. *The Washington Report on Middle East Affairs*, April, 51–52.

Archibold, R.C. (2007). A city's violence feeds on Black-Hispanic rivalry. *The New York Times*, 17 January.

Anti-Defamation League (ADL) (2005). *Anti Defamation League state hate crime statutory provisions*. Available online at: http://www.adl.org/learn/hate_crime_laws/state_hate_crime_statutory_provisions_chart.pdf. accessed on 1 December 2005.

Balboni, J. and McDevitt, J. (2001). Hate crime reporting: Understanding police officer perceptions and the role of the victim. *Justice Research and Policy*, 3(1): 1-27.

Barnes, C.A. (1983). *Journey from Jim Crow: The Desegregation of Southern Transit* Columbia University Press.

Bjorgo, T. (2003). Violence against ethnic and religious minorities. In W. Heitmeyer and Hagan. J. (eds.) *International Handbook of Violence Research* (pp.785-800). Dordrecht/Boston/London: Kluwer Academic Publishers.

Browning, S., Cullen, F., Cao, L., Kopache, R. and Stevenson, T. (1994). Race and getting hassled by the police: A research note. *Police Studies*, 17: 1-11.

Bureau of Justice Statistics (2005). *Criminal Victimization, 2005*. Washington D.C.

California Department of Fair Employment and Housing (2003). *Responding to Hate: Rights, Remedies, and Prevention Strategies*.

California Department of Justice. (2006). *Hate Crimes in California 2005*. Sacramento, Ca.: Author. Cordner, G., Williams, B. and Zuniga, M. (2001) *Vehicle Stop Study: Final Report*. San Diego, Ca.: San Diego Police Department.

Craig, K. M. (1999). Retaliation, Fear, or Rage: an Investigation of African American and White Reactions to Racist Hate Crimes. *Journal of Interpersonal Violence*, 14(2), 138-151.

Davis, R. C. and Henderson, N. J. (2003). Willingness to report crimes: The role of ethnic group membership and community efficacy. *Crime and Delinquency* 49 (4): 564-80.

Donziger, S. A. (ed.). (1996). *The Real War on Crime: The Report of the National Criminal Justice Commission*. New York: Harper Perennial.

Eck, J., Liu, L., Growette Bostaph, L. (2003). *Police vehicle stops in Cincinnati: July 1 – December 31, 2001*. Available online at: http://www.cincinnati-oh.gov/police/downloads/police_pdf6937.pdf, accessed on 15 February 2007.

Farrell, A., McDevitt, J., Bailey, L., Andresen, C., and Pierce, E. (2004). *Massachusetts Racial and Gender Profiling Study*, Institute on Race and Justice, Report to Massachusetts Executive Office of Public Safety.

Federal Bureau of Investigation (FBI) (2006). *Hate Crime Statistics, 2004*, Washington, DC: US Department of Justice.

Federal Bureau of Investigation (FBI) (2005). *Crime in the United States, 2004*, Washington, DC: US Department of Justice.

Finkelman, Paul (ed.) (1992). *Lynching, Racial Violence, and the Law*. New York: Garland Press.

Flowers, R. B. (1990). *Minorities and Criminality*. New York: Praeger.

Fridell, L. Lunney, B., Diamond, D., and Feagin, J. R. (2000). Racist America: Roots, current realities, and Kubu. (2001). *Racially Biased Policing: A Principled Response*. Washington D.C.: Police Executive Research Forum.Future Reparations. Routledge (UK).

Hacker, A. (1992). *Two Nations: Black and White, Separate, Hostile, Unequal*. New York: Ballantine.

Harris, D. (1999). *Racial Profiling on our Nation's Highways: An American Civil Liberties Special Report.*

Helly, D. (2004). Are Muslims discriminated against in Canada since September 2001? *Canadian Ethnic Studies*, XXXVI (1), 24-47.

Ibish, H. (2004). Acts of evil: An analysis of Hate Crime Reports, *Covert Action Quarterly*, 77 (Fall), 26-29.

Kennedy, R. (1997). *Race, Crime, and the Law*. New York, Vintage.

Lamberth, J. (2003). *Racial profiling study and services: A Multi-jurisdictional Assessment of Traffic Enforcement and Data Collection in Kansas*. Washington, D.C: Police Foundation.

Landsdowne, W. (2000). *San Jose Vehicle Stop Demographic Study*. San Jose, CA: San Jose Police Department.

Lee, K. S. (2002). Building intergroup relations after September 11. *Analyses of Social Issues and Public Policy*, pp.131-141.

Levin, B. Extremism and the Constitution: How American's Legal Evolution Affects the Response to Extremism. *American Behavioral Scientist*, 45(4): 714-755.

Levin, J., and McDevitt, J. (1993). *Hate Crimes: The Rising Tide of Bigotry and Bloodshed*. New York: Plenum Press.

Ludwig, J. (2003). Americans See Racial Profiling As Widespread, *Gallup Poll Tuesday Briefing*, 13 May, available online at: http://www.gallup.com, accessed on July 28, 2004.

Ma,, C. R. (1993). *Unequal Justice: a Question of Color*. Bloomington: Indiana University Press.

Marshall, I. Haen (ed.). (1997). *Minorities, Migrants, and Crime. Diversity and Similarity across Europe and the United States*. Thousand Oaks: Sage.

Marshall, I. Haen. (2007). Immigrant communities and the police, in J. Greene (ed.), *Encyclopedia of police sciences* (pp.649-654) Third edition, Routledge.

McDevitt, J., Balboni, S. and Bennett, S. (2000). *Improving the quality and accuracy of bias crime statistics nationally: An assessment of the first ten years of bias crime data collection*, Washington D.C.: Bureau of Justice Statistics.

McDevitt, J., Cronin, S., Balboni, J., Farrell, A., Nolan, J. and Weiss, J. (2003). *Bridging the information disconnect in bias crime reporting*. Washington DC: Bureau of Justice Statistics.

Misch, G., Evangelou, T., and Burke, C. (2004). Pathways to tolerance: Changing attitudes of youth at risk of committing hate crimes. San Diego, California: San Diego Association of Governments, Anti-Defamation League, San Diego Regional Planning Agency.

Nielsen, M. O. and Silverman, R. A. (eds.). (1996). *Native Americans, Crime, and Justice*. Boulder, Colorado: Westview Press.

Parrillo, Vincent N. (1996). *Diversity in America*. Thousand Oaks, California: Pine Forge Press.

Perry, B. (2002). Defending the color line: Racially and ethnically motivated hate crime. *American Behavior Scientist*, 45(1): 72-92.

Phillips, S. and Grattet, R. (2000). Judicial rhetoric, meaning-making, and the institutionalization of hate crime law. *Law and Society Review* 34(3): 567-606.

Ramirez, D., McDevitt, J., and Farrell, A. (2000). *A resource guide on racial profiling data collection: Promising practices and lessons learned*. Washington D.C.: Department of Justice.

Ross, J.I. and Gould, L. (eds.) (2006). Native Americans and the criminal justice system, Boulder, CO: Paradigm Publishers.

Shafter, B. E. (ed.). (1991). *Is America Different? A New Look at American Exceptionalism*. Oxford: Clarendon Press.

Shapiro, H. 1988. *White Violence and Black Response: From Reconstruction to Montgomery*. Amherst: University of Massachusetts.

Shively, M. (2005). *Study of Literature and Legislation on Hate Crime in America*, Bethesda, MD: Abt. Associates Incorporated.

Tennessee Bureau of Investigation (2003). *2003 Hate Crime Report*. Nashville, TN: Tennessee Bureau of Investigation.

Wakeling, S., Jorgensen, M. and Michaelson, S. (2001). Policing on American Indian reservations. *National Institute of Justice Journal*, 3-7 January.

Walker, S., Spohn, C. and Delone, M. (2000). *The Color of Justice: Race, Ethnicity and Crime in America.* Second edition. Belmont, Ca.: Wadsworth pubs.

Webb, G. (1999). D.W.B. *Esquire*, April.

Welch, M. (2006). *Scapegoats of September 11th. Hate Crimes & State Crimes in the War on Terror.* Brunswick, NJ and New York: Rutgers University Press.

Weitzer, R. (1999). Citizens' perceptions of police misconduct: Race and neighborhood contexts. *Justice Quarterly*, 16: 819-846.

Wilson, W. J. and Taub, R. P. (2007). *There Goes the Neighborhood: Racial, Ethnic, and Class Tensions in Four Chicago Neighborhoods and their Meaning for America.* New York: Random House.

Wisconsin v. Mitchell, 508 U.S. 47 (1993).

Helpful websites

http://www.ojp.usdoj.gov/bjs/cvictgen.htm – Bureau of Justice Statistics.

http://www.fisk.edu/index.asp?cat=24 – Fisk University Race Relations Institute.

http://150.174.33.57/isrr/ – Institute for the Study of Race Relations, Virginia State University.

www.racialprofilinganalysis.neu.edu/ – Racial Profiling Data Collection Resource Centre at Northeastern University.

Epilogue

John Winterdyk and Georgios Antonopoulos

There are a few issues and/or trends that are evident from the current collection. The first one is that the countries included have different experiences of minority ethnic groups and migrants. We have, for instance, countries that have been subjugating autochthonous populations such as Australia and the United States, and colonial powers on one hand, and relatively inexperienced countries like Greece on the other, where the victims of racism are primarily migrant groups. This of course does not exclude the racist victimization of groups that are citizens of the country (e.g., Greek Roma in Greece). This presents significant challenges when trying to compare the phenomenon of racist vicitimization (and not only) among these countries, which not only have different means and methods of dealing with their minorities and different infrastructures but also define the 'receptors' of the phenomenon differently. In addition, "there's more to racism than black and white", to borrow Martinez's (2001: 272) title. In countries such as the United States there is primarily a case of victimization of *racial* groups, whereas in countries, for example, of continental Europe there is more of a case of victimization of *ethnic* groups. This, of course, is neither to suggest that white minorities are not victimized as representatives of the group they belong to in the United States, nor that non-whites are victimized in continental Europe.

As is evidenced in other comparative based research and/or discourse, there are a number of *problems* when it comes to studying the phenomenon of racist victimization in an international/comparative context. Even though the chapters are not presented in a comparative context, the objective of the reader is to provide an opportunity for comparison around an issue that transcends national borders. Perhaps the most evident challenge upon reading any of the chapters is the different definitions used to define racist victimization between different countries. Despite the fact that racist violence has a long history throughout the world irrespectively of the differences of specific geographic contexts, the definition of racist victimization has been a contested issue (Baker, 1994; FitzGerald and Ellis, 1989; and Webster, 1995). According to Hamm (1994: 174) "crimes motivated by a victim's race, ethnicity, or religion are defined at least nine different ways in… different nations around the world". As Björgo and Witte (1993) note, these definitions and labels can vary from racist violence, racial violence, anti-Semitic violence, anti-immigrant violence, violence against the foreigners etc. This is evident in the current collection as well. In addition, other common terms are used to define the study of discriminatory practices and attitudes towards marginalized groups and characterize the phenomenon such as 'racial vilification' (see Frances Reid and Smith, 1998), 'racial hatred', 'hate crime', 'bias crime' and 'prejudice-related violence' (see Box 1 in the introduction). Moreover, different countries have different ways of classifying the victims of racism and minority ethnic groups. In Australia, for example, Aboriginal status is a self-designation by the respondents, however this is not the case for the United States, where the term 'Black' refers to persons with specific ancestral origins from the sub-Saharan Africa (Gall and Lucas, 1996; also see Chapter 1). In so doing, it serves to illustrate the challenge of addressing the subject matter not only at a national level but also within an international level. In this collection, rather than impose a generic term familiar to the editors of this collection, we decided to allow the contributing authors to use whatever term they thought would fit their context better as opposed to imposing terminology that may not be congruent with their perspective(s).

In addition, to using different terminologies and classifications (see Box 1 in the Introduction to this collection), countries have also differed widely in how they have responded to racist victimization. For example, as reflected in the readings some countries use human rights legislation to address hate/racist victimization (e.g., Canada, Chapter 2), while others rely on civil legislation (e.g., Greece, Chapter 6).

Related to the above is the definition of violence through the prism of conventional victimization. In Britain, before the introduction of the 1998 *Crime and Disorder Act*, the agencies concerned with defining the phenomenon of racist violence used to do so within a strict legalistic framework focusing on the act of racist violence itself rather than in the wider socio-economic context in which racist violence takes place (Webster, 1995; see also Bowling, 1999). But as Sampson and Phillips (1992) have found, racist victimization is not *an* incident of victimization but something of a repeated condition. In some countries, such as France, there is no recognition of the particular phenomenon (see Chapter 4 for further details). As noted earlier, in Canada the Department of Justice does not collect; in a reliable manner, information pertaining to hate crime in spite of the fact that there have been an increasing number of such incidents reported in the media in recent years and that as recently as 1993 the *Hate Crime Statistics Act* (Bill C-455) was introduced into Parliament. But, the Act never got past first reading. In countries like Greece not only is there not a standardized data collection (see Institute of Race Relations, 2005) but there is also official reluctance to accept that such a phenomenon exist. For example, Antonopoulos (2006), who interviewed police officers in Greece, found that having they attempted to make the point of absence of racist violence in the country clear their responses were classified into three general categories:

a. Having no interest in the nature or motives of racist violence.
b. Viewing racist violence as an act of self-defence on the part of the Greeks.
c. Viewing racist violence as an act of violence of migrants directed towards the Greeks.

Conversely, since 1990, the United Nations under the Hate Crime Statistics Act, has been collecting hate crime statistics and Britain derives its hate crime data from the British Crime Survey.

Establishing the 'racist' motive of the offender(s) is an important issue when discussing and researching racist victimization. According to Smith (1994) there are two approaches to this, either accepting the victims' view as correct, or drawing conclusions from the accounts available. The fact remains however, that both approaches could not possibly be as valid as the view of the perpetrators who are in the position to clarify whether or not there was a racist motive. Although in Britain after the publication of the Macpherson Report (Macpherson, 1999) establishing whether there has been a racist motive in a criminal activity, which in consequence constitutes the starting point for the police investigation, depends on the view of the victim as well as the perceptions of those who have witnessed the racist victimization or reported the racist victimization to the police on behalf of a third person, this is not the case in other contexts. And although research on prejudice, discrimination and racist victimization grows, research on the perpetrators and why they victimize others who are perceived as representatives of a certain group, is still in an embryonic stage (see Hall, 2005; see also Cashmore and Jenkins, 2001). This is further illustrated in this collection as research is absent in some of the countries and in those that research on perpetrators does exist, numerous questions remain unanswered.

Finally, there is the issue of 'dark figure' of crime which primarily comes as a result of deteriorated relationships and mistrust between the police (and other state conveyors) and minority ethnic groups, fear that racist victimization will not be taken seriously, or fear of reprisal on the part of the perpetrator. This affects – to an extent – the quantification of the extent of racist victimization and any data that is available is at best speculative. Yet, the need for more reliable statistics is not only important to better inform and educate the public but to also assist the criminal justice system and community to more efficiently and effectively allocate its resources. At present, the extent, nature and quality of information and statistics on racist victimization is wanted at both a national and international level.

In-spite of the diversity in how the countries in this collection define and operationalize racist victimization, the phenomena tends to have a long history in of the countries represented. Yet, the interest in the scientific study of racist victimization and efforts to address the plight has only developed more recently (Hall, 2005). The extent to which the countries have attempted to address racist victimization in their respective countries remains quite diverse. It appears that the degree to which countries have active agendas to curb and/or understand racist victimization is related to a variety of factors and pressures. There is a disparity between how the countries presented in this collection perceive themselves, notably as liberal, tolerant and hospitable to foreigners countries which respect their cultural diversity, and on the other hand the way the minority ethnic groups in these countries view themselves, notably as excluded and victimized, with their victimization taking numerous forms, criminal, racist and economic. Moreover, there is a huge difference on the research conducted on the subject of racist victimization based on the acceptance of a country as multicultural, the experience of a country with minority ethnic groups, the funds available for research, etc. For example, research on the topic in Greece in much different in nature to that in England and Wales (as is also apparent in this collection) because Greece became a country of *immigration* only in the 1990s, and research funds are incomparably less in the particular country than in England and Wales.

Responding to Racist Violence

Although racist victimization and 'conventional', criminal victimization are in many respects similar and occupy many common elements, they are simultaneously different. Racist victimization and hate crime in general "possess dynamic racial, political, ideological and cultural dimensions that magnify their impact on victims and on the communities in which they occur" (Kelly and Maghan, 1998: 222). Related to this is the fact that racist victimization is, as Ben Bowling (1999) suggests, "a social process". The fact that the state agencies and particularly the police and other criminal justice agencies view racist victimization as incidents that have nothing to do with each makes understanding and dealing with the phenomenon even more complicated and difficult.

When it comes to policy recommendations we suggest programmes established and initiatives undertaken towards police training on the needs of the migrant communities, and the needs of the victims of racist violence. Again depending on the experience of each context of minorities the degree of sensitization of the police and other criminal justice agencies to minorities' problems differs. Certainly more experienced countries have a lot of lessons to give. Finally, it is an imperative that the community is included when responding to racist victimization. The countries presented in this edited collection largely ignore the community and especially the minority community when responding to racist victimization as well as other issues relating to ethnicity and crime (with some exceptions, of course).

Research: Some Recommendations

As with any edited collection or authored books several gaps exist. In fact, given that this anthology represents one of a few efforts to examine a concept (i.e., racist victimization) that lacks a clear or uniform definition, we can only assume that this collection leaves more issues and questions regarding the nature, extent, and responses to racist victimization unanswered than answered. Our recommendations in respect to the criminological/victimological research on the topic stems a) from the gaps of the current collection, and b) from the gaps of the general criminological/ victimological research. Specifically, it is recommended: more research on the topic of racist victimization be conducted in order for the "sequence of interactions" (Hagan and Palloni, 1999: 619) in more 'experienced' and more 'inexperienced' context to be revealed. We would suggest that the need for the more 'inexperienced' context is greater.

An additional observation gleaned from the chapters is general lack of research/ information on the victims of racist victimization. Given that the body of related research on victims of crime has grown considerably in recent years, it would be useful for researchers to focus on the victims of racist victimization. It would be instructive and pedagogically sound to be able to provide reliable information on the type and nature of harm resulting form racist victimization as well as provide a clearer understanding on the group the victim belong too. For example, it would be interesting not only to learn why France has been reluctant to mobilize for ethnic and racial rights but also see how the new EU initiatives to fight xenophobia might impact the attitudes and perspectives of the French populace towards people of different racial and/or ethnic background. Our recommendation was also conveyed by several of the contributors. In addition, research should focus on the perpetrators of racist violence and should unravel – at least to an extent – the dynamics that lead to the racist victimization process. Thus far, the existing criminological theory has been largely inadequate in explaining the racist victimization process (see Perry, 2003).

What is also suggested is (additional) research on the media representation of ethnic minorities and migrants in the local and national media, and whether and –if so – how, and the extent to which this representation affects the racist victimization of minorities. The Internet, which has provided new possibilities of communication in relation to ethnicity-related issues in recent years (see Whine, 2003), should be included in an integrated media analysis. Very importantly, the representation of the victimization of minorities should be researched as this may be related to the actual victimization of minorities. We believe that an integral part of this analysis should be an attempt towards the analysis of the way the public receives the information provided by the media, and the way they 'decode' the meanings provided. For example, additional research on police attitudes and practices in relation to minorities in a country, the way(s) these reinforce each other as well as on the extent to which certain police attitudes and practices lead to the victimization of minorities What is also suggested is research on the police response to the racist victimization of minorities, as well as on the victimization of minorities *by* the police.

With respect to the limitations in the general criminological/victimological research on the racist victimization it is suggested: additional research on racist victimization in contexts that are largely neglected such as the rural context (see, however, Chakraborti and Garland, 2004) as well as research on the racist victimization of minority and migrant inmates in the prison, and the experience of a differential treatment between majority and minority inmates. The latter is a relatively neglected aspect of racist victimization. For example, there is absence of adequate research on the victimization of minorities by individuals, groups or networks that take advantage of the position of minorities in a host society, and the victimization of minorities by employers. In addition, we feel that there must be an emphasis on the perpetrators of racist violence. We are inclined to concur with Bowling (1999: 305) who has argued that "an effective response to violent racism now requires a shift away from the victimological perspective, which has characterized the development of policy thus far".

Drawing on the diverse range of perspective presented in this collection, we believe that comparative research, possibly by an international team of researchers, on the issues relating to minority ethnic groups and crime is necessary in order for the conceptual and methodological problems to be overcome to a significant extent, and for us to have a clearer picture. The above does not of course mean that we have to 'denounce' criminologists (and other social scientists) who conduct research on geographically, temporally, and socially limited contexts, since comparative research has two levels with the first one being non-comparative. In general terms it is an imperative that the racist victimization becomes a priority in the research agenda of the social scientists in all countries.

References

Antonopoulos, G. A. (2006) 'Greece: Policing Racist Violence in the 'Fenceless Vineyard', *Race & Class,* 48(2), 92-100.
Baker, D. (1994). *Reading Racism and the Criminal Justice System.* Toronto: Canadian Scholars' Press.
Björgo, T. and Witte, R. (1993) 'Introduction'. In Björgo, T. and Witte, R. (1993) (Eds.) *Racist Violence in Europe.* (pp.1-16) London: Macmillan.
Bowling, B. (1999) Violent Racism: Victimisation, Policing and Social Context. Revised Edition New York: Oxford University Press.
Cashmore, E. and Jenkins, J. (eds) 'Conclusion'. In Cashmore, E. and Jenkins, J. (eds) Racism: Essential Readings. (pp.408-413) London: Sage.
Chakraborti, N. amd Garland, J. (eds) (2004) *Rural Racism.* Cullompton: Willan.
FitzGerald, M. and C. Hale. (1996). *Ethnic Minorities, Victimization and Racial Harassment.* Research Findings No.39 London: Home Office.
Frances Reid, S. and Smith, R.G. (1998) 'Regulating Racial Hatred', *Trends and Issues in Crime and Criminal Justice*, No. 79 Canberra: Australian Institute of Criminology.
Gall, T.L. and Lucas, D.M. (1996) *Statistics on Crime and Punishment.* Detroit, MI.: Gale Research Inc.
Hagan, J. and Palloni, A. (1999) 'Sociological Criminology and the Mythology of Hispanic Immigration and Crime', *Social Problems*, 46(4), 617-632.
Hall, N. (2005) *Hate Crime.* Cullompton: Willan.
Hamm, M. (1994) 'Conceptualising Hate Crime in a Global Context'. In Hamm, S. (ed.) *Hate Crime: International Perspectives on Causes and Control.* (pp.173-194) Cincinnati, OH.: Anderson.
Institute of Race Relations (2005) 'Protecting Ethnic Minorities', *European Race Bulletin,* No.53, 15-30.
Kelly, R.J. and Maghan, J. (1998) 'Epilogue'. In Kelly, R.J. and Maghan, J. (eds) *Hate Crime: The Global Politics of Globalisation.* (pp.221-235) Carbondale, Il.: Southern Illinois University Press.
Macpherson, Sir William of Cluny (1999) *The Stephen Lawrence Inquiry.* Cmnd 4262-1 London: HMSO.
Martinez, E. (2001) 'There's More to Racism Than Black and White'. In Cashmore and Jenkins, J. (eds) *Racism: Essential Readings.* (pp.272-276) London: Sage.
Perry, B. (ed.) (2003) *Hate and Bias Crime: A Reader.* New York: Routledge.
Sampson, A. and Phillips, C. (1992) *Multiple Victimisation: Racial Attacks on an East London Estate.* Crime Prevention Unit Series Paper No. 36, London: Home Office.
Smith, D.J. (1994) 'Race, Crime, and Criminal Justice'. In Maguire, M., Morgan, R. and Reiner, R. (eds.) *The Oxford Handbook of Criminology.* (pp.1041-1117) New York: Oxford University Press.

Webster, C. (1995) 'Researching Racial Violence: A Scientific Realist Approach'. Paper presented in the British Criminology Conference, Loughborough University, 18-21 July.

Whine, M. (2003) 'Race Hate on the Internet: The Legal Position in the UK', *Searchlight*, November, p.10.

Index

Aborigines, Australia 21–22, 31
Ainu, Japan 173–74
Annual Reports on Organized Crime, Greece 145
anti-discrimination legislation
    Australia 33–34
    Canada 62–63
    European Union 108, 114, 118
    France 97–100, 107–8
    Germany 114
    Greece 147–48, 158
anti-racist organizations, France 105–6
anti-Semitism
    Australia 32–33
    Canada 56
    France 89–90, 93, 97–98, 103
    Germany 113
Anti-Terrorism Act (2005), Australia 28
Anti-terrorism, Crime and Security Act (2001), Britain 71
anti-trafficking legislation 148
Arabic Council (AAC), Australia 37
assimilation policy 21
asylum legislation 155–56
Audit of Anti-semitic Incidents, Canada 56
Australia 11–12, 19–21
    anti-Semitism 32–33
    court cases 26, 27–28, 34
    cyber-racism 32–33
    ethnic groups 21–22, 28–29, 31–32
    immigration 22–23, 30, 34–35
    incident reporting 23–26
    institutional racism 25, 35–36
    legislation 21–22, 28, 31, 33–37
    race riots 29
    racial violence 24–26, 31–32
    racism 23–25, 27–28, 29–30

bias crime, *see* hate crime
Britain 12
    Crime Surveys (BCS) 78–80
    ethnic groups 68–69, 73–77, 78–80
    incident reporting 70–71, 76, 78–82
    institutional racism 69–70, 71, 82–83
    legislation 71–73
    MacPherson inquiry 67, 69–71, 83
    police discrimination 4–5, 71, 75
    race riots 73, 75
    racial violence 73–74, 75–76, 210, 211
    racist offenders 74, 75–76, 77–78, 83
    Stephen Lawrence murder 67, 69–70
    victims, crime risk 79–81
Burakumin, Japan 176–77

Canada 12
    anti-Semitism 56
    court cases 49–50
    crime statistics 54–58
    discrimination 47–49
    hate crime 44–45, 46, 49–53, 54–58, 63, 210
    immigration 43–44
    incident reporting 55
    institutional racism 44, 47, 56–57, 63
    legislation 44, 45–48, 49–53, 62–63
    racist offenders 58
    victims, impact on 58–62, 63
Charter of Rights and Freedom (1982), Canada 44, 47, 52, 63
convenient enemies 118
court cases 26, 27–28, 34, 49–50, 202
Crime and Disorder Act (1998), Britain 71
crime statistics 5, 6, 211
    Canada 54–58
    Germany 120–21, 122–27
    Greece 151–55
    Japan 180
    United States of America 192–98
Crime Surveys (BCS), Britain 78–80
Criminal Code, Canada 45, 46, 49–53, 63
criminal victimization 2, 212
    Canada 46, 49–53, 54–58, 63, 210
    Germany 114–17, 119, 120, 123–24, 126–27, 128
    Greece 144, 145–47
    United States of America 193–98
cyber-racism 32–33

discrimination 3, 4–5

Canada 47–49
France 99–100, 103, 104, 106–7
Greece 147, 154–55, 157, 158
Japan 173, 174–75, 176–77, 180–81
United States of America 185–89, 200–201, 204
Division of Human Rights (DHR), Greece 152–54

enforcement measures, Greece 146, 149
Ethnic Diversity Survey (EDS), Canada 55–56, 57–58, 59
ethnic groups 1–2, 209
    Australia 21–22, 28–29, 31–32
    Britain 68–69, 73–77, 78–80
    France 89, 92, 93, 96, 107
    United States of America 185–88, 197–98, 200–201, 204
ethnic youth 31–32, 96, 203
European Union, legislation 108, 114, 118

France 12, 93, 95, 212–13
    Algerian war 94
    anti-racist organizations 105–6
    anti-Semitism 89–90, 93, 97–98, 103
    crime statistics 100–102
    discrimination 99–100, 103, 104, 106–7
    ethnic groups 89, 92, 93, 96, 107
    hate crime 100–103
    immigration 92
    institutional racism 91, 99, 104–5
    legislation 97–100, 104, 107–8
    race riots 96
    racial violence 89, 90, 93–94, 95
    racism 91–93, 107
    racist crime 93, 95–96, 100–103
    racist offenders 102–3
    victims, crime risk 89–90, 95–96, 103
    xenophobia 93, 96, 100–102

Gayssot Law (1990), France 98
General Social Survey (GSS), Canada 55, 56, 57, 58
genocide 4, 45, 49–50, 113
Germany 12
    anti-Semitism 113
    crime statistics 120–21, 122–27
    genocide 113
    hate crime 114–17, 119, 120, 123–24, 126–27, 128
    immigration 124–25
    legislation 114–17
    racial violence 117–19, 120, 121, 122–23, 126–27, 128–29, 130–32
    racism 113, 119–20
    racist offenders 126–27
    victims, crime risk 129–30
    xenophobia 114, 119, 120, 123–24, 126–27, 128
governmental racism 34–35, 44, 169–70
Greece 12–13
    crime statistics 151–55
    discrimination 147, 154–55, 157, 158
    enforcement measures 146, 149
    The Greek Ombudsman 147, 151–54
    hate crime 144, 145–47, 210
    illegal immigration 146, 149–50, 156
    immigrant criminality 144, 145–47
    immigrant legislation 149–50, 157–58, 159, 160–61
    immigrant victimization 140–41, 144–45, 147, 148, 155, 159–60
    immigration 140–41, 142–43, 144, 150–51, 159
    incident reporting 151–52
    institutional racism 144–45, 154–55, 160–61
    legislation 141, 147–50, 155–56, 158
    negative stereotyping 144, 159, 160
    racial violence 156–57, 158
    racism legislation 147–48
    regularization programs 149–50
    xenophobia 144, 156–57
Greek Ombudsman, The 147, 151–54

Hagan v. Trustees 26
hate crime 3, 212
    Canada 44–45, 46, 49–53, 54–58, 63, 210
    France 103, 104
    Germany 114–17, 119, 120, 123–24, 126–27, 128
    Greece 210
    United States of America 193
    victims, crime risk 79–81, 89–90, 95–96, 103, 129–30
    victims, impact on 58–62, 63, 129–30, 196–98
Hate Crime Pilot Survey, Canada 54–55, 57, 58

Hate Crime Statistics Act (HCSA) (1990), United States of America 13, 191, 192
Human Rights Act (1977), Canada 44, 47–48
Human Rights and Equal Opportunity Commission (HREOC), Australia 24–25, 26, 29–30, 33, 35

illegal immigration, Greece 146, 149–50, 156
immigrant criminality 144, 145–47, 179–81
immigration
    Australia 22–23, 30, 34–35
    Canada 43–44
    France 92
    Germany 124–25
    Greece 140–41, 142–43, 144, 150–51, 159
    United States of America 185–89
incidents, reporting of 197–98
    Australia 23–26
    Britain 70–71, 76, 78–79
    Canada 55
    Greece 151–52
    United States of America 192–93
institutional racism 3, 4–5
    Australia 25, 35–36
    Britain 69–70, 71, 82–83
    Canada 44, 47, 56–57, 63
    France 91, 99, 104–5
    Greece 144–45, 154–55, 160–61
    Japan 169–70
    United States of America 185, 186–87, 198–201
internet racism 32–33, 34
Ishihara, S. 178–80
islamophobia 119

Japan 13, 170–72
    crime statistics 180
    discrimination 173–77, 180–81
    immigrant criminality 179–81
    institutional racism 169–70
    legislation 169, 177–78
    racist crime 169–70
    stereotyping 181

Koreans, Japan 175–76

Law against Racism (1990), France 98

Law against Racism and Anti-Semitism (1972), France 97
Lawrence, Stephen, murder of 67, 69–70
League for Human Rights of B'nai Brith Canada 56, 57
legislation 210, 212
    Australia 21–22, 28, 31, 33–37
    Britain 71–73
    Canada 44, 45–48, 49–53, 62–63
    European Union 108, 114, 118
    France 97–100, 104
    Germany 114–17
    Greece 141, 147–50, 155–56, 158
    Japan 169, 177–78
    United States of America 190–92, 199, 201–3
Lellouch Law (2003), France 98

MacPherson inquiry 67, 69–71, 83
Mugesera v. Canada (Minister of Citizenship and Immigration) 49–50
Multiculturalism Act (1988), Canada 47, 63

Nakasone, Y. 170–71
National Advisory Commission on Human Rights (CNCDH), France 100–101
National Crime Victimization Survey (NCVS), United States of America 193
National Inquiry into Racial Violence, Australia 32

Okinawans, Japan 175
Ontario Human Rights Act (1962) 44

Pacific Solution 34–35
perpetrators, *see* racist offenders
police discrimination
    Britain 4–5, 71, 75
    France 99, 104–5
    Greece 154–55, 158
    Japan 180–81
    United States of America 198–201
Police Multicultural Advisory Bureau (APMAB), Australia 36, 37
polysemic racism 91
prejudice 3
profiling 1–2, 28, 198–200, 201

race 4, 119
race riots 29, 73, 75, 96

Racial Discrimination Act (1975), Australia 33
racial victimization 2, 3, 54, 189–90, 209
racial violence 2–3, 117–18
    Australia 24–26, 31–32
    Britain 67, 69–70, 73–74, 75–76, 210, 211
    France 89, 90, 93–94, 95
    Germany 117–19, 120, 121, 122–23, 126–27, 128–29, 130–32
    Greece 156–57, 158
    United States of America 196–98
racism 2, 3, 4, 60–61
    Australia 23–25, 27–28, 29–30
    France 91–93, 107
    Germany 113, 119–20
    United States of America 186–87, 188–89, 203
racist crime 4, 5, 63, 210–11
    France 93, 95–96, 100–103
    Japan 169–70
    Stephen Lawrence murder 67, 69–70
    victims, crime risk 79–81, 89–90, 95–96, 103, 129–30
    victims, impact on 7, 8, 58–62, 63
racist offenders 189–90, 213
    Britain 74, 75–76, 77–78, 83
    Canada 58
    France 102–3
    Germany 126–27
racist society 188–89
Roma discrimination, Greece 147

Saskatchewan Bill of Rights Act (1947) 44
secondary victimization 62
Snowy Mountains Hydro-Electric scheme 23
Special Committee on Hate Propaganda in Canada (1965) 45
Statistics Canada surveys 55–59
stereotyping 32, 144, 159, 160, 181

Steven Hagan v. Australia 26
sweep operations, Greece 146, 149

Toben v. Jones 34
trafficking 4, 145, 148, 158

Uniform Crime Reporting (UCR) Program, United States of America 192
United States of America 13, 204–5, 210
    crime statistics 192–98
    discrimination 185–89, 200–201, 204
    ethnic groups 185–88, 197–98, 200–201, 204
    hate crime 190–91, 193–98, 196–98, 204
    immigration 185–89
    incident reporting 192–93, 197–98
    institutional racism 185, 186–87, 198–201
    legislation 190–92, 199, 201–3
    profiling 198–200, 201
    racial violence 196–98
    racism 186–87, 188–89, 203
    victims, impact on 196–98

victim impact statements (VIS) 8
victimology 5–8, 121
victims
    crime risk 79–81, 89–90, 95–96, 103, 129–30
    impact on 7, 8, 58–62, 63, 129–30, 196–98

Western Aboriginal Legal Services Limited v. Jones 27–28
White Australia Policy 23
Wisconsin v. Mitchell 202

xenophobia 3
    France 93, 96, 98
    Germany 114, 119, 120, 123–24, 126–27, 128
    Greece 144, 156–57